House

est Gate

ABLE

1939

The President and Mrs. Roosevelt

request the pleasure of the company of

Mr. Mellett

at dinner

Tuesday evening, December the thirteenth

at eight o'clock

1938

the United States,

Doct. Thorntons

ursday

next.

er is requested.

Miss Lane

requests the honor of

the Messrs Washington

company on Thursday evening

Oct 4th at 9 o'clock

Executive Mansion

The

the United States

the company of

Mrs. Heintzelman

tion in honor of

esty the King of

waiian Islands

evening December 18th

nine o'clock.

Mrs. Taft

At Home

afternoon

from five until seven o'clock

IN AND OUT OF THE WHITE HOUSE

an intimate glimpse into the social and
domestic aspects of the presidential life

IN AND OUT OF
THE

...from Washingto

WILFRED FUNK, INC. • NEW YORK

WHITE HOUSE

the Eisenhowers

Ona Griffin Jeffries

2

ACKNOWLEDGMENTS

It is my pleasure to extend thanks to the following friends who have been helpful in the preparation of this book: To Lowell Mellett, former editor of the Scripps-Howard Newspaper Alliance and the Washington *Daily News,* a great man, a great editor, and a great believer in freedom of the press; to Col. Robert S. Allen, columnist and lecturer, and his wife, Ruth Finney, columnist for the Scripps-Howard newspapers and special correspondent for the San Francisco *Daily News;* to Mrs. Henrietta Nesbitt, and others in official capacity, who made possible an authentic picture of White House life during Franklin D. Roosevelt's administration and the beginning of Harry S. Truman's.

To the Library of Congress, and particularly to Dr. Elizabeth G. McPherson of the Manuscript Division; Edwin A. Thompson, head of the Reader Service; Frederick Kline, head of the Issue Desk; Miss Virginia Daiker, Mr. Carl E. Stange, and Messrs. Hirst D. Milhollen and Milton Kaplan (co-authors of *Presidents on Parade*), of the Prints and Photographs Division; and Mrs. K. Lillian Takeshita, Reference Librarian of the Japanese section, Orientalia Division.

To the District of Columbia Public Library, especially Mrs. Helen R. Thompson, Coordinator Central Library Reference Service; Miss Georgia Cowan, Chief of the Biography Division; Miss Edith Ray Saul, Chief of the Washingtoniana Division; and Mr. Marchal E. Landgren of the Art Division. To Mrs. Ruth Pratt, Librarian at the Takoma Park, Maryland, Library. To Mrs. Margaret Brown Klapthor, Associate Curator, and Mr. Charles G. Dorman, Assistant Curator, Division of Political History, Smithsonian Institution, and to Mrs. Jewell S. Baker, Administrative Assistant, National Collection of Fine Arts. To Miss Josephine Cobb, Archivist in Charge, Still Picture Branch of the Audio-Visual Record Division, National Archives; to Mr. Stanley W. McClure, Assistant Chief Park Historian, and Mrs. Carol J. Smith, Chief, Information Section, National Capital Parks.

To Mr. Laurence Gouverneur Hoes, President, James Monroe Memorial Foundation; to Mrs. Kathleen Sproul, writer and editor, and Margaret Davis, Associate Director of Public Relations, George Washington University, without whose encouragement this work probably would not yet be finished; to Mrs. Katharine Kennedy Everett, my editor, who has done a wonderful job; to Mrs. Maibelle Lemon, who kept a sharp eye out for political views that *would* pop up. To Mrs. Lelah Magan Kendrick, fellow member of my chapter of the Daughters of the American Revolution, who suggested the title for the book.

My debt of gratitude is great indeed to the late William Philip Simms, Foreign Editor of the Scripps-Howard newspapers; to the late Raymond Clapper, the great political columnist, and his wife, Olive; to the late Thomas L. Stokes, another top-honor political journalist; and to the late George W. Morris, correspondent for the Memphis, Tennessee *Commercial Appeal*.

The preparation of this work has been a tremendous task, but a wonderful one! Not one minute of the years spent on research is begrudged, and this book is offered with the hope that my readers will share, as I did, in the experiences of White House life down through the history of our country.

CONTENTS

INTRODUCTION

Since the beginning of our history as a nation, Americans have had a very special interest in both the informal and the official social life of our capital. Indeed, many of our social customs have been modeled on those of official Washington, and especially on those established by presidential families.

Social customs, like language, are constantly changing; the so-called "rules" of etiquette (whose purpose is to make the world a more pleasant place to live in) both reflect and are shaped by the times. As this book shows, every one of our Presidents has made changes in White House etiquette to suit the times he lived in. During George Washington's administration, when his official residence was in New York, he called a Cabinet-level conference to determine etiquette for the new government and its leaders. Today the housekeeping staff of the White House, which copes with Easter egg rolling as well as congressional dinners, is supplemented by the huge Protocol Staff of the State Department in order to manage the visits of foreign dignitaries and heads of state.

Mrs. Jeffries has done a remarkable job of gathering material for IN AND OUT OF THE WHITE HOUSE. It is high time that such a history appeared.

New York   *The Emily Post Institute*

IN AND OUT OF THE WHITE HOUSE

I

A Tenable System
of Etiquette

George and Martha Washington

Washington was at Mount Vernon when courier Charles
Thomson, secretary of Congress under the Articles of Confederation, arrived April 14, 1789, to deliver the summons
of his election as President of the United States. Two days
later the General, accompanied by Mr. Thomson, Colonel
David Humphreys, and Tobias Lear, left Mount Vernon by
carriage for New York, arriving there after a triumphal tour
on Thursday, April 23, one week before the inauguration
was to take place.

The President-elect was at once escorted to the temporary
palace of the President. This, the former home of Walter
Franklin, was one of the handsomest edifices in the city, and
was located at Number 3 Cherry Street. Here Colonel Humphreys took charge of putting the house in order and making
final preparations for the inauguration.

The whole city was astir early Thursday morning, April
30, 1789. At nine o'clock bells summoned the people to church

to join in prayer; the air was gay with the rhythms of martial bands. People from all walks of life, traveling by foot, horseback, coach, carriage, and boat, were flocking to New York for a glimpse of their first President.

At the stroke of noon the inaugural procession formed in front of the mansion where the President-elect was staying. Heading the parade were military troops, followed by committees of the Senate and House of Representatives, and department heads under the Confederation. Washington's coach, drawn by four white horses and surrounded by a uniformed escort, came next, and Colonel Humphreys and Tobias Lear followed in the carriage which had brought Washington from Mount Vernon. Various foreign ministers and distinguished citizens brought up the rear.

Washington and his entourage alighted two hundred yards from Federal Hall, marched between lines of troops standing at attention, and entered the Senate Chamber. Here the President-elect, after a formal welcome by the Congress, strode to the outside balcony to take the oath of office before a great concourse of people. He bowed several times to the cheering crowd, then seated himself beside a table covered with a crimson cloth, on which lay a Bible lent by St. John's Masonic Lodge.

A hush fell as Washington rose to his feet. John Adams stood to his right and Robert B. Livingston, Chancellor of the State of New York, to his left. With great dignity, the chancellor asked the President-elect: "Do you solemnly swear that you will faithfully execute the office of President of the United States, and will, to the best of your ability, preserve, protect, and defend the Constitution of the United States?"

Slowly, Washington repeated the oath. Then, bending to kiss the Bible held before him on a crimson cushion, he said in a firm voice, "So help me God."

Immediately Chancellor Livingston turned to the people and cried: "Long live George Washington, President of the

HARPER'S BAZAR

A Repository of Fashion, Pleasure, and Instruction.

Vol. XXII.—No. 19.
Copyright, 1889, by Harper & Brothers.
All Rights Reserved.

NEW YORK, SATURDAY, MAY 11, 1889.

TEN CENTS A COPY.
WITH SUPPLEMENTS.

H. A. Ogden, '89.

Domestic arrangements at Mount Vernon and the slowness of coach travel prevented Martha Washington's arrival in New York for the inauguration. The ball was postponed for one week, but Martha was delayed four! This drawing from Harper's Bazar shows Washington at the ball "leading Mrs. Maxwell in the minuet."

United States!" The crowd cheered; the American flag with its thirteen stars waved proudly from the cupola; guns boomed and bells rang. Notables on the balcony returned to the Senate Chamber to hear the new President deliver his inaugural address. Then the procession re-formed and moved down Broadway to St. Paul's Chapel of Trinity Parish, where special services were held. The historic day ended with a succession of dinner parties and fireworks.

The inauguration ceremonies were barely over when Washington was besieged by callers. Some had legitimate business; others, curious to see what the new President looked like, simply wanted to shake his hand. They came at all hours of the day, even before breakfast, disrupting his household and leaving him little time for official duties.

When John Adams suggested that the President hold levees, somewhat after the European fashion, Washington, according to Jefferson, "resisted them for three weeks," mainly because he was loath to adopt any custom that smacked of royalty. As the situation became critical, however, the President sent Vice President John Adams a questionnaire covering these problems: his necessary exclusion from company; weekly visits of compliment; receiving businessmen; official dinners; anniversary entertainments; his informal social visits and how he should be distinguished on such occasions in his private character; his appearance at tea and other social events; and the making of occasional tours over the country to study its resources, its needs, and its people.

A Cabinet conference was called, which Vice President John Adams, Alexander Hamilton, James Madison, John Jay, and Colonel Humphreys, Washington's master of ceremonies, attended. Using the questionnaire as a basis, "a tenable system of etiquette" for the President's Palace was drawn up, according to which the President would return no visits; invitations to dinner would be given only to official persons and strangers of distinction; and visits of courtesy

This drawing of the first President's Palace, located at Number 3 Cherry Street in New York, was obviously made some years after the nation's capital had been moved. Earlier sketches show an intact roof-railing, several trees, a side entrance, and (of course) no signs.

would be confined to Tuesday afternoons. Foreign ministers, heads of departments, and members of Congress, however, were to be received on other occasions, and the President was to be accessible to persons whose business was important.

Washington's levees, stag affairs held on Tuesdays between three and four in the afternoon in the large dining room of the presidential mansion, were attended without invitation. It was generally understood that it was the President of the United States, not George Washington the man, who was being visited.

As the guests entered they saw the tall, erect figure of the President, surrounded by members of his Cabinet, standing before the fireplace. His powdered hair was worn gathered behind in a silk bag; his coat and breeches were of black velvet, and his silver knee and shoe buckles glittered in the firelight. A dress sword sheathed in a polished white leather scabbard protruded from underneath his coat; he wore a white vest and yellow gloves, and carried a cocked hat under his arm.

Guests were introduced by Washington's first Secretary, Tobias Lear. Washington rarely forgot the name of a person who had once been introduced to him, often delighting those who met him the second time by addressing them by name. He never shook hands, even with his most intimate friends. According to Rufus Griswold, author of *The Republican Court, or American Society in the Days of Washington,* "The visitor was received with a dignified bow and passed on to another part of the room." At a quarter past three the door was closed; the gentlemen present moved into a circle, and the President (beginning at his right) proceeded to exchange a few words with each. When the circuit was completed, Washington resumed his first position; as the visitors were ready to leave they approached him, bowed, and retired.

The President himself described the levee in a letter to his friend, Dr. Stuart:

Gentlemen, often in great numbers, come and go, chat with each other, and act as they please. A porter shows them into a room and they retire from it when they choose, with ceremony. At their first entrance they salute me, and I them, and as many as I can I talk to.

The one levee Washington failed to hold was the one which would have taken place on Tuesday before New Year's Day, 1790. Since New Year's Day fell on Friday, the regular day for Mrs. Washington's reception, it was decided to combine the two levees and hold a single reception from noon to three o'clock. This established a precedent for New Year's Day that continued to the Franklin D. Roosevelt administration, although it was always dropped temporarily during wars.

Martha Washington, who remained at Mount Vernon to supervise the packing, arrived in New York on May 27, 1789, four weeks after her husband's inauguration. The following day the President gave an informal dinner in her honor, inviting *en famille* Vice President Adams, Governor George Clinton of New York, the ministers of France and Spain, the governor of the Western Territory, the Speaker of the House, and others. Senator Paine Wingate of New Hampshire, one of the guests, wrote that "the dinner was the least showy of any he had seen given by the President. There was no clergyman and the President himself said grace upon taking his seat. He dined on leg of mutton, as it was his custom to eat only one dish. After dessert a single glass of wine was offered each guest." When the dinner was over, the President sat at the table for ten or fifteen minutes; he then joined Mrs. Washington and the ladies for coffee, leaving his secretaries to tarry with the convivial diners.

Martha Washington, as observant as her husband in matters of dress and decorum, was almost as much admired as he, and there probably never has been a busier First Lady. The principal ladies of New York City lost no time in paying their respects to the amiable consort of the President. Calling was the foremost social observance, not only for the ladies but for the men as well. Senator William Maclay of Pennsylvania wrote three days after Mrs. Washington's arrival:

> The gentlemen of Congress have, it seems, called on Mrs. Washington and all the congressional ladies. Speaker Synkoop and self called on Mrs. Morris half after ten. Not at home. Left our cards. . . . Being in the lady way, we called to see Mrs. Langdon and Mrs. Dalton. Found Mr. Langdon; the Ladies abroad. . . .

Mrs. Washington began returning calls the third day after arriving in the city. A neighbor who lived across the street from the presidential mansion wrote that a footman first knocked loudly on the door to announce his mistress. Then, in company with Mr. Lear, the First Lady entered.

The Washingtons held a reception on July 4, 1789, which Senator Maclay described in his *Journal:*

> Independence Day was celebrated with much pomp. The Cincinnati [a society of officers of the Continental Army] assembled at St. Paul's Church, where an oration was pronounced by Colonel Hamilton in honor of General Greene. The Church was crowded. The Cincinnati had seats allotted for themselves; wore their eagles at their button-holes, and were preceded by a flag. The oration was well delivered; the composition appeared good, but I thought he should have given us some account of his virtues as a citizen as well as warrior, for I supposed he possessed them, and he lived some time after the war, and I believe commenced farming.

On July 29, 1789, the notation, "Mrs. Washington will be at home every Friday, at eight o'clock p.m., to see company," appeared in the papers. Full dress was mandatory for her drawing-rooms, and it was "the usage of all persons in good society to attend." Abigail Adams, wife of the Vice President, took the place of honor at Mrs. Washington's right on these occasions. Mrs. Adams wrote to her daughter, Abby, in 1790:

My station is always at the right of Mrs. Washington. I find it sometimes occupied, but on such occasions, the President never fails to see
that it is relinquished for me, and having removed ladies several times,
they have now learned to rise up and give it to me!

An English visitor, describing Mrs. Washington's drawing-
room, wrote that a "nice-looking and well-dressed servant"
received guests at the door and turned them over to an army
officer, who ushered them into the drawing room. The First
Lady was "matronly and kind, with perfect good breeding.
She at once entered into easy conversation, asked how long
I had been in America and how I liked the country."

The President, who always attended his wife's drawing-
rooms as a private gentleman, usually wore black knee breeches
and a colored coat, then the height of fashion. The coat best
recalled was brown (his favorite color), with bright buttons.
He also liked gray. He carried neither hat nor sword.

Washington, who liked people and enjoyed talking with
them, was popular with the ladies—particularly the younger
ones, who had little opportunity of seeing him except at social
affairs. They made the most of such opportunities by trying
to engage him in animated conversation, and while the President accepted their adulation gracefully he was always careful not to neglect other guests. Some of the ladies enjoyed
special privileges; when the widows of Generals Nathanael
Greene and Richard Montgomery took leave, Washington
personally conducted them to their carriages. Other unaccom-
panied ladies were escorted to their conveyances by his secretaries.

According to George Washington Parke Custis (Martha
Washington's grandson) it was customary to serve "refreshments of all kinds" at these social functions. Specific beverages
and foods mentioned are coffee, tea, punch, lemonade, cakes,
and sweetmeats. Robert Lewis, the President's nephew and
third secretary, and Thomas Nelson, son of Governor Thomas

Nelson of Virginia, also a third secretary, kept busy seeing to it that the table was well supplied, the guests well served, and that things moved smoothly.

After the government moved to Philadelphia in December, 1790, receptions and levees continued to be brilliant. "I should spend a very dissipated winter," wrote Abigail Adams, "if I were to accept one-half the invitations I receive." Another correspondent wrote: "I never saw anything like the frenzy which has seized upon the inhabitants here. They have been half mad ever since this city became the seat of Government, and there is no limit to their prodigality." The President and Mrs. Washington continued their Fourth of July and New Year's Day receptions, at which they usually served wine, punch, and cakes.

Henry Wansey, an English manufacturer, who breakfasted with Washington and his family on the eighth of June, 1794, was greatly impressed with the President, who was then in his sixty-third year but had little appearance of age. Wansey wrote:

> [Mrs. Washington] made tea and coffee for them; on the table were two small plates of sliced tongue and dry toast, bread and butter, but no broiled fish, as is generally the custom. Miss Eleanor Custis, her granddaughter, in her sixteenth year, sat next to her, and next, her grandson, George Washington Parke Custis, two years older. There were but few slight indications of form; one servant only attended who wore no livery.

Mrs. Washington struck him as something older than the President, although he understood they were both born the same year. She was "short in stature, rather robust, extremely simple in her dress, and wore a very plain cap, with her hair turned under it."

When the Continental Army made its headquarters in New York during the Revolution, Washington and his officers had frequently dined at a tavern operated by Samuel Fraunces, a

In 1782 Count Adam Philippe Custine presented a set of china to George Washington. This bowl from the set is now in the U. S. National Museum. Count Custine was quartermaster general of the French forces in America from 1778 to 1783, and was present at the surrender of Yorktown.

West Indian of French descent called "Black Sam" because of his complexion. Washington had great confidence in Black Sam, and good reason to be grateful to his daughter, Phoebe, who kept house for him at the time. Phoebe had saved the General's life in 1776 by exposing a plot by one of his guards to poison him. So, when he was elected to the Presidency, Washington asked Black Sam to recommend a steward. Black Sam, unable to find anyone whom he considered capable of the task, accepted the stewardship himself, because of his deep devotion to Washington. Four days after Washington's inauguration, the following notice appeared in the New York papers:

> Whereas, all servants and others appointed to procure provisions or supplies for the household of The President of the United States will be furnished with monies for these purposes: Notice is therefore given, that no accounts, for the payment of which the public might be considered as responsible, are to be opened with any of them.
>   May 4th, 1789
>   SAMUEL FRAUNCES, Steward of the Household.

Although ambitious and fond of display, the new steward was not unmindful of the dignity of his position. Clad in black silk knee breeches and white ruffled shirt, his black hair carefully powdered, he would announce: "Dinner is served *up*!" During the meal he stood with his back to the sideboard, his shoe-button eyes following the footmen as they attended to the needs of the guests.

Black Sam, extravagant only insofar as delicacies for his beloved employer were concerned, watched the expense records, which he submitted weekly, with an eagle eye. The cost of food for the presidential table in New York ranged from $143 to $165 weekly, exclusive of wines and liquors, which amounted to $1700 during the seventeen months Washington remained in that city. The President himself, let it be said, was all his life a temperate man.

Black Sam, who received an annual salary of $150, resigned when his wife, who ran her own tavern, insisted that she could no longer manage alone. He was succeeded by Mr. and Mrs. John Hyde, who received respectively $200 and $100 annually. But the two combined could not match Black Sam's efficiency. Hyde thought himself above the tasks in which Sam had taken such pride; also, his food bills were much larger. "Fraunces," Washington wrote, "besides being an excellent cook, knew how to provide genteel dinners. He gave aid in dressing them, prepared the dessert, made the cakes and did everything that is done by the new steward and his wife together."

The upshot of this was that Black Sam returned to Washington's household in Philadelphia in April, 1791, at $300 a year—twice his original salary—and remained with the President for the rest of his administration.

When the President and his family moved to Philadelphia they took along two of their New York footmen, James and Fidas, and their wives. Washington ordered liveries for the footmen in the colors of his coat of arms—white with "trimmings and facings of scarlet and a scarlet waistcoat." They were paid eight dollars a month, and the speed and efficiency with which they carried out their duties are said to have made a deep impression on the guests.

Fifteen employed white servants and about seven slaves made up the household staff. Maids and washerwomen, who were paid four dollars a month in New York, had their wages increased to five dollars when the government moved to Philadelphia.

Washington tried vainly in New York and Philadelphia to find a cook on a par with Uncle Harkless (Hercules) at Mount Vernon, and was finally compelled to send for him. Uncle Harkless became the celebrated dandy of the President's kitchen. George Washington Parke Custis said he was at his greatest when preparing the congressional dinner on Thursday. "The order and discipline observed in so bustling a scene were surprising," he wrote, and "assistants flew in all directions executing his orders while he seemed to be everywhere at the same time."

A congressional or "publick" dinner was given every Thursday at four, and private dinners on other days at three o'clock. Once the food was placed on the dinner table Uncle Harkless' labors were ended and Black Sam took over. Shortly after Uncle Harkless left the kitchen he would emerge from his quarters dressed for his evening promenade in linen "of exceptional whiteness and quality" which set off his black silk knee breeches and waistcoat and long black cotton stockings. His shoes were always highly polished, the buckles so large they covered a considerable portion of his foot. His blue cloth coat was adorned with a velvet collar and bright metal buttons, and a long watch chain dangled majestically from a fob. To complete the picture of elegance, he wore a black cocked hat and carried a gold-headed cane.

Apparently all this glory was too much for Uncle Harkless, for when Washington's Presidency ended he ran away, and was never seen again, although Washington searched many months for him. Of his disappearance, Washington wrote:

> The running off of my cook has been a most inconvenient thing to this family; and what renders it more disagreeable is, that I had resolved never to become the master of another slave by purchase, but this resolution I fear I must break. . . . I have endeavoured to hire black or white, but am not yet supplied.

Washington looked upon his five young secretaries as members of the family; each served in some capacity in connection with the presidential household. Their salaries varied according to their duties. Tobias Lear, first secretary, a graduate of Harvard, was paid $800 a year; in addition to his regular work, he supervised the household staff and also issued dinner invitations.

The handsome Major William Jackson, third secretary,

delivered the invitations. On July 5, 1790, Maclay wrote: "Jackson gave me this day the President's compliments and an invitation to dinner on Thursday." The Major was paid $600 annually.

Colonel David Humphreys, second secretary, a poet and writer of note with a master's degree from Yale, drew the same salary as Major Jackson: $600. Acting as master of ceremonies, he is credited with having established the rules of precedence. The Colonel, who had served as aide-de-camp to Washington, knew the General so well that it was said he even looked and acted like him. Tall, broad-shouldered, and handsome, well trained for the post which called for tact and a knowledge of diplomacy, he had served as Secretary to the American Commission for Negotiating Commerce Treaties in Europe and lived with the polished Jefferson in Paris, where he was received in the best social and literary circles in the French capital. He wrote General Washington from Paris on July 17, 1785:

> My public character puts it in my option to be present at the King's Levee every Tuesday, & after the Levee to dine with the whole Diplomatic Corps at the Cte de Vergennes—it is curious to see forty or fifty Ambassadors, Ministers or other strangers of the first fashion from all the nations of Europe, assembling in the most amicable manner & conversing in the same language; what heightens the pleasure is their being universally men of unaffected manners & good dispositions. . . .

Thomas Nelson and Robert Lewis, the latter a nephew of the President and aide to Mrs. Washington, were paid $300 a year as junior secretaries.

It was only a short time before Washington became President that the Dutch fashion of alternating men and women at the table became fashionable. The year before the first inauguration John Trusler wrote in his "Honors of the Table" that the fashion of having ladies seated at one end of the

dinner table and the gentlemen at the other was being super-
seded by alternating a gentleman with a lady.

Seating arrangements at Washington's table depended upon
circumstances. The President and his secretaries did the carving and serving, and occupied places where they could see and
wait on guests to best advantage: the President at the center
of one side, a secretary on the opposite side (when Mrs.
Washington did not occupy that space), and a secretary at each
end of the table.

A favorite dessert served at Washington's dinners was
"Trifle." Here, from Mary Randolph's *The Virginia House-
Wife,* is the recipe:

TRIFLE

Put slices of Savoy cake (sponge) or Naples biscuit at the bottom
of a deep dish; wet it with white wine, and fill the dish nearly to the
top with rich boiled custard; season ½ pint of cream (heavy) with
white wine and sugar; whip to a froth—as it rises, take it lightly off,
and lay it on the custard; pile it up high and tastily decorate it with
preserves of any kind, cut so thin as not to bear the froth down by
its weight.

RICH CUSTARD

Scald one quart milk, one-half cup sugar and a good pinch of salt.
Beat six eggs and add half cup cold milk to them, stir and add gradu-
ally to hot milk mixture. Cook over water until custard coats spoon.
Add flavoring when cold.

Washington felt that his table decorations should be in
keeping with the dignity of his office, so he had his silver
melted and recast into "more elegant and harmonious forms"
and stamped with the family crest. Its value at that time is
said to have been $30,000.

Instead of the usual *epergne* or castor, Washington preferred a mirrored plateau as a centerpiece. He wrote Gouver-

The mirrored plateau purchased by Washington is far less ornate than the Monroe plateau, which is still in use in the White House. The Washington plateau is now at Mount Vernon; shown here are three of its nine sections.

neur Morris, then minister to France, asking him to purchase one for him. His letter, dated New York, October 13, 1789, reads in part:

> Will you then, my good Sir, permit me to ask the favor of you to provide and send to me by the first Ship, bound to this place, or Philadelphia, mirrors for a table, with neat and fashionable but not expensive ornaments for them; such as will do credit to your taste. The mirrors will of course be in pieces that they may be adapted to the company (the size of it I mean); the aggregate length of them may be ten feet, the breadth two feet. The frames may be plated ware, or anything else more fashionable but not more expensive. If I am defective recur to what you have seen on Mr. Robert Morris's table for my ideas generally. Whether these things can be had on better terms and in a better style in Paris than in London I will not undertake to decide. I recollect however to have had plated ware from both places, and those from the latter came cheapest; but a single instance is no evidence of a general fact.

The plateau, which cost Washington 468 livres, or $90 in American money, duly arrived. It was in nine sections, easily adjustable to the size of the table. Theophilus Bradbury, in a letter to his daughter, described the ornament as he saw it at a dinner given in the President's Palace on Christmas Eve, 1795:

> Last Thursday I had the honor of dining with the President in company with the Vice-President, the Senators, the Delegates of Massachusetts, and some other members of Congress, about 20 in all.
> In the middle of the table was placed a piece of table furniture about six feet long and two feet wide, rounded at the ends. It was either of wood gilded or polished metal, raised about an inch with a silver rim around it like that around a tea board; in the center was a pedestal of plaster of Paris with images upon it, and on each end figures, male and female, of the same. It was very elegant and used for ornament only. The dishes were placed all around. . . .

The plateau shown on the table in the Mount Vernon picture contains three of the original nine sections. The old Waterford candelabra on the plateau belonged to Washington.

Perhaps the best available description of one of Washington's "publick" dinners is that given by Senator William Maclay of Pennsylvania about four months after Washington's first inauguration, and before the plateau had been ordered. The guests included Vice President and Mrs. Adams; the Governor and his wife; Mr. Jay and wife; Mr. Langdon and wife; Mr. Dalton and a lady "perhaps his wife," the Senator wrote; and a Mr. Smith, Mr. Basset, Senator Maclay, and two secretaries, Lear and Lewis.

> The President and Mrs. Washington sat opposite each other in the middle of the table, the two secretaries, one at each end. It was a great dinner, and the best of the kind I ever was at. The room, however, was disagreeably warm.
>
> First was the soup; fish, roasted and boiled; meats, gammon, fowls, etc. This was the dinner. The middle of the table was garnished in the usual tasty way, with small images, flowers (artificial), etc. The dessert was, first apple-pies, puddings, etc.; then ice creams, jellies, etc.; then water-melons, musk-melons, apples, peaches, nuts. [According to De Voe's Market Book, 1866, other fruits available in Washington's time were lemons, limes, nectarines, wild plums, prunes, oranges, pineapples, sickle pears, berries, and olives.]
>
> It was the most solemn dinner ever I sat at. Not a health drank; scarce a word said until the cloth was taken away. Then the President, filling a glass of wine, with great formality drank to the health of every individual by name round the table. Everybody imitated him, charged glasses, and such a buzz of "health, sir," and "health, madam" and "thank-you, sir," and "thank-you, madam," never had I heard before. . . . The ladies sat a good while, and the bottle passed about; but there was a dead silence almost. Mrs. Washington at last withdrew with the ladies.
>
> I expected the men would now begin, but the same stillness remained. The President told of a New England clergyman who had lost a hat and wig in passing a river called the Brunks. He smiled, and everybody else laughed. He now and then said a sentence or two on some common subject, and what he said was not amiss. . . . The President kept a fork in his hand, when the cloth was taken away,

I thought for the purpose of picking nuts. He ate no nuts, but played with the fork, striking on the edge of the table with it. We did not sit long after the ladies retired. The President rose, went up stairs to drink coffee; the company followed. . . .

George Washington Parke Custis confirmed Senator Maclay's story that the President, with old-fashioned courtesy, drank to the health of each guest, and that this one toast was to everyone: "All Our Friends."

The custom of toasting guests, or host, in wine originated as a gesture of friendship; strangers never toasted each other. Toasts, once started, kept on until host and guests ended up under the table, although seasoned hands sometimes managed to walk home. When the French revolutionary Jacques Pierre Brissot de Warville, who after a visit to this country astounded his compatriots by wearing his hair unpowdered and assuming Quaker dress, visited the United States, Washington told him that people were drinking less; that guests were no longer forced to drink, and it was not fashionable to send them home inebriated.

Benjamin Franklin is credited with one of the most clever toasts ever proposed by an American. The great Quaker, then minister to France, was dining with the English and French ambassadors. The Englishman rose and proudly said: "England—the Sun whose beams enlighten and fructify the remotest corners of the earth!" The Frenchman, glowing with national pride, toasted: "France—the Moon whose mild, steady, cheering rays are the delight of all nations, consoling them in darkness and making their dreariness beautiful!" Franklin, with his quaint humor, responded: "George Washington—the Joshua who commanded the sun and moon to stand still, and they obeyed him."

The President's sixty-fifth birthday, February 22, 1797, was both a happy and a sad occasion, according to author Rufus Griswold:

Washington's state dinner service was white Sèvres china with a gold rim.
The matching bowl shown is Angoulême china. It was not until Wilson's
administration that American ware was purchased for formal service.

The sixty-fifth anniversary of the birthday of Washington was celebrated with an unusual but saddened enthusiasm. Everyone felt that
it was the last occasion of the kind on which he would be present in
Philadelphia. The ships in the harbor displayed their gayest colors;
the bells of the churches every half hour during the day rang merry
peals, and the members of Congress and official characters and private
citizens waited on the President at his residence to offer in person
their homage and congratulations. In the evening there was a ball at
the amphitheatre. Both the President and Mrs. Washington attended.

Washington declined a third term—he would not have survived it. The last dinner he gave as President was held in
Philadelphia on the day before John Adams' inauguration.
As many guests as could be seated at the President's table
were invited. Among them were President-elect Adams and
his wife, Abigail, Alexander Hamilton, Thomas Jefferson,
Bishop William White, and the heads of the diplomatic mis-
sions and their wives, including British Minister and Mrs.
Robert Liston.

During the dinner "much hilarity prevailed," wrote the
Episcopalian Bishop White, Chaplain to Congress, but on removal of the cloth it was "put to an end by the President—
certainly without design. Having filled his glass, he addressed
the company, with a smile on his countenance, saying: 'Ladies
and gentlemen, this is the last time I shall drink your health
as a public man. I do it with sincerity, and wishing you all
possible happiness.' "

When he had finished, the Bishop, happening to glance at
Mrs. Liston, wife of the British minister, saw tears stream-
ing down her cheeks.

George Washington returned to Mount Vernon—now a national shrine—to enjoy its domestic ease. In 1800, a few
months after his death, the Federal Government was firmly
established in the city of Washington, and the President's Palace, still incomplete, received its first occupants—John and
Abigail Adams.

Huntington's The Republican Court in the Time of Washington was painted long after Washington's death. Portraits served as models for the personages, and formal clothing of the day was added. Abigail Adams is at the extreme left; John Jay and Alexander Hamilton stand between her and Martha Washington. The President, near the center, is easily recognizable.

II

The First White-House Hosts

John and Abigail Adams

The President's Palace—like the Capitol—was still under construction when President John Adams and his wife, Abigail, moved into it. Three and a half years of his four-year term had already expired for the second President. However, since Congress was due to reconvene, for the first time in Washington, on November 17, 1800, it was imperative that the President take up residence in the Federal City.

Adams had left Philadelphia, the temporary capital, in May, arriving in Washington on the third of June. Abigail, in the meantime, had gone home to Braintree (now Quincy), Massachusetts, for the summer. She rejoined her husband in November. When they moved into the Executive Mansion, Abigail found only six of the rooms habitable (a rather broad term, as the walls were newly plastered, the fireplaces were cold, and the rooms were damp), and of these six rooms two were used as offices by the President and his secretary.

George Washington had selected the site for the new man-

sion on a plan for the "Federal City" designed by the French
engineer Pierre L'Enfant. The location of the Federal City
itself had been settled by compromise after years of rivalry
for this honor between North and South. James Hoban, an
Irish-born architect, designed the house, and its cornerstone
was laid on October 13, 1792.

The plan of the building provided for reception rooms on
the first floor and the President's apartments on the second.
On the first floor were the East Room, nearly forty feet wide
and seventy-nine feet long (the full width of the building),
to be used for public receptions. The adjoining Green Room,
considerably smaller, was designated in the original plans as
the "Common Dining Room"; the centrally situated Oval
Room (now the Blue Room) was indicated as the "Drawing
Room." It opened onto the Green Room on the east and the
Red Room on the west side of the entrance. The Red Room
is traditionally used by the First Lady when she receives guests,
but it served John Adams as an "anti-chamber" to the Cabinet Room, which was located in the southwest portion of
what is now the State Dining Room. Today's family dining
room was the "Public Dining Room" in the early days; it
adjoins the State Dining Room on the west end of the building.

The entrance was then on the south side, and led into the
Oval Room. The north ends of the Green, Oval, and Red
Rooms opened onto the corridor running from the East
Room to the State Dining Room.

At the time the Adamses moved in, Abigail needed all her
ingenuity, tact, charm, and housewifely skill to meet the demands of her role as First Lady. Accustomed as she was to
"Richmond Hill," their beautiful New York residence during
Adams' Vice Presidency, and to the other comforts of Philadelphia, she found the President's Palace barnlike and inhos-
pitable. Not a single apartment, not even the East Room
(which she put to use for drying clothes), was finished. The
grounds were rough and muddy. The house had no water

The building on the left is the Executive Mansion on High Street in Philadelphia, seat of the Government from December, 1790, to May, 1800, when John Adams moved into the new mansion in Washington. The building to the right, at the Sixth Street corner, was the house of Robert Morris.

supply—and so, of course, no bathroom—and there was no
wood for the fireplaces. Coal was available, but grates were
not—"nor," wrote Abigail at the time, "were there enough
'lusters' or lamps, so candles were stuck here and there for
light—neither the chief staircase nor the outer steps were
completed, so the family had to enter the house by temporary
wooden stairs and platform." Servants were on hand, but
there were no bells to summon them!

At that time the capital, later to be dubbed the "City of
Magnificent Distances," had a population of only three thousand, with a scattering of about four hundred and fifty houses,
the greater number of which were in Georgetown. Travel was
by coach and carriage, mostly over foot- and cow-paths. Ladies
drove three and four miles to call on Mrs. Adams, and often
carried or sent gifts of meat, vegetables, yeast, and milk.
George Washington Parke Custis, Mrs. Washington, and
Mrs. Lewis sent a haunch of venison by a servant, together
with a congratulatory letter and a special invitation to visit
them at Mount Vernon. Abigail soon found the greater part
of her time being spent returning calls, sometimes as many
as fifteen a day.

The ladies became impatient for Mrs. Adams to hold a
drawing-room, but her tea china, over half of which had been
broken or stolen in transit from Philadelphia, had to be replaced before Abigail could arrange this.

On New Year's Day, 1801, the President's Palace was formally opened to the public. Abigail, in brocade and velvet,
sat in a chair and greeted her guests. The President, dressed
in black velvet, silk stockings, silver knee and shoe buckles,
and high stock collar, his hair powdered and tied in a queue,
stood at her side. After the guests paid their respects to the
President and Mrs. Adams they were served refreshments
and entertained by the Marine Band, which made its official
debut at that same housewarming.

The Adamses received in the Oval Room, where furniture

The obscure white building at the upper left is the Executive Mansion in 1799, the year before John and Abigail Adams moved in. It was some years before the scene changed appreciably; the first landscaping of the mansion grounds was done in Jefferson's time.

upholstered in crimson damask had been placed. Logs crack-
ling merrily in the open fireplace, a piano, a harp, and a guitar
which the hosts had brought with them, an Aubusson rug, little
side tables, and damask draperies, all combined to bring
warmth and cheer to the big room. Only Abigail's closest
friends knew the careful planning that had gone into the refreshments: tea, coffee, punch, and wine; cakes and tarts
baked in the ovens on each side of the huge kitchen fireplace;
curds and creams, jellies, trifles, floating island, syllabub,
sweetmeats, fruits.

Abigail soon found that her experience abroad—her husband had been commissioner to France and minister to Hol-
land and England—had more than prepared her to meet the
exigencies of taking up residence in the new "Federal City,"
as Washington was then called.

Born in Massachusetts, the daughter of a Weymouth minister, Abigail was a capable housekeeper. In Paris she had
found the servant problem far more complicated than in
America. There, each servant had his special department from
which he refused to deviate. The Adamses had had to hire
a coachman, a maître d'hôtel (who graciously offered to act
as footman to save the expense of another servant if his mistress would buy him a "gentleman's suit" in lieu of livery);
a gardener; a *frotteur* to take care of the floors; a charwoman,
and a laundress. Abigail had brought along two of her own servants, who served as *valet de chambre* and *femme de chambre,*
and, according to their mistress, this couple was worth more
than a dozen of the others. The Adamses had even had to hire
their own hairdresser; powdered hair being the fashion, they
found it cheaper to employ someone than to have this cosmetic
service done outside.

John Adams—unlike George Washington—had never been a
wealthy man; during his stay abroad the United States Government had been forced to curtail expenses, and Adams had found
his salary reduced from 2,500 to 2,000 guineas a year. Abi-

Abigail Adams is one of the most prominent First Ladies in American history. This is a silk-screen reproduction of a portrait by Christian Schussele.

gail, hard put to it to keep expenses down, eliminated suppers and attended as few functions as possible. She found formal dinners (which averaged one a week) quite expensive, costing approximately one guinea per guest. There were always from fifteen to twenty, and occasionally twenty-seven, guests, but Abigail, who considered such dinners important, wrote: "More is to be performed by way of negotiation many times at one of these entertainments, than at twenty serious conversations."

The Adamses' guest list, impressive by American standards, usually included such dignitaries as the Marquis de Lafayette, the Chevalier de la Luzerne, Messrs. Franklin and Jefferson, diplomats and high-ranking Frenchmen and, occasionally, their wives. And, of course, there was the indispensable Colonel Humphreys, then secretary to the American Commission.

Abigail disliked French etiquette, which required the newcomer to make the first call; her inherent honesty rebelled at elaborate compliments which she thought stupid. The dancing in the French theaters shocked her, and at first she was ashamed to be seen watching the dancers—though she admitted that the costumes and the beauty of the performers were "enchanting." Eventually, as she became accustomed to the productions, she wrote: "I now see them with pleasure."

The Adamses were popular in Paris, and it was with regret that their French friends saw them depart for London, where Adams was to be stationed as the first American Minister to the Court of St. James's.

Arriving in London May 28, 1785, after eight months in Paris, Abigail was quick to sense the antagonism of the English toward the "Colonials" from America. "The Tory venom," she wrote, "has begun to spit itself forth in the public papers; bursting with envy that an American Minister should be received here with the same marks of attention . . . which are shown to the ministers of any other foreign power."

King George III and his queen, however, showed no outward resentment over the loss of their American colonies when John Adams was presented to them. When Abigail and Abby, her daughter, were received at court and Lord Onslow introduced the King, the eyes of that monarch brightened with interest. Abigail had removed her white glove in order to shake hands, but "His Majesty saluted my left cheek," Abigail wrote, "then asked me if I had taken a walk today. I could have told his Majesty that I had been all the morning preparing to wait upon him; but I replied: 'No, Sire.' 'Why? Don't you love walking?' he said."

When Abigail was presented to the Queen, she sensed that her Majesty was slightly embarrassed at meeting so recent an enemy. She herself, she wrote, was conscious of "a disagreeable feeling," although everything was "said affably with the ease and freedom of old acquaintance." The Queen politely inquired: "Mrs. Adams, have you got into your house? Pray, how do you like the situation of it?"

The Princess Royal, observing the full drawing room, did her mother one better. She looked at Abigail compassionately and inquired if she were not much fatigued.

Of the Prince of Wales, Mrs. Adams wrote: "His Highness looked much better than the King. He is a stout, well-made man and would look very well if he had not sacrificed so much to Bacchus."

Later, when the Adamses attended the ball given in honor of the Queen's birthday, Colonel Humphreys, in a letter dated February 11, 1786, wrote General Washington: "In honour of America Mrs. Adams appeared to good advantage, being an extremely decent Lady and that Miss Adams, in beauty and real taste in dress, was not excelled by any young lady in the room."

Card playing was then fashionable in both England and France, the players usually going in for high stakes. On April 5, 1786, Abigail attended a party for two hundred at the Swedish minister's. She described it as "a stupid rout" in a letter to her sister, Mrs. Cranch. Although she observed that three large rooms were filled with card tables, she was opposed to gambling for high stakes and had made up her mind not to participate in a game. But hardly was the curtsying over when she was asked by the hostess: "Whist, cribbage or commerce?" and before she quite realized it, Abigail was sitting at a table with three strangers.

"The lady who was against me," she wrote, "started the game at half a guinea apiece. I told her I thought it full high; but I knew she designed to win, so I said no more but expected to lose." To her surprise, Abigail won four games straight. "I paid for the cards, which is the custom here," her letter continued, "and left her to attack others."

Lady Luck seems to have dogged the footsteps of the charming Abigail. On the eve of a dinner for the diplomatic corps —invitations had gone out ten days before—her good friend Captain Hay returned from the West Indies bringing a gift of a hundred-and-fourteen-pound turtle. "Though it gave us a good deal of pain to receive so valuable a present," Abigail wrote, "we could not refuse it without affronting him. And it certainly happened in a most fortunate time!"

Mrs. Adams liked England and felt at home with the English, among whom she had many friends. She liked the similarity of American and English etiquette, particularly "when she was called on as a stranger" instead of having to make the first call, as in Paris. However, it was her opinion that an American would appreciate a diplomatic post there far more after the antagonisms of the war had worn off.

Before leaving Europe, Mrs. Adams wrote:

> I have learned to know the world and its value; I have seen high life; I have witnessed the luxury and pomp of state, the power of riches and the influence of titles, and have beheld all ranks bow before them as the only shrine worthy of worship. Notwithstanding this, I feel that I can return to my little cottage, and be happier than here, and, if we have not wealth, we have what is better, integrity.

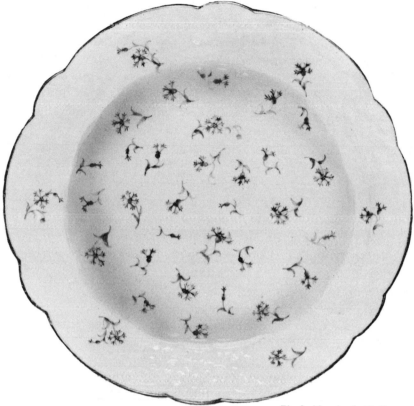

This white Sèvres china decorated with blue cornflowers was used for state dinners in the White House during John Adams' administration. It is now in the collections of the U. S. National Museum.

Abigail Adams, the first wife of an American minister to be introduced at the Court of St. James's and the first President's Lady to reside in the President's Palace, also had the distinction of being the mother of a President. Though her residence at the mansion was a short one (Thomas Jefferson was to take over the President's Palace within four months after the Adamses moved in), Abigail has gone down in history as one of the most brilliant women of her time and one of the most charming of America's First Ladies.

In contrast to Abigail's warmth, grace, and gentle dignity, John Adams was sometimes described by eyewitnesses as "cool and wary." He liked the pomp of royal etiquette, and his "grasping of titles" was called by observers of the time *"Nobiliamania."* Senator Izard of South Carolina, after describing Adams' air, manner, and deportment (and personal figure in the chair), concluded by applying to him the descriptive mock title, "Rotundity." On occasion, members of the House of Representatives lampooned Adams before his face with the satiric nickname of "Bonny Johnny Adams."

A somewhat dour but doubtless candid eyewitness portrait of Adams is given by William Maclay, a Scotsman and lawyer from Pennsylvania, who, nettled because Adams did not possess the "sedate and easy air" he associated with a person of Adams' exalted position in the nation, complained that Adams (in the chair) would "look on one side, then on the other, then down on the knees of his breeches, then dimple his visage with the most silly kind of half-smile, which I cannot well express in English. The Scotch-Irish have a word that hits it exactly—smudging."

After that first big reception at the mansion the Adamses did little formal entertaining, for Adams had failed in his bid for reelection and Thomas Jefferson was due to enter the President's House March 4, 1801. But when Abigail Adams returned to Massachusetts she left behind a social system which even the unceremonial Jefferson could not permanently upset.

III

The Pell-Mell System

Thomas Jefferson

Thomas Jefferson succeeded to the Presidency on the fourth of March, 1801. He was the first President to be inaugurated in the new city of Washington, which had become the capital of the nation only the year before. At that time the city on the Potomac was still a wilderness of unpaved roads and scattered houses. The President's Palace stood unfinished in the middle of an open field.

Jefferson, whose service to the new nation as Governor of Virginia and as Secretary of State under President Washington had uniquely equipped him for the presidential office, was fifty-seven years old and a widower when he succeeded John Adams. At the time of his inauguration he was living in the Conrad boarding house on the west side of New Jersey Avenue, between B and C Streets, one block from the Capitol grounds. It was his express desire that this first presidential inauguration in the "Federal City" be kept simple and devoid of ceremony.

At an early hour on Wednesday, the city of Washington presented a "spectacle of uncommon animation, occasioned by the addition to its usual population of a large body of citizens from the . . . adjacent districts," the *National Intelligencer* tells us (March 6, 1801). A discharge from the Company of Washington Artillery ushered in the day; at about ten o'clock the Alexandria Company of Riflemen, with the company of artillery, paraded in front of the President's lodgings.

At high noon Jefferson—tall, raw-boned, freckled, his sandy hair now snow-white—wearing his usual dress, that of a plain citizen without any distinctive badge of office, left the boarding house in the company of five or six of his fellow boarders (who happened to be senators and representatives). He walked up New Jersey Avenue to the Capitol, where he was met by a Committee of the Senate. To a thundering blast of artillery he entered the Senate Chamber, where were assembled the Senate, members of the House of Representatives, and as many citizens as could crowd in. All present rose as Jefferson, followed by Secretaries of the Navy and Treasury, entered; then Aaron Burr, who had taken his seat in the Senate as Vice President the day before, vacated his chair to Jefferson. After a few moments of silence, the new President rose and began to speak.

"Friends and fellow citizens . . ." The manner in which he delivered the speech was "plain, dignified, and unostentatious; the style . . . chaste, appropriate and eloquent; the principles . . . pure, explicit and comprehensive," the *National Intelligencer* reported. When the cheers and ovation following his address had subsided, Jefferson seated himself again for a short period. He then rose and walked to the clerk's table, where the oath of office was administered by Chief Justice John Marshall (who was, incidentally, a cousin of Jefferson's).

After congratulations by friends and statesmen Jefferson is

said to have walked back to his lodgings accompanied by the Vice President, the Chief Justice, and various heads of departments and citizens. At dinner he occupied his usual seat at the foot of the table. Outside, the new capital city was vociferously celebrating with "festivities and illuminations."

It was the middle of March before Jefferson could bring himself to give up his rooms in Conrad's crowded lodging house on Capitol Hill and move to the still-unfinished President's Palace, which he promptly rechristened "President's House."

One of the new President's acts was to abolish levees and drawing-rooms and limit public ceremony to the traditional Fourth of July and New Year's Day receptions. He even refused to celebrate his own birthday—April 13—with the customary ball. Instead, he began preparations for the "only birthday which he wished to commemorate"—that of the Declaration of Independence.

The dawn of Saturday, July 4, 1801, was announced in Washington by a "salute from the frigates," upon which all ordinary business was suspended. The doors of the unfinished President's House stood open for Jefferson's first reception; the worn and faded furniture which had been used by George and Martha Washington was polished and tastefully arranged. The grounds outside the President's House (sometimes used as a pasture for foraging herds) were colorful with tents and booths as crowds thronged in from the city and nearby country districts. It was to be, as one eyewitness wonderingly reported, "a day of joy to our citizens and of pride to our President!" In the distance—far down Pennsylvania Avenue, "beyond the alder bushes"—the faint sound of martial music announced the first of the great historic processions that were to pass along that thoroughfare.

Inside the President's House, Jefferson stood surrounded by his guests of honor: five chiefs of the Cherokee tribe who had come to Washington on a mission and who, in their feathered attire, mingled in colorful dignity with the civil and military officers, foreign diplomats, and citizens of Washington and Georgetown who had come to celebrate the nation's birthday.

Some time after the company had assembled, Colonel Burrows, at the head of the Marine Corps, saluted the President and struck up a new song, "The President's March." As the band began to play, a handsome naval officer, Captain Tingey, commandant of the newly-established Washington Navy Yard, began to sing. Soon the crowds outside began to echo the words, and the new song—now known as "Hail Columbia"—which had been specially written for the occasion, caught the fancy of the guests so much that "many rose, fell in behind the band and joined in a grand march through the rooms and corridors of the White House, returning at last to the place from which they had started to resume their feast of good things." At intervals the band played martial and patriotic airs, then "fired sixteen rounds in platoons, and concluded with a general *feu-de-joie.*"

Jefferson, his manners "good, natural, with a frank and friendly . . . expression on his red, freckled face," invited the company of about one hundred into the dining room, where four large sideboards covered with refreshments such as cakes, wine, and punch waited. The celebration lasted from noon until about three o'clock.

Jefferson's democratic spirit and natural kindliness of heart soon won the love and admiration of all who met him. He mingled freely with all citizens and conversed with any that came his way, and opened the house to all comers each morning. He introduced the custom of shaking hands instead of bowing. His dinner invitations read, "Th. Jefferson invites," instead of "The President of the United States invites" (which Washington had used). If Jefferson saw a guest seemingly at a loss in the gay company, he would give him special attention until he had overcome his diffidence.

Jefferson refused to celebrate his own birthday with a ball. The "only birthday which he wished to commemorate" was that of the United States, so on July 4, 1801, he gave his first public reception. The President's House was still unfinished, and the open field surrounding it was still in use as a pasture.

Jefferson's desire to carry on the American tradition of true democracy once led him to invite his butcher to dinner. The man appeared with his son in tow; he had heard, he explained, that one of the guests was ill, and since there would be an extra plate, he thought he might as well bring his son along. Without raising an eyebrow, the President introduced the butcher and his son to his distinguished guests, and kept an eye on them during the meal to be sure they were well served.

Jefferson's wife, the beautiful Martha Wales Skelton, had died at the age of thirty-three, leaving him with two little girls: Martha, later to become Mrs. Thomas Mann Randolph, and Mary, who married her cousin, John Wayles Eppes. Mary, the younger, was inclined to be shy and retiring, but the Paris-educated Martha tried to spend as much time as she could with her father and served as his official hostess on occasion, though she had twelve children to care for. Her eighth child, James Madison Randolph, was the first child born in the White House.

President Jefferson soon established his own system of etiquette, referring to it as the "pell-mell" system. The formalities which had prevailed during the Washington and Adams administrations were abolished and no distinction of persons was recognized at the White House. In fact, in order to nullify the question of rank and protocol, he introduced a circular table, so that no guest could outrank another.

Jefferson's decision to abolish the levee and the drawing-room is said to have caused an uproar among the Washington elite. A delegation of women who called to protest took him by surprise, but he received them courteously, listened gravely to their complaints, and then, with the famous Jefferson charm, explained his position. He was a widower, living in the President's House (more or less as a bachelor) with his two congressmen sons-in-law and his secretary. His lady callers were so entranced with his manners they left completely mollified.

Thomas Jefferson and Patrick Henry, while young lawyers, spent many hours together playing violin duets. Jefferson continued his interest in the violin throughout his life, and was considered a fairly good musician. Below is the piano in use in the Executive Mansion during his tenure.

Actually, the "pell-mell" etiquette system aroused so much bitterness in diplomatic circles that the new British minister and Mrs. Merry, accustomed to the old school of etiquette, decided that they had been insulted on their first visit to the President's House shortly after Jefferson came into office.

It all began when dinner was announced and the President offered his arm to Mrs. James Madison—his honored hostess when his daughter was not there. Secretary of State Madison then offered his arm to the lady next to him, and other Cabinet members followed suit as the bewildered Englishman, unaware of the new custom, stared in amazement. Guests had found their way to the dining room before he realized what had transpired and offered his arm to Mrs. Merry. After a similar experience at the Madisons, the minister and Mrs. Merry were so incensed that no apology had been offered, or even considered necessary, that they refused to accept further invitations from Jefferson and the Madisons. Jefferson, whose rule was "first come, first served," promptly forgot the matter.

Jefferson's penchant for French and Italian cookery, a taste developed while serving as Treaty Commissioner to France from 1785 to 1789, brought the wrath of Patrick Henry upon his head. The President, Henry declared, was "a man unfaithful to his native victuals." Even after he left France, his secretary, who remained behind, sent him a mold for macaroni, his favorite Italian dish.

During his Presidency, Jefferson employed a French steward, Etienne Lemaire, who did the buying, and a French chef, Julien. He had brought back Petit, who served as his valet in Paris, with him when he returned to America. He also brought eleven servants from Monticello, including two Negro slaves, Edy and Fanny, who were to be instructed in French cooking by the chef, and Annette, his Virginia cook who knew just how he liked batter cakes, fried apples, and hot breads served with bacon and eggs at breakfast.

The President took his desserts seriously; among the many

Martha Jefferson Randolph, the President's elder daughter, sometimes served as his official hostess. She had twelve children; her eighth, James Madison Randolph, was the first child born in the Executive Mansion.

recipes he brought back from France was one for ice cream, or "cream-ice" as it was originally called by the Parisian artist who first served it to the duc de Chartres in 1774. The delicacy was not unknown in America, for Martha Washington had purchased a "cream machine for ice" in 1784 for use at Mount Vernon, and according to William Maclay the delicacy was served along with the desserts during Washington's administration. While in Philadelphia, Mrs. Washington purchased molds for more attractive serving, but she did not, insofar as is known, leave a recipe. So to Jefferson goes the credit of popularizing ice cream as a White House dessert, for he served it so often that Washington hostesses followed suit. Sometimes it was brought to the table in the form of small balls enclosed in cases of warm pastry. By 1812 ice cream took precedence over other desserts. Mrs. Seaton, wife of the owner of the *National Intelligencer,* wrote at the time: "Pastry and puddings are going out of date and wines and ice creams coming in." Jefferson's table also provided dishes as American as the flag itself. His persimmon beer recipe was so highly recommended by one of his close friends that it was printed in the first issue of the *American Farmer,* dated April 2, 1819.

MR. JEFFERSON'S PERSIMMON BEER

Gather the persimmons perfectly ripe and free from any roughness, work them into large loaves, with bran enough to make them consistent, bake them so thoroughly that the cake may be brown and dry throughout, but not burnt, they are then fit for use; but if you keep them any time, it will be necessary to dry them frequently in an oven moderately warm. Of these loaves broken into a coarse powder, take 8 bushels, pour over them 40 gallons of cold water, and after two or three days draw it off; boil it as other beer, hop it; this makes a very strong beer. By putting 30 gallons of water to the same powder, and letting it stand two or three days longer, you may have a very fine small beer.

Jefferson's pound cake, and his sponge cake which he always

had on hand to serve with wine, were as famous as his persimmon beer. The pound cake was a great Southern favorite; the identical recipe is found in both *The Virginia House-Wife*, by Mary Randolph (a cousin of Thomas Jefferson's) and *Martha Washington's Rules for Cooking*, by Ann Marshall.

POUND CAKE (Monticello)

One pound of unsalted butter, rub soft as cream; have ready a pound of flour, a pound of powdered sugar. Add 12 eggs well beaten. Put alternately into butter and sugar and the froth of eggs, continuing to beat well until all the ingredients are in and cake is light. Add some grated lemon peel, a nutmeg and a gill of brandy. Butter the pan and bake. Serve with melted butter, sugar and wine as a sauce, or dry with wine.

MONTICELLO SPONGE CAKE

One dozen eggs, whites and yolks beaten separately; one pint of sugar; one pint of flour; juice and grated rind of one lemon. Mix yolks, sugar, flour and lemon; add whites. This is a good cake.

(Martha Jefferson)

While Jefferson was in residence at the President's House he kept in constant touch with affairs at Monticello. His grandchildren had to be as thoroughly schooled in the art of cooking as they were in Latin, music, and French. Many of his favorite recipes which he collected from friends and from Messieurs Lemaire, Julien, and Petit were copied in his own fine hand and made up in individual booklets for his granddaughters to take with them as brides to their new homes.

Although a light eater, Jefferson was one of the great connoisseurs of his day. Nothing but the best available was good enough for his guests. He entertained so extensively that his bills at the Georgetown markets frequently averaged fifty dollars a day. Often he accompanied Etienne Lemaire to the market, hoping to find some delicacy he particularly desired.

He was fond of olives, figs, mulberries, crabs, oysters, partridges, venison, pineapple, and light wines. His marketing was not confined to Georgetown. He kept wagons moving from Baltimore, Richmond, and Monticello to pick up foods not obtainable in Georgetown.

History records his wine bill for his two terms in office as $10,000, the greater part of which was spent during the first four years. Coffee and tea were served after big dinners— coffee as a settler and tea, usually green, to awaken and excite the senses after they had been lulled by wine.

John Adams, a onetime close friend who never forgave Jefferson for defeating him in his run for reelection, and who criticized him for wasting so much time entertaining, wrote:

> I held levees once a week that all my time might not be wasted by idle visit. Jeffersons whole eight years were a levee. . . . I dined a large company once or twice a week; Jefferson was for liberty and straight hair; I thought curled hair just as democratic.

Jefferson realized the value of the dinner table for political discussions—as did our First President, who frequently took advantage of such occasions. In fact, it was at Jefferson's table when he was Secretary of State that it was finally settled that the capital city would be located on the banks of the Potomac, and that it would be called "Washington."

To preclude the danger of being overheard by talkative servants, Jefferson invented "dumbwaiters" (tiered tables) to hold everything necessary for the meal. He also installed revolving shelves in the wall between the small dining room and the pantry. These were operated by the touch of a spring; the shelves loaded with food would swing into the dining room and those stacked with empty dishes would move outward into the pantry.

Jefferson took great pride in the floors of the President's House. On the day of a dinner a green canvas cover would be spread over the dining-room floor to protect it from grease or anything that might happen to be dropped from the table. The canvas was removed after dinner.

Jefferson usually rose at dawn. He is said to have bathed his feet in cold water every morning in the belief that this kept off colds. He wrote and read until breakfast, spent some hours in the afternoon playing the violin, riding horseback (six or eight miles a day), gardening, or taming birds; at one time he had a tame mockingbird which he allowed the freedom of his rooms. He drank water only once a day, a single glass, when he returned from his horseback ride.

He is said to have preferred French cooking "because the meats were more tender"; he ate heartily of vegetables but little meat, and never drank strong liquors; malt liquors and cider were his table drinks.

The President enjoyed entertaining savants and men of letters; distinguished foreigners were received with informal but generous hospitality. Two famous persons who visited the capital city during Jefferson's Presidency were Jérôme Bonaparte, who spent a great deal of time in Washington, and Baron Alexander von Humboldt, the German explorer and scientist. Bonaparte, the youngest brother of Napoleon, was the lion of the day in social circles; attentions were showered upon him from all sides. Young and impressionable, he succumbed to the charms of Miss Elizabeth Patterson of Baltimore, whose father, the president of the Bank of Baltimore, was the wealthiest man in Maryland.

Baron von Humboldt was a "charming Prussian baron." Mrs. Madison tells us "all the ladies say they are in love with him, notwithstanding his lack of personal charms. He is the most polite, modest, well-informed and interesting traveler we have ever met, and is much pleased with America."

Perhaps the social event that eclipsed all others in Jefferson's administration was the reception given for the Ambassador from Tunis, who arrived in "silk robes, a plaster-of-Paris turban, and slippers that curved at the toes." All Washington buzzed about his "taking off the slippers in order not to defile the sacred floors of the President's Palace," and about his taking off the turban to show the assembled Osage Indian chiefs in full ceremonial regalia that "his head was shaved just like theirs!"

In Jefferson's administration, the first landscaping of the White House grounds was done, and plans were developed for the addition of the north and south porticoes. The east and west terraces, which Jefferson himself is said to have planned—the architect for the project was Benjamin H. Latrobe—made provision for service quarters on each side of the house, stables, saddle rooms, an ice house and a hen house.

Toward the end of Jefferson's eight-year administration he grew weary of company, and of the dinners that began at four and lasted until nightfall. When he stepped aside to make way for James Madison he said, "I am now a very happy man."

IV

The Golden Age
of Queen Dolly

James and Dolly Madison

For weeks before the inauguration of James Madison in 1809 stagecoaches rumbled over roads from New England to the Carolinas, all heading toward the new capital city. One tavern keeper declared he saw as many as three coaches pass in a single day. Madison's inauguration brought the greatest influx of people that Washington had seen up to that time.

Dolly Madison, the "brilliant, sunny-hearted, witty little Quakeress from Philadelphia," who had on occasion acted as hostess for Jefferson in the Executive Mansion after Jefferson had made "Jemmy" Madison his Secretary of State, stepped into her role as First Lady with elegance and a delightful dignity.

The new President, who had entered Princeton College at the age of eighteen and carried such a heavy schedule that for months he had slept only three hours a day, had married Dorothy Payne Todd, the widow of a Philadelphia lawyer, in September, 1794.

Dolly was forty years old when she entered the White House as First Lady. Washington Irving described her as "a fine, portly, buxom dame, who has a smile and a pleasant word for everybody . . . but as for Jemmy Madison—ah! poor Jemmy! He is but a withered little apple-John."

But Jemmy was famous, and Dolly was an astute politician who exercised her graciousness, charm, and femininity to further her husband's career; she was careful never to make an enemy. Her political dinners were well timed and well served, and she had an amazing memory for names and faces. Above all, Dolly had a natural vivacity that drew people to her as to a magnet.

Her costume for her husband's inauguration was comparatively simple—for Dolly. According to Mrs. Samuel Harrison Smith, wife of the publisher of the *National Intelligencer,* she wore a plain cambric dress with a long train, without handkerchief, and a bonnet of purple velvet and white satin with white plumes. "Today, after the inauguration, we all went to the Madisons—we had to wait near a half-hour before we could get in, house filled, parlours, entry, drawing room and bed-room. Near door of drawing room Mr. and Mrs. Madison received."

Madison was the first President to give an Inaugural Ball in Washington. The new First Lady's gown for the occasion was magnificent; it had been ordered long beforehand. To Dolly, this was truly a great occasion. Her costume of "handsome light yellow or buff velvet, full as was the fashion of the day, and with a long train," and her turban (a headgear for which she was famous) of buff velvet combined with white satin and topped off by a bird of paradise which came from Paris and would have done a maharajah credit, gave her a regal appearance. Her jewels were pearls.

Extra fiddlers had come all the way from New York to play for the guests. Socialites from New York, Boston, Baltimore, and Philadelphia joined Washington élite at the ball, which also drew many members of the diplomatic corps, Cabinet officers, and Justices of the Supreme Court.

Dolly was escorted to supper by the French minister, and sat in sparkling grace between him and the British minister at the center of the table, opposite her husband. She and the President left the ball immediately after supper.

The Madison administration's eight years in the White House became known as "The Golden Age," mainly because of Dolly's style of entertaining and the lavishness of her gowns, jewels, and turbans (on which she is said to have spent $1,000 a year). Her evening shoes were fabulous. The average lady of her class would have had three pairs; Dolly had a dozen. There were slippers of gold and of silver and slippers heavily beaded or buckled, all designed to show to best advantage her tiny feet.

The principal change made in the President's House at the beginning of the Madison administration was in the drawing room, which she had decorated in yellow satin and hung with damask draperies of yellow. (Yellow was Dolly Madison's favorite color.)

To improve house service, Dolly had bells installed in every room, increased the number of servants to thirty—Jefferson had had fourteen—and gave Jean Pierre Sioussant (who had worked for British Minister Merry) the position of master of ceremonies.

Dolly made it a practice to serve refreshments to all visitors, regardless of their business or the brevity of their stay. During the first year of her husband's administration she surprised and delighted the new British minister by interrupting his conference with the President by sending in a Negro servant with glasses of punch and seed cake. She also introduced the comforting practice of serving bouillon at afternoon receptions when the weather was cold and dreary—and her layer cake is famous to this day!

Here are the three recipes:

SEED CAKE

1 lb. butter	1 lb. flour
6 eggs	¾ oz. caraway seeds
¾ lb. sifted sugar	1 wineglass of brandy

Pounded mace, and grated nutmeg to taste

Beat the butter to a cream; dredge in the flour; add the sugar, mace, nutmeg and caraway seeds, and mix these ingredients well together. Whisk the eggs, stir into them the brandy, and beat the cake again for 10 minutes. Put it into a tin lined with buttered paper, and bake it from 1½ to 2 hours.

(This cake is equally nice made with currants, and omitting the caraway seeds.)

DOLLY MADISON'S BOUILLON

Four pounds of juicy beef, one knuckle of veal, two small turnips, two small carrots, one soup bunch, one small pod of red pepper, two small white onions, salt, six quarts of water. Simmer for six hours, then strain through a fine sieve. Let stand overnight to congeal. Skim off all the grease; put in a kettle to heat and just before serving, add sherry to taste.

DOLLY MADISON'S LAYER CAKE

The whites of eight eggs beaten stiff, two and a half cups of sugar, one small cup of butter, one cup of milk, three quarters of a cup of cornstarch, three cups of flour, two and a half teaspoonfuls of vanilla. This amount makes four layers.

CARAMEL (for between layers)

Three cups of brown sugar; one cup of sweet cream; butter the size of an egg; one teaspoon of vanilla just before removing from the fire. Cook in double boiler for twenty minutes. If not as much as desired add sugar.

Receptions held on New Year's Day and on the Fourth of July are said to have brought "sturdy patriots from near and far." The one held on January 1, 1813, was one of the most imposing ever held in the Executive Mansion, according to biographers. The French minister arrived in a huge coach that resembled a great golden ball on wings. His footmen were resplendent in gold livery and gilded swords. The clothing of the guests was "rich and elegant" and the affair "widely attended."

Dolly apparently outdid her own former magnificence on that occasion, for she wore a gown of rose-colored satin trimmed in ermine, and a velvet turban of the same shade ornamented with a jeweled crescent and white ostrich plumes.

It was about this time that Samuel Harrison Smith sold the *National Intelligencer* to William Seaton and his brother-in-law, Joseph Gales, of Raleigh, North Carolina. These young gentlemen (Seaton was only twenty-four and Gales about the same age) turned the paper from a triweekly into a daily. Seaton's pretty young wife, Sarah (Joseph's sister), became the unofficial society reporter, a position formerly held by Mrs. Smith. Her letters to her mother in Raleigh have since been of inestimable value to historians. The first of these, written October 12, 1812, shortly after her arrival in Washington, informs us:

> That afternoon the first drawing-room of the season was held at the White House. William was much solicited to attend, but like a good husband, preferred remaining at home with his wife, as I have not yet been presented to her Majesty and it not being etiquette to appear in public 'till that ceremony is performed.

Once this had been rectified, Mrs. Seaton's prolific letter writing established a record of the doings of the vivacious Mrs. Madison that was to delight writers of a future day.

Here is her description of tea:

It is customary to breakfast at nine, dine at four and drink tea at eight. I am more surprised at method of taking tea here than any other meal. In private families, if you step in of an evening, they give you tea and crackers, or cold bread; and if by invitation, unless the party is very splendid, you have a few sweet-cakes, macaroons from the confectioners. This is the extent. Once I saw a ceremony of preserves at tea; but the deficiency is made up by the style of dinner.

And of the "style of dinner," she wrote:

On Tuesday, William and I repaired to the "palace" between four and five o'clock, our carriage setting us down after the first comers and before the last. It is customary, on whatever occasion, to advance to the upper end of the room, pay your obeisance to Mrs. Madison, curtsey to his highness, and take a seat, after this ceremony being at liberty to speak to acquaintances or amuse yourself as at another party. The party already assembled consisted of the Treasurer of the United States; Mr. Russell, the American Minister to England; Mr. Cutts, brother-in-law of Mrs. Madison; General Van Ness and family; General Smith and daughter from New York; Patrick Magruder's family; Col. Goodwine and daughter; Mr. Coles, the private secretary; Washington Irving, the author of "Knickerbocker" and "Salmagundi"; Mr. Thomas, an European; Mr. Poindexter, William R. King, and two other gentlemen, and these, with Mr. and Mrs. Madison and Payne Todd, her son, completed the select company.

Mrs. Madison very handsomely came to me and led me nearest the fire, introduced Mrs. Magruder, and sat down between us, politely conversing on familiar subjects, and by her own ease of manner making her guests feel at home. Mr. King came to our side, sans ceremonie, and gayly chatted with us until dinner was announced. Mrs. Magruder, by priority of age, was entitled to the right hand of her hostess, and I, in virtue of being a stranger, to the next seat, Mr. Russell to her left, Mr. Coles at the foot of the table, the President in the middle, which relieves him from the trouble of receiving guests, drinking wine, etc. The dinner was certainly very fine, but still I was rather surprised as it did not surpass some I have eaten in Carolina. There were many French dishes and exquisite wines, I presume, by the praises bestowed upon them; but I have been so little accustomed to drink that I could not discern the difference between sherry and rare old Burgundy madeira. Comment on the quality of the wine seems to form the chief topic after the removal of the cloth and during the dessert, at which by the way, no pastry is countenanced. Ice creams, macaroons, preserves and various cakes are placed on the table, which are removed for almonds, raisins, pecan nuts, apples, pears, etc. Candles were introduced before the ladies left the table, and the gentlemen continued half an hour longer to drink a social glass.

Meantime Mrs. Madison insisted on my playing on her elegant grand piano a waltz for Miss Smith and Miss Magruder to dance, the figure of which she instructed them in. By this time the gentlemen came in, and we adjourned to the tea room; and here in the most delightful manner imaginable I shared with Miss Smith, who is remarkably intelligent, the pleasure of Mrs. Madison's conversation on books, men and manners, literature in general, and many special branches of knowledge. I never spent a more rational or pleasant half hour than that which preceded our return home. On paying our compliments at parting we were politely invited to attend the levee the next evening. I would describe the dignified appearance of Mrs. Madison, but I fear it is the woman altogether whom I should wish you to see. She wears a crimson cap that almost hides her forehead, but which becomes her extremely and reminds one of a crown from its brilliant appearance, contrasted with the white satin folds and her jet-black curls.

Ceremonious dinners were given to the members of the Cabinet and to the diplomatic corps, but Mrs. Madison delighted in small dinner parties made up of her intimate friends, mixed with distinguished guests who happened to be in the city. She selected her guests with care both for the sake of congeniality and in order to keep her social gatherings as free from ceremony as possible.

At such affairs, servants were plentiful. Slave waiters from neighboring plantations were hired at thirty-five cents each for the evening, and one was assigned to each guest at the dinner table. Food was so plentiful at Mrs. Madison's dinners that Mrs. Merry thought her table "more like a harvest-home."

The first marriage in the White House took place during Madison's administration. Mrs. Madison's sister, Lucy Payne Washington, widow of Phillip Steptoe Washington, married

Thomas Todd of Kentucky, then Justice of the United States Supreme Court, on March 11, 1811. Dolly, according to Charles Bagot, the new British minister, apparently stole the show, for he described the First Lady as "looking every inch the queen."

The "most profuse" ball given in Washington up to January, 1813, was not held at the White House. It was given by the Secretary of the Treasury, Albert Gallatin, at his residence. According to Mrs. Seaton, Gallatin went all out as far as food was concerned. Wrote the twenty-three-year-old Sarah:

> I am sure not ten minutes elapsed without refreshments being handed. 1st, coffee, tea, all kinds of toast and warm cakes; 2nd, ice-creams; 3rd, lemonade, punch, burgundy, claret, curacao, champagne; 4th, bonbons, cakes of all sorts and sizes; 5th, apples, oranges; 6th, confectionery, denomination divers; 7th, nuts, almonds, raisins; 8th, set supper, composed of tempting solid dishes, meats, savory pasties garnished with lemon; 9th, drinkables of every species; 10th, boiling chocolate. . . . The assembly was more numerous, more select, and more elegant than at any time ever before seen in the city.

The War of 1812 had little effect on presidential entertaining until the British burned the Executive Mansion on August 24, 1814. There is an interesting, if confusing, story connected with the arrival of the British. According to an English writer named Gleig, they "found a bountiful dinner spread for forty guests. This they concluded was for the American officers who were expected to return victorious from the field of Bladensburg." (Naturally, the British soldiers ate the dinner before plundering the mansion and setting it afire!) This story has since been pronounced absolutely false, and Mrs. Madison's letter to her sister dated August 23 would indicate that the preparation of a large dinner was the last thing she would have concerned herself with at such a time. In part, her letter reads:

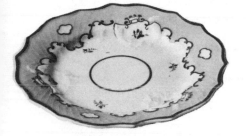

Decorated in blue and gold, this tea set served Dolly Madison during her career as First Lady. The set is now in the collections of the U. S. National Museum in Washington.

Tuesday, August 23, 1814.

Dear Sister:

My husband left me yesterday to join General Winder. He enquired anxiously whether I had the courage or firmness to remain in the President's house until his return tomorrow, or succeeding day, and on my assurance that I had no fear but for him and the success of our army, he left me, beseeching me to take care of myself and of the Cabinet papers, public and private.

I have since received two dispatches from him, written with pencil; the last is alarming, because he desires that I should be ready at a moment's warning, to enter my carriage and leave the city; that the enemy seemed stronger than had been reported. . . . I am accordingly ready . . .

Wednesday morning, twelve o'clock. Since sunrise, I have been turning my spy-glass in every direction and watching with unwearied anxiety, hoping to discover the approach of my dear husband and his friends; but, alas, I can descry only groups of military wandering in all directions, as if there was a lack of arms, or of spirits, to fight for their own firesides.

Three o'clock. Will you believe it, my sister, we have had a battle, or a skirmish, near Bladensburg, and I am still here within sound of the cannon! Mr. Madison comes not; may God protect him! Two messengers, covered with dust, come to bid me fly; but I wait for him. . . .

Her letter continues with details of the preparation: the wagon loaded with valuables, the removal of General Washington's picture from the wall, the "two gentlemen of New York" to whom the portrait was entrusted, her own preparations for departure.

It would seem that no thought could have been given to preparing a large dinner; but Paul Jennings, a slave belonging to Mr. Madison, published a book in 1865 entitled *A Colored Man's Reminiscences of James Madison,* in which he corroborates in some detail Gleig's story of the feast. Many of his statements conflict with Dolly Madison's, and it is not possible to overlook the fact that he probably wrote his reminiscences many years after the event; however, he was there, and he says, "I set the table myself."

This photograph of Octagon House was taken in 1936, but the building has not changed in appearance since James and Dolly Madison moved in in 1814 after the burning of the Executive Mansion.

While the destruction of the Executive Mansion was generally mourned, those who had looked askance at what they considered the wastefulness and extravagance of the Madison administration expressed their opinions, one of which was:

> The destruction of the President's House cannot be a great loss in one point of view, as we hope it will put an end to drawing-rooms and levees; the resort of the idle and the encouragers of spies and traitors.

These critics were to be disappointed, however, for although Dolly and her husband now lived in closer quarters at the Tayloe house—which was known as the "Octagon House" —there was no letup in entertaining, according to Mrs. Seaton:

> The winter will be extremely gay and decked with the splendor of polished manners . . . and the drawing-rooms will sparkle . . . Mr. Jefferson's granddaughter, Miss Randolph, will lead the van in accomplishments and beauty. . . . There is every reason to expect a crowded and interesting winter, as it will be the first meeting of Congress since the peace. Mrs. Madison tells me that there will be a great many foreigners of distinction here.

During the last year of "Jemmy" Madison's first term as President, one professional observer, Mrs. Seaton, gave this description of Washington life:

> Ladies of fifty years of age [at a state ball] were decked with lace and ribbons, wreaths of roses and gold leaves in their false hair, wreaths of jasmine across their bosom, and no kerchiefs! [Though] the splendid dress of these antiquated dames of the *beau monde* adds to the general grandeur, it certainly only tends to make the contrast still more striking between them and the young and beautiful. . . . This incongruity of dress extends to young girls, and is equally incompatible with general propriety. Madame Joseph Bonaparte is a model of fashion, and many of our belles strive to imitate her, but without equal *éclat* as she has certainly the most transcendently beautiful back and shoulders that ever were seen. . . . It is the fashion for most of

the ladies a little advanced in age to rouge and pearl, which is spoken of with as much *sang-froid* as putting on their bonnets. Mrs. Monroe paints very much, and has besides, an appearance of youth which would induce a stranger to suppose her age to be thirty: in lieu of which, she introduces them to her daughter and even her granddaughter, eighteen or nineteen years old. . . . Mrs. Madison is said to rouge; but not evident to my eyes, and I do not think it is true, as I am well assured I saw her color come and go at the naval ball, when the Mace-donian flag was presented to her by young Hamilton. Mrs. C. and Mrs. G. paint excessively, and think it becoming; but with them it is no deception, only folly, and they speak of it as indispensable to a decent appearance.

Madison's inauguration for his second term—on March 4, 1813—took place in a crowded capital city. In giving his address, the President's "voice was so low and the audience so very great that scarcely a word could be distinguished. On concluding, the oath of office was administered by the Chief Justice, and the little man was accompanied on his return to the Palace by the multitude; for every creature that could afford twenty-five cents for hack-hire was present," wrote Mrs. Seaton.

The majority of the respectable citizens then offered him their congratulations, ate his ice creams and bonbons, drank his Madeira, made their bows, and retired, leaving him "fatigued beyond measure with the incessant bending to which politeness urged him, and in which he never allows himself to be eclipsed, returning bow for bow, even to those ad infinitum of Serrurier and other foreigners."

The story is told that Dolly Madison offered her snuff box to the French ambassador, and, as he stooped over it with courtly grace, whipped out a red bandanna and a marvelous lace handkerchief!

James Madison went out of office before the new Executive Mansion was ready for occupancy, and the next President, James Monroe, came into office in 1817.

V

Tempest in the Social Teapot

James and Elizabeth Monroe

James Monroe was the first President to occupy the rebuilt mansion after its burning by the British; it was not ready for him, however, until the autumn of 1817, months after his inauguration. In the meantime he lived at 2017 Eye Street, N.W.

Shortly before Monroe's inauguration, Congress had appropriated money for refurnishing the Executive Mansion. All of the pieces used since Washington's Presidency had been destroyed in the fire nearly three years before. Reconstruction of the Executive Mansion itself had begun in 1815 under the direction of James Hoban, the original designer. It was a monumental job, since the entire building had been destroyed except for its exterior sandstone walls and the interior brickwork. Even these were seriously damaged, ironically, by an act of nature: the walls were still hot when a heavy rain came pouring down on them, resulting in extensive cracking. It was at the time of this restoration that the outside walls of the Executive Mansion were painted white.

The East Room was still unfinished when the Monroes moved into the White House in December of 1817. The President and his wife were, however, determined that the mansion should have all the accoutrements of gracious living so, over and above Congress' appropriation, they sold their own collection of fine French pieces to the government and ordered additional furniture, china, and silver—both ornaments and essentials—from France. Each piece was chosen with a connoisseur's eye not only to comfort and beauty, but to the lasting service and enjoyment of future occupants of the White House.

When his two-term administration ended in 1825, Monroe repurchased his original possessions from the government at the price he had received for them, and today a large number of these pieces can be seen at the James Monroe Law Office Museum in Fredericksburg, Virginia, which was opened by Laurence Gouverneur Hoes, Monroe's great-great-grandson, and his mother, Mrs. Rose Gouverneur Hoes, who inherited the furniture. Mrs. Hoes was also the founder of the collection of "Dresses of the First Ladies of the Land" now in the United States National Museum, she herself collecting up through the Coolidge administration.

The sun shone bright on the morning that Monroe took his oath of office, out of doors before a crowd of eight thousand persons, the largest inaugural crowd up to that time. But clouds gathered when the new First Lady courageously refused to be bullied into continuing customs which she considered burdensome and unnecessary. Among these was the practice established by Dolly Madison (and often regretted) of making the first call. Elizabeth Kortright Monroe refused not only to make the first call, but to return calls, a chore she relegated to her lovely elder daughter, Mrs. George Hay.

So bold a flaunting of tradition brought the wrath of so-cially-conscious, party-loving Washington upon Elizabeth Monroe's head. This upsetting of an old custom proved "bit-

"To the Honourable James Monroe, Esquire, from His Friends and Admirers Associated, London, 1803," reads the inscription on this tray made
in 1794–1795 by Peter and Ann Bateman, Silversmiths. The Sheffield punch
bowl was probably presented to Monroe when he was minister to England
(1803–1807). The silver ladle, initialed "M," was made in Edinburgh in 1806.

ter to the palates of all our old citizens," Mrs. Seaton wrote, and the "petty and provincial Washington" of that day took revenge on Mrs. Monroe, who "had the good sense to see that life would be intolerable to any woman in her place who undertook to return all the calls made upon her." To this day the same custom prevails—much to the credit of Mrs. Monroe, who stood firm despite the criticism heaped on her.

President Monroe actually made the social question the subject of a formal Cabinet consultation, because he received a complaint that the wife of the Secretary of State, Mrs. John Quincy Adams, neglected her duty in omitting to make the first call on the wives of senators and representatives in Congress. When the Cabinet was not able to reach an agreement as to "the right and wrong of this profound subject," the Secretary wrote the President that he would be "unworthy of confidence if I had a heart insensible to social obligations"; that he had been "five years a member of the Senate, and thought I knew the duties and privileges of a Senator's wife"; that "formality does not appear to me congenial to the republican simplicity of our institutions"; and finally, that unless the President overruled him, "Mrs. Adams could not take upon herself the responsibility of making first calls."

The straw that broke the camel's back was the marriage of Elizabeth's younger daughter, seventeen-year-old Maria, to the socially prominent Samuel L. Gouverneur of New York, Mrs. Monroe's nephew. Washington society, agog over the coming nuptials of the first President's daughter to be married in the White House, had planned several large balls, the first one to be given by the Commodore Stephen Decaturs. When, in February, Mrs. Seaton wrote that the wedding was to be "entirely private," and later asserted the reason was to be found "in the question of precedence and etiquette," the storm broke.

The wedding took place on March 9, 1820. John Quincy Adams wrote in his diary:

Samuel Lawrence Gouverneur of New York was this day married to Maria Hester Monroe. . . . There has been some further question of etiquette upon this occasion. The foreign Ministers were uncertain whether it was expected they should pay their compliments on the marriage or not, and Poletica, the Russian Minister, made the inquiry of Mrs. Adams. She applied to Mrs. Hay, the President's eldest daughter who has lived in his home ever since he has been President but never visits at the houses of any of the foreign Ministers, because their ladies did not pay her first calls. Mrs. Hay thought her youngest sister could not receive and return visits which she herself could not reciprocate, and therefore that no foreign Minister should take notice of the marriage, which was accordingly communicated to them.

After the wedding Mrs. Seaton wrote:

The New York style was adopted at Maria Monroe's wedding. Only attendants, the relatives and a few old friends of the bride and groom witnessed the ceremony. . . . The bridesmaids were told their company and services would be dispensed with until the following Tuesday, when the bride would receive visitors. Accordingly, all who visit at the President's paid their respects to Mrs. Gouverneur, who presided in her mother's place on this evening while Mrs. Monroe mingled with the other citizens. Every visitor was led to the bride and introduced.

The bridal festivities received a check about two weeks later, when Commodore Stephen Decatur was killed in a duel with Commodore James Barron. The *National Intelligencer* expressed the shocked sorrow of the Capital City:

Mourn Columbia! for one of the brightest stars has set, a son without fear and without reproach.

Commodore and Mrs. Decatur had given their ball, but invitations sent out by Commodore Porter, Van Ness, and others were remanded. Even the announcement of Maria's wedding was simplified to a modest notice in the papers:

> Married on Thursday evening last in this city by the Rev. Mr.
> Hawley, Samuel Lawrence Gouverneur, Esq. of New York to Miss
> Maria Hester Monroe, youngest daughter of James Monroe, President of the United States.

Washington society, outraged at being deprived of the most important event of the season, the first wedding of a President's daughter in the White House, expressed its annoyance by practically boycotting the Monroes during their entire first term. Even as early as December 18, 1819, practically three months before the wedding, Mrs. Seaton wrote: "The drawing-room of the President was opened last night to a beggarly row of empty chairs. Only five females attended, three of whom were foreigners."

The snub extended to Mrs. Adams. She had invited a large number to her home the previous week. Only three attended. The President fared no better; those attending his dinners usually comprised only personal friends and political supporters. John Quincy Adams, Secretary of State, worked to his wits' end trying to restore peace among the ladies, but it was not until Monroe's second term that society's resentment simmered down and the drawing-rooms and receptions were well attended.

The New Year's Day reception of 1821 drew the biggest crowd that had ever attended a White House function. The President, with his wife and two daughters, stood near the door to greet their guests as they entered. Samuel Lawrence Gouverneur, the President's private secretary, and George Hay, his elder daughter's husband (who prosecuted Aaron Burr at his trial for treason) were much in evidence.

But even this gracious gesture failed to stop the criticism of a few die-hard faultfinders. Monroe's knee breeches, silk hose, and silver-buckled shoes were described as "old-fashioned" in an era of pantaloons (trousers), which had come into fashion during Jefferson's administration. Monroe continued to wear this type of Revolutionary clothing until his death on July 4, 1831. He was known as the last of the "Cocked Hats."

The First Lady, however, was lovely in black velvet and pearls, her hair piled high in fashionable puffs and ornamented with ostrich plumes. "She was," Mrs. Seaton wrote, "discreetly rouged and very youthful looking to be the mother of grown daughters." Mrs. Hay wore crimson velvet, and Maria, as befitted a bride, was exquisite in white satin trimmed in silver lace. Both girls wore necklaces of pearls, and ostrich plumes in their hair. Wine was served on large silver salvers.

In the Monroe household, dining was a fine art. The dinner hour was six o'clock and the food superb. They preferred French cookery and the French style of serving, although it was "a little Americanized," according to author James Fenimore Cooper, who was a frequent guest at the Monroe table. Cooper wrote:

> Some of the guests prefer to help themselves but usually the dishes are handed around.
>
> Of attendants there were a good many. They were neatly dressed, out of livery, and sufficient. To conclude, the whole entertainment might have passed for a better sort of European dinner party, at which the guests were too numerous for general or very agreeable discourse, and some of them too new to be entirely at their ease. Mrs. Monroe arose at the end of the dessert, and withdrew, attended by two or three of the most gallant of the company. No sooner was his wife's back turned than the President reseated himself, inviting his guests to imitate the action. After allowing his guests sufficient time to renew, in a few glasses, the recollections of similar enjoyment of their own, he arose, giving the hint to his company that it was time to rejoin the ladies. In the drawing room coffee was served, and every one left the house before nine.

Monroe's table was formal and beautifully appointed. Like Washington, he preferred the mirrored plateau (*surtout de table*) as a centerpiece, and ordered one from France at a cost of six thousand francs. It was valued at two hundred dollars in an "estimate of furniture in the President's House" at the time. Matching candelabra, fruit *epergnes,* and vases for flowers were also ordered.

The plateau is in seven pieces. Extended its full length, it is thirteen and a half feet long and two feet wide. The rim is bronze decorated in garlands of fruit and vines. At equidistant intervals around the rim are figures of Bacchus and Bacchantes upholding crystal vases for flowers and crowns for candles. These are removable, allowing for varied decorations.

The plateau, silver plated when purchased but later gilded by Van Buren, was referred to as a "silver waiter" by Mrs. Smith Thompson, wife of Monroe's Secretary of the Navy, who, in describing a dinner party, wrote:

> We had the most stylish dinner I have been at. The table was wider than we have and in the middle was a large, perhaps silver, waiter with images like some Aunt Silsbee has, only more of them. Vases filled with flowers made a very showy appearance as the candles were lighted when we went to the table. The dishes [meaning dishes of food] were silver and set around this waiter. The plates were handsome china [President Monroe had ordered enough china to serve thirty people], the forks silver and so heavy you could call them clumsy things.

Monroe had a recipe for a non-alcoholic mint julep:

MINT JULEP

½ pint grape juice
½ pint orange juice
½ cup chopped mint
1 pint charged water
Juice of 6 lemons or limes

Mix fruit juice and mint and stand on ice one hour. A dash of sugar to taste. Add water and pour into glasses half filled with ice. A sprig of mint in each glass and serve at once.

Oak Hill

In refurbishing the White House after it was burned in 1814, Monroe purchased this mirrored surtout de table from France for six thousand francs. The plateau, still in use, is in seven pieces and measures nearly fourteen feet full length. The Bacchanalian figures are removable.

The above recipe was given to the author by Mr. Laurence Gouverneur Hoes, whose mother had copied it, with others, from the Monroe recipes as they appeared in Martha Jefferson Randolph's manuscript cookbook. Mrs. Samuel Laurence Gouverneur, Monroe's granddaughter, had borrowed the book from Mrs. Randolph's daughter; Mrs. Hoes was only fourteen at the time—too young, she wrote, to appreciate the book's value.

James Monroe established for the diplomats a protocol described by his Secretary of State as "exceedingly formal and stately." Jefferson and Madison had permitted social visits, but Monroe received diplomats only at private audiences upon request, and at the drawing-rooms and diplomatic dinners held once or twice during the winter. Like the European sovereigns, he received standing. Ministers were required to appear in court dress.

The stately etiquette upon which Monroe insisted had favorable repercussions abroad, although it was resented in Washington. The British and French had long awed lesser nations by such tactics; now, equaled at their own game, they developed a wholesome respect for our young nation and from then on ceased to refer to us as "Colonials."

When the Monroes left the White House and retired to Oak Hill, Virginia, they were far more popular than when they entered.

The porcelain chocolate cups and saucers are the only known remaining pieces of Monroe's official china. The only known pieces of plate still extant are the cruet stand, circa 1819, maker unknown, and three silver caps made in London by Joseph Wilson at approximately the same time. The pair of Sheffield candlesticks, circa 1795, bear the Monroe family crest.

VI

Puritan Heritage vs.
Popular Parties

John Quincy and Louisa Adams

On March 4, 1825, John Quincy Adams took the oath of office as the sixth President of the United States. The White House, which had welcomed his father as its first occupant, now opened its doors to Abigail's and John's son and his wife, the former Louisa Catherine Johnson, daughter of the American consul in London, whom he had married in 1797.

Adams, whose diplomatic career had started at the age of fourteen, when he was appointed to a post as secretary to the minister to Russia, was known as "Old Man Eloquent." He and the new First Lady lost no time in "taking the chill" off the White House. Both, no doubt, felt that the adoption of the Monroe social policies was a "must," since Monroe had been able to quell Washington's tempest in the social teapot.

Though he was punctilious in matters of etiquette, the new President's doors were open to all. Both he and Louisa Adams had practically grown up in European courts; he had crossed the ocean four times by the age of twelve, and by seventeen had traveled over the greater part of Europe. Louisa, who was born in London of an English mother and American father whose home was in Maryland (her uncle had been governor of that state and a signer of the Declaration of Independence), had received every educational advantage. She could read French, English, and Greek literature, wrote verse, loved music, and had a cultivated voice. Biographers give her no credit for beauty, but her charm was enviable—though "she was just too retiring and scholarly to be a popular First Lady."

The President's heritage of the simple, devout, and intelligent traits of his Puritan family and his love of gardening, horseback riding, and swimming no doubt explain why he chafed under his duties as the nation's host. He entered in his diary February 20, 1828:

> This evening was the sixth drawing-room. Very much crowded; sixteen Senators, perhaps sixty members of the House of Representatives and multitudes of strangers—among whom were the Institutors of Deaf and Dumb from Philadelphia, New York and Hartford. The heat was oppressive and these parties are becoming more and more insupportable to me.

However, when the President and Mrs. Adams did entertain it was usually lavish. The most outstanding party of their career was a ball given January 8, 1824—when Adams was Secretary of State under Monroe—honoring General Andrew Jackson on the anniversary of his victory at New Orleans. It was noted as one of the most brilliant entertainments that had ever been seen in Washington.

Mrs. Adams is described as "elegantly but not gorgeously" dressed; her headdress and plumes were "tastefully arranged." Eight hundred guests attended. The ladies climbed up on chairs and benches to see the General. To help them get a better view, Louisa Adams gracefully took the General's

This portrait of Mrs. John Quincy Adams was done by Charles Bird King.
The harp, music books, and music stand were owned by Mrs. Adams.

arm and promenaded with him through the apartments.

At ten o'clock the doors of a spacious dining room were opened to disclose the table loaded with "refreshments of every description, served up in elegant style, of which the company were invited to partake without ceremony."

President and Mrs. Adams held a levee every other Wednesday evening. E. Cooley, in his *Etiquette at Washington City,* published in 1829, describes the etiquette of the levee thus:

Gentlemen and ladies both attend, arrive about 8:00 and leave around 10:00. No lady goes by herself, but sometimes one gentleman waits on two but most commonly only one. They mostly all stand, or move around the rooms; the ladies always resting on the left arm of the gentleman, when he attends to only one. The guests, on arrival, find the President and his Lady standing in the upper part of the same room (saloon), but at some distance apart with some of their particular friends at their side. The guests all make their way through the crowd, toward the President, and salute him; and those of his acquaintance shake hands with him, and then pass on to salute his Lady.

There is no established rule, or formal regulation for the support of order, more than that which prevails in other assemblages of fashionable and genteel people, in other places of the city.

There are three large furnished rooms, besides the two antichambers (the middle one is round, and is called the saloon) where the President and his Lady receive their guests; which are generally all so full, that it is with much delay, and edging difficulty, that a gentleman can get through to the upper end of the saloon to salute the President.

The company is treated with coffee, tea and a variety of cakes, jellies, ice-cream, and white and red wine, mixed and unmixed, and sometimes other cordials and liquors, and frequently with West India fruit; all of which are carried about the rooms amongst the guests, upon large trays by servants dressed in livery; each one takes from it what he pleases, when an opportunity offers, which, at some of the fullest levees, may not happen very often; not because there is any scarcity of refreshment, but the difficulty the waiters find in making their way through the crowd with their trays. . . . After some part of the company have retired, so as to give more room for the waiters to move freely about the rooms with refreshments, everyone is furnished bountifully; which shows that the articles were not wanting so much as an opportunity of presenting them freely to the guests.

At the President's levees there is commonly no other amusement but conversation, so that those who happen to be quite strangers, are merely spectators; and at every levee there are many of that class, so that the novelty, or the presumed honour of being one of a party of the highest order in the United States, are all the inducements that an entire stranger has to go there.

Mr. Adams usually arose between four and six o'clock, according to the season, and took a ride on horseback or a walk to the Potomac river, where he bathed. He entered in his diary on April 13, 1827:

> I have already been tempted by the prevailing warm weather to bathe in the Potomac, but have been deterred by the catarrh still hanging on me, and by the warnings of physicians, whose doctrines are not in harmony with my experience. I took, however, for this morning's walk the direction of the river, and visited the rock whence I most frequently go into the river. It is yet adapted to the purpose; but all trace of the old sycamore tree, which was near it, and blew down the winter before last, is gone. There is yet one standing a little below, but it is undermined with every high tide, and must be soon overthrown. . . .

The rock under the sycamore tree was the point from whence John Quincy Adams probably gave the most embarrassing interview of his career. According to *Ladies of the Press,* by Ishbel Ross, the indomitable and termagant Anne Royall, a newspaper woman, pursued him to the river early one morning to get a story. Finding the President clad only in his skin, she parked herself "on his clothes as he bathed . . . and refused to budge until he had answered her questions."

Old books about Washington make mention of Anne. In 1903 there were still those who could recall the crazy hag with the sharp, strident voice. Wearing thick worsted mittens from which "claws protruded," always carrying her green cotton umbrella and her newspaper subscription book, she was a poor, ludicrous figure. Her green calash dress in summer and shabby shawls and cloak in winter rendered all the more striking the wrinkled, swarthy, rawboned face of this woman who had struggled so bravely against hard times. To Washington she was a freak—a combination of town character and town nuisance—loved in the one aspect and hated in the other. She was an aggressive person with no mind for clothes, and if she had been clothes-minded, she had no money to buy them.

"I can see her now tramping through the halls of the old Capitol, umbrella (it was a large green one) in hand, seizing upon every passerby, and offering her book for sale," wrote John Forney in his *Anecdotes of Public Men*. Any public man who refused to buy was certain of a severe philippic in her newspaper.

"We have the famous Mrs. Royall here," wrote Justice Story to Mrs. Story, on the eighth of March, 1827, "with her new novel, 'The Tennesseans,' which she has compelled the Chief Justice and myself to buy to avoid castigation. I shall bring it home for your edification."

Sarah Harver Porter, in her book, *The Life and Times of Anne Royall,* states that Adams really "liked and respected the courageous woman whom he had known since the week of her arrival." Mrs. Porter's book also contains a letter addressed by Anne to John Quincy Adams in which she saluted him as "Most Valued Friend," and ended with "Your grateful friend." The President once called Anne a "Virago errant in enchanted armor," but the Adamses were very nearly the only people of any importance who treated Anne Royall with courtesy. Others coldly shut the door in her face, but Adams took her in, subscribed to her forthcoming book, agreed to do his best for her pension (which she finally did succeed in getting) and, above all, asked her to call on Mrs. Adams.

Short, bald, and rotund, Adams had none of the social graces. A man who usually began his day by reading two or three chapters of the Bible, with Scott's and Hewlett's Com-

*During his administration John Quincy Adams used this china, which he pur-
chased in Germany. Shown here is a Royal Meissen state service dinner plate.
The two saltcellars are from Mrs. John Adams' blue and white Saxony dinner set. These may be seen today in the White House china room.*

mentaries, he was "cold, aloof, self-centered, suspicious and censorious in his relations with all the world, but in his family relationship he was one of the most affectionate and devoted of sons, husbands, and fathers," says Bennett Champ Clark in his *John Quincy Adams*. He was "negligent, sometimes even slovenly in his dress; a proficient linguist; had a penchant for emphasizing the gloomy aspect of events and cared nothing for society, although he had passed so many years in the most fashionable European courts that he was as completely master of the intricacies of etiquette and social conventions as of diplomatic punctilio."

Benjamin Perley Poor, a noted journalist of his day, tells us in his *Reminiscences* that during Adams' administration the Washington assemblies were ceremonious and exclusive. Admission was obtained only by cards of invitation, issued after long consultation among the committeemen—and, once inside the exclusive ring, the "beaux and belles bowed to the disciplinary rule of a master of ceremonies." No gentleman, whatever his rank or calling, was permitted on the floor unless in full evening dress, with "pumps, silk-stockings, and flowing cravat, unless he belonged to the Army or Navy, in which case complete regimentals covered a multitude of sins."

The *Reminiscences* of "Perley" continue:

> "Minuet de la cour" and stately "quadrille," varied by the "basket dance," and, on exceptional occasions, the exhilarating "cheat," formed the staple for saltatorial performance, until the hour of eleven brought the concluding country dance when a final squad of roysterers bobbed "up the middle and down again" to the airs of "Sir Roger de Coverly" or "Money Musk." The music was furnished by colored performers on the violin, except on great occasions when some of the Marine Band played an accompaniment on flutes and clarinets. The refreshments were iced lemonade, ice-cream, Port wine, negus, and small cakes, served in a room adjoining the dancing hall, or brought in by colored domestics, or by the cavalier in his own proper person, who ofttimes appeared upon the dancing floor, elbowing his way to the lady of his adoration, in the one hand bearing well filled glasses, and in the other a plate heaped up with cakes.

The Washington Star

This drawing by Bob Hoke appeared in the Washington Star with the caption, "President John Quincy Adams was a student of astronomy and had a telescope mounted on the White House roof to study the stars."

The costume of a lady was a classic in scantiness, especially at balls and parties. The fashionable ball-dress was of "white India crape and five breadths, each a quarter of a yard wide which came to the ankles, elaborately trimmed with a dozen or more rows of narrow flounces. Silver or cotton stockings adorned with embroidered 'clocks,' and thin slippers were ornamented with silk rosettes and tiny buckles."

When in full dress, men wore "dress-coats with enormous collars and short waists, well-stuffed white cambric cravats, small-clothes, or tight-fitting pantaloons, silk stockings and pumps."

John Quincy Adams is credited with having proposed the first toast ever drunk at a dinner in the President's House. It was on September 6, 1825 (Lafayette's birthday), when Lafayette was the "Nation's guest." Adams rose, and as the scarlet-coated Marine Band broke softly into the *Marseillaise,* he bowed to his distinguished guest, saying: "The Twenty-Second of February and the Sixth of September."

To this Lafayette responded gallantly: "The Fourth of July, the birthday of liberty in both hemispheres."

The last New Year's Day party to be given by John Quincy and his wife took place on January 1, 1829. Mrs. Seaton wrote: "On no former occasion have we witnessed a greater crowd, nor have we ever seen the annual tributes of good feeling offered with more apparent sincerity on the one hand, or received with more evident satisfaction and cheerfulness on the other. . . ."

The election of Jackson disappointed Adams, and he showed it by staying away from Jackson's inauguration ceremonies. He left the Executive Mansion on the third of March, 1829. The next day, the booming of cannon announcing that Jackson had taken the oath of office found Adams, aloof and bitter, on a horse, taking his daily ride.

VII

Old Hickory
and the Social Whirl

Andrew Jackson

Twenty thousand admirers, arriving in everything from fringed buckskin and coonskin capes to formal attire, poured through the doors of the White House, and when the rooms became packed with them they crashed through the windows. They wrecked furniture, spilled food on expensive rugs, ripped draperies, and even tore one another's clothing as they surged forward for a closer glimpse of their hero.

Andrew Jackson, a frontiersman, simple in heart and manner, whose military exploits at Talladega, the Horseshoe, and New Orleans had made him the idol of the people, had generously offered to share his triumph with the nation at a reception after his inauguration on March 4, 1829. But the new President had not anticipated that his devotees would almost tear him limb from limb in their intoxicated demonstrations of affection! Appalled, he finally managed, with the help of a cordon of friends, to elude the horde and escape through a rear door. Eventually the merrymakers were coaxed

89

outside by the device of tubs of punch set up on the lawn.

Other receptions that took place during Jackson's eight years in office were more decorous, although they lacked the polish and formality of those of many earlier administrations. His wife, Rachel Donelson Robards, whom he married in 1791, had died three months before he took office, and he had little heart for ceremonious entertaining the first year. Conscious, however, of his obligations, he delegated the duties of hospitality to Mrs. Emily Donelson, wife of Major Andrew Jackson Donelson, his wife's nephew, whom they had adopted as a child. The auburn-haired Emily, who came to the Executive Mansion as a raw country girl from Tennessee, developed within a short time into one of the most charming and capable of White House hostesses. Her husband became the President's secretary.

Major William B. Lewis (a former neighbor and confidante) and his family also took up residence in the spacious Executive Mansion at the request of the lonely President, and Major Lewis was made Second Auditor of the Treasury. His pretty daughter, Delia, was married in the White House in 1833 to Alphonse de Pageot, then Secretary of the French legation and later French minister to the United States. The wedding was notable for its simplicity. Guests were limited to members of the diplomatic corps, the President's Cabinet, Justices of the Supreme Court, and a few personal friends and relatives.

The popular Mary Easten (a young cousin of Mrs. Jackson's whom she had planned to bring with her to the White House, and a great pet of the General's), had been married in the mansion in April, 1832, to Lucius J. Polk, a relative of James K. Polk.

Although Andrew Jackson was a soldier, accustomed to the privations and hardships of army life, there was nothing spartan about the food served in the Executive Mansion. An hour before dinner, wine and "whets" were placed on a table in

Auburn-haired Mrs. Emily Donelson, the wife of Mrs. Jackson's nephew, served as Andrew Jackson's official White House hostess. Rachel Jackson had died of angina pectoris three months before her husband took office.

the Red Room. The meals were prepared by Michael Anthony Guista, a French chef whom John Quincy Adams had employed in Amsterdam in 1814 and whom he regretfully relinquished when he left the White House. Jackson also brought several of his best slaves from the Hermitage.

Levees were held every other Thursday during the time Congress was in session. Mrs. Freemont, daughter of Senator Benton of Missouri, who attended one at Jackson's insistence when she was quite young, wrote:

> President Jackson at first had suppers at the general receptions, but these had to be given up. He had them, however, for his invited receptions of a thousand or more. It was his wish that I should come to one of these great supper-parties, and I have the beautiful recollection of the whole stately house adorned and ready for the company (for I was taken early and sent home after a very short stay); the great wood-fires in every room, the immense number of wax lights softly burning, the stands of camellias and laurestina banked row upon row, the glossy dark-green leaves bringing into full relief their lovely wax-like flowers; after going all through this silent waiting fairyland, we were taken to the State Dining-Room, where was the gorgeous supper-table shaped like a horseshoe, and covered with every good and glittering thing French skill could devise, and at either end was a monster salmon in waves of meat jelly.

Meat jelly, or "savory jelly," as it was also known, was a great favorite in those days. Indeed, it had often been served during Washington's time. The author offers the following recipe (taken from Mary Randolph's cookbook) for savory or meat jelly, and for "fish a-la-daub":

SAVORY JELLY

> Put eight or ten pounds of coarse lean beef, or the same of a forequarter of veal into a pot with two gallons of water, a pound of lean salt pork, three large onions, chopped, three carrots, a large handful of parsley and any sweet herb that you choose, with pepper and salt. Boil it very gently, reduce to two quarts; strain it through a sieve.

Next day, take off the fat, turn out the jelly and separate it from the dregs at the bottom, put it on the fire with a half pint of white wine, a large spoon of lemon pickle and the whites and shells of four eggs beaten; when it boils clear on one side, run it through the jelly bag.

FISH a-la-DAUB

Boil as many large white perch as will be sufficient for the dish; do not take off their heads and be careful not to break their skins; when cold, place them in the dish, and cover them with savory jelly broken. A nice piece of rockfish is excellent done in the same way.

Mary Randolph also made a *blanc mange* fish in jelly. In this case she used hogs' feet to make a very light-colored and perfectly transparent jelly.

FISH IN JELLY

Fill a deep glass dish half full of jelly; have as many small fish-moulds as will lie conveniently in it, fill them with blanc mange; when they are cold, and the jelly set, lay them on it as if going in different directions; put in a little more jelly, and let it get cold to keep the fish in their places, then fill the dish so as to cover them.

Mrs. Washington's "Goldfish in Jelly" is very similar to Mrs. Randolph's, except that she gilded the fish with gold-leaf after they were firm and let them dry before adding the jelly.

During Jackson's eight years in office three children were born to his pretty niece. Jackson, who, like his wife Rachel, had bemoaned the fact that they had no children of their own, welcomed the youngsters with all the affection of a doting grandfather. However, they came very near being born in Tennessee, for Emily, despite her youth, was strong-willed. She clashed with her uncle over the gorgeous and controversial Peggy O'Neal, who has gone down in history as the only woman ever to wreck a President's Cabinet.

Peggy O'Neal was the daughter of a Washington tavern-keeper who played host to many important members of Congress. A tavern in those days was similar to a hotel today; Peggy, red-haired and beautiful, was a great favorite of the boarders, among them John H. Eaton, who was a Senator from Tennessee in 1818 and took lodging at the O'Neal tavern. When the Senator first met Peggy she was the wife of John Timberlake, a ship's purser.

During her husband's frequent long absences at sea, Senator Eaton escorted the beautiful Peggy to social functions, thus stirring up considerable gossip. When, in 1828, Timberlake, then on duty in the Mediterranean, committed suicide aboard ship, scandal-mongers laid it to grief over his wife's "unfaithfulness." Some biographers reason, "He was short in his accounts"; others, "He could not conquer his habits of excessive drinking."

Whatever the cause, Eaton's continued residence at the tavern led to accusations that he and Peggy were living together. After Timberlake's death the Senator consulted his dearest and closest friend, President-elect Andrew Jackson, on the propriety of marrying her.

General Jackson, who had lived at the same tavern five years after becoming senator, was quite fond of Peggy. He thought her amiable and intellectually above average (she had attended Mrs. Hayward's Seminary in Washington and Madame Day's School in New York), and had once written his wife that Mrs. Timberlake "plays on the piano delightfully & every Sunday evening entertains her pious mother with Sacred music to which we are invited." He sanctioned the marriage, hoping it would be a means of discrediting the rumors.

The wedding took place on January 1, 1829. Shortly afterward the President-elect appointed Senator Eaton his Secretary of War, thus placing Mrs. Eaton in the highest social circle of Washington. The female element of capital society, however, refused to accept Peggy, and her own explosive temper did nothing to ease the situation. She had accidentally, or otherwise, bumped into the wife of a governor at a ball and the scene that followed only served to arouse further hostility toward her. Mrs. Donelson, out of respect for her uncle, had made a courtesy call upon Mrs. Eaton, but flatly refused to accept her. Shortly afterward, when Emily became ill on a trip down the Potomac and Mrs. Eaton offered her the use of her smellling salts, Emily coldly and pointedly refused. Peggy rushed to Jackson, who ordered his niece to either accept the lady or return to Tennessee. She and her husband returned to Tennessee. But in about six months Jackson, who loved and sadly missed them, asked them to come back.

By this time the Eaton affair had waxed so intense that Martin Van Buren, then Secretary of State, tendered his resignation as a hint that Eaton do likewise. He complied, after first talking it over with his wife.

President Jackson had felt all along that his enemies, led by Vice President John C. Calhoun, were using Mrs. Eaton as a political weapon against him, just as they had used attacks on his wife's virtue during his Presidential campaign. His bitterness and resentment over the treatment which he felt had hastened his beloved Rachel's death caused him to champion Peggy, who, he was convinced, was the essence of virtue and, like Rachel, a political victim. The stalwart old Hero of New Orleans, it is reported, often wore a look of pain on his thin features at this time, partly, no doubt, due to sufferings caused by old war wounds and rheumatism, but partly, too, from his sense of betrayal toward those who had slandered his wife, an act which he never forgave. Determined not to let his enemies triumph, he made Eaton Governor of Florida, and at the same time bluntly ordered Secretaries Barry, Branch, and Ingham, whose wives were openly hostile to Mrs. Eaton, to resign.

But Peggy didn't like Florida. She missed the social life of the nation's capital, disliked the Florida climate, and found herself as strongly ostracized there as she had been in Washington. So Jackson appointed Eaton minister to Spain, and to everybody's relief Peggy went with him.

President Jackson's friends celebrated the eighth of January, 1835, by giving a grand banquet. It was not only the anniversary of the battle of New Orleans, but on that day the last installment of the national debt had been paid. Colonel Benton presided, and when the cloth was removed he delivered a speech. "The national debt," he exclaimed, "is paid!"

General Jackson liked the physical excitement of a horse race, and he was always to be seen at the races at the National Course, just north of Washington. He also enjoyed cock-fighting; this was, in fact, one of his favorite home amusements.

Up to Jackson's time the Washington newspapers contained very little of what has since then been known as local news. A parade, an inauguration, or the funeral of a distinguished person would receive brief mention. The first "Society Letters," as they were called, were written from Washington by Nathaniel P. Willis to the New York *Mirror*. Willis also introduced to Washington steel pens, made by Joseph Gillott at Birmingham, which he brought back from England. Up to this time, goose-quill pens had been used exclusively.

In 1832 Jackson sent Buchanan to the Court of St. Petersburg, in Russia, and in 1834, upon his return, Buchanan called at the White House with a charming English lady whom he desired to present to the President. Leaving his friend in the reception room, Buchanan entered Jackson's private quarters and found Old Hickory unshaved, unkempt, in his dressing gown, with his slippered feet on the fender before a blazing wood fire, smoking a corncob pipe. When Buchanan stated his object to Jackson, the General told him he would be very glad to meet the lady. But Buchanan, shocked at the idea of the President meeting a lady in such attire, asked if the President didn't intend to change his costume, whereupon the Old Warrior rose, his long pipe in his hand, and, deliberately knocking

This covered silver bowl, owned by President Andrew Jackson, is now in the collections of the U. S. National Museum.

the ashes out of the bowl, said to his friend: "Buchanan, I want to give you a little piece of advice, which I hope you will remember. I knew a man once who made his fortune by attending to his own business. Tell the lady I will see her presently."

Buchanan, who became President in 1856, often stated that this remark of Jackson's had humiliated him more than any he had ever received. He walked slowly downstairs to meet his fair charge, and in a short time President Jackson entered the room, attired in a full suit of black, cleanly shaved, with his stubborn white hair forced back from his face, and, advancing to the beautiful Englishwoman, saluted her with almost kingly grace. As she left the White House she exclaimed to her escort, "Your republican President is the royal model of a gentleman."

Andrew Jackson had the knack of winning and keeping friends without courting the people. His "strict integrity, generous nature, high honor, military character and history, were the chief elements of his prestige," according to one observer.

Dr. J. C. Hall, a well-known physician in Washington who attended General Jackson on several occasions, testified to the Old Hero's kindness to everyone, especially his servants. Once, when smallpox broke out among them, and nearly everybody else fled, the President remained in the White House and "waited on black and white with unremitting attention," according to John Forney, in his *Anecdotes*.

The following story, titled "Recollections of a character of Jackson's time," was written for the *Evening Star* July 20, 1901:

> In the days that are gone, when beauty bright my heart's chain wove, when Roger Weightman, Jo. Gales and William W. Seaton were mayors of Washington . . . Washington City was "truly rural," a "rus in urbe."
>
> . . . Andrew Goddard, retired dry goods merchant on 7th Street and the writer were recalling memories of those old times together

the other day in his handsome home on 18th Street, N.W. Andrew is just three weeks and three days younger than the writer, having been born on the 4th of March 1829, the date of Andrew Jackson's inauguration, after whom he was named A.J. We both recollect well the tall Roman nose and bristling pompadour hair, his gray blue eyes, fierce as an eagle's and gentle as a lamb's; bushy eyebrows, gathered like a gathering storm, and then dispersed like summer clouds in smiling sunlight. Yes, "by the eternal," we both remember him. We both agreed, too, that it required a lunatic like Randolph to dare to lay hold of that Cyrano proboscis and pull it, for which the General promptly knocked the aggressor down with his hickory shilalah.

If we remembered Old Hickory, of course we well remember his satellite, Jemmy Maher, the gardener. Jemmy was more Irish than "the Masther" whom he adored. Jemmy had a rich brogue and "a janius for *dhrawing* the liquor and a janius for *dhrinking* it, too." Sometimes Jemmy would be rather the worse for it, when it happened to get the better of him. After one or two of these occasions which had been reported at the White House, with exaggerations no doubt, the President reluctantly sent for the culprit.

"How is this, Jemmy?" began the Executive, with one of his De Bergerac scowls. "What is this they are telling me of you, sir? They say you are drunk half the time or half drunk all the time, and are neglecting your duties, sir. Now, by the eternal—"

"Oh, don't, now, please don't, now, gineral, darling," interrupted Maher. "Jist hear me, now, only wan word, and listen to raison. Phy does your honor's rivirence pay any attintion to what the blaggards does be spakin' ag'in me? Phy, your honor, gineral, dear, if I was to moind the laste in the wurreld the dommed lies they does be telling me all the time about you, gineral, I wud believe that you ought to be hung on a gallows in front of the jail, begad!"

The brows relaxed and Jemmy was sent back to the trees, flowers and shrubbery, which he loved next to the General and his own family.

Jackson, like all Presidents, past and present, received his share of gifts, many of them food in one form or another. He had been seven years in office when a constituent sent him a cheese weighing fourteen hundred pounds. The President ordered it put in the White House cellar for aging and ripening. Shortly before going out of office he invited the public to share in his gift. Then, as always, the people responded with enthusiasm, some coming from as far away as Baltimore and Annapolis.

Shops and offices were closed and all roads led to the White House. The jamboree that followed was almost as hectic as Jackson's first inaugural reception. The President's rough-and-ready admirers practically dedicated the White House in cheese! They ground it into the carpets, smeared it on the walls and furniture and even on the draperies. When the guests finally departed, gorged with cheese, their pockets bulging, all that remained—besides a state of chaos—was the empty wooden stand on which the cheese had rested. President-elect Martin Van Buren, viewing the debris, grimly determined to exclude the public from the Executive Mansion during his administration.

The White House was modernized during Jackson's administration, at a cost of $45,000. For the first time, water was piped in—spring water from Franklin Park—and the East Room came into full use.

The north portico was also finished at this time, and, since the south portico had been completed in 1824, this was the final step in repairing the destruction wrought by the British in 1814.

Jackson received, as a gift from a constituent, a cheese weighing fourteen hundred pounds. Shortly before going out of office he invited the public in to share his gift. This sketch from Perley's Reminiscences *indicates the informal nature of the affair.*

VIII

Keep the Public Out

Martin Van Buren

Cheer after cheer went up from the crowds surging up Pennsylvania Avenue on March 4, 1837, as General Jackson, who had risen from his sick bed against the advice of his physician, came into view, riding at the side of President-elect Van Buren. Their carriage was an elegant phaeton constructed of oak from the original timber of the frigate *Constitution,* which had been made at Amherst, Massachusetts, and presented to the old hero by sixty admirers.

The sun gleamed on the highly varnished wood and on the panels on either side, which represented "Old Ironsides" under full sail. Four iron-gray carriage horses, General Jackson's own, drew the phaeton from the White House to the Capitol.

As soon as Van Buren had kissed the Bible, the pledge of his acceptance of the powers and responsibilities of his new office, General Jackson advanced and shook his hand vigorously and the Marine Band struck up "Hail to the Chief." President Van Buren and ex-President Jackson were then escorted back to the White House, through which, for three hours, the American public surged.

At four o'clock in the afternoon the members of the diplomatic corps, in brilliant formal dress, called in a body. Don Calderón de la Barca, who at that time was dean of the diplomats, presented a congratulatory address. In his reply, Van Buren made his only known *lapsus linguae,* according to Perley in his *Reminiscences;* he addressed the diplomats as the "Democratic Corps." It wasn't until after his attention had been directed to his mistake that he corrected himself and stated that he had intended to say "Diplomatic Corps."

In the evening, two inaugural balls kept the overcrowded city in a whirl. "There was no rest for the weary limbs that night," Perley tells us. The leading hotel was Gadsby's; the chief amusement centers were gambling houses and a mediocre theater. There were no public halls, except Carusi's. "Visitors went from boarding-house to hotel and from hotel to private residence, seeking lodgings in vain. 'Beds! Beds! Beds!' was the general cry. Hundreds slept in the market-house on bundles of hay, and a party of distinguished Bostonians passed the night in the shaving chairs of a barber shop!"

In the November following Van Buren's inauguration, his eldest son, Colonel Abraham Van Buren, a West Point graduate who had served with distinction in the Mexican War, and who also served as his father's private secretary, was married to Miss Angelica Singleton, daughter of a wealthy South Carolina planter, Robert Singleton. A relative of Dolly Madison, Angelica had been educated in Philadelphia and had passed the preceding winter in Washington in the family of her relative, Senator Preston.

President Van Buren's wife, Hannah, had died nineteen years before his entrance into the White House as our eighth President. Angelica fitted as perfectly into her new role as White House hostess at the New Year's Day reception in 1839 as she fitted into the royal-blue velvet gown she wore,

Two inauguration balls were held on March 4, 1837, and the city of Washington was deluged with visitors unable to find accommodations. This sketch from Perley's Reminiscences *depicts "a party of distinguished Bostonians" passing the night in a barber shop.*

which may be seen today at the Smithsonian Institution. Hoops had come into fashion, and they did full justice to Angelica's tiny waist as they billowed out the elegant folds of her ten-yard skirt. Her "rare accomplishment, superior education, beauty of face and figure, grace of manner, and vivacity in conversation, assured her social success."

During Van Buren's administration, the White House was refurnished in the most expensive manner, and a "code of etiquette established which rivalled that of a German principality." The polar opposite of Andrew Jackson, Van Buren refused to tolerate what he termed the "offensive scenes" Jackson had endured from his rough-and-ready admirers. Nor would he countenance the wear and tear on White House furniture caused by those previous lusty and inconsiderate guests.

Hardly had he been in office a week before he ordered the Executive Mansion repainted and redecorated (he even had the Monroe table service gilded) and the furniture reupholstered. He discontinued the practice of serving food at public receptions, prohibited eating or drinking in the mansion except at the table, and discontinued public receptions, except those which fell on New Year's Day and the Fourth of July—holidays with which even he dared not interfere.

While his arbitrary methods and keep-the-public-out policy roused a storm of protest (which he grandly ignored) it must be stated in fairness to Van Buren that he did make an attempt, in his own fashion, to restore the cordial relations between the Administration and top echelons of Washington society which had been ruptured during Jackson's tenure.

He gave numerous small, elaborate dinner parties, at which guests were carefully screened for their importance, and made it a point to attend dinners given by members of his Cabinet. Ex-President John Quincy Adams (then a member of the House of Representatives), the widow of President Madison, and the widow of Alexander Hamilton each formed the center of a pleasant little coterie, and Van Buren often expressed his

*Van Buren was a widower. His daughter-in-law, the former Angelica Single-
ton, acted as his official hostess. In this portrait by Henry Inman she poses
with a bust of the President.*

desire that the members of his Cabinet and their principal subordinates each give a series of intimate dinner parties and evening receptions during the successive sessions of Congress.

The city on the Potomac, which had by now grown to a population of forty thousand, was intensely cold during the winter holidays of 1839. The streets and avenues were miserably lighted and almost impassable. Even in good weather travel was difficult on the swampy, rutted roads, but now—"Snow lay deep on the ground; sleighs were the ordinary conveyances; Senators and Congressmen generally huddled into ordinary boarding houses, in which a sort of Gipsy life was led. The only creditable buildings were the Capitol, the President's house and the Departments," wrote John Forney, a newspaper publisher and editor. The dinners added a needed sparkle to a cheerless city, but they were oh, so much alike! according to one eyewitness—guests at different houses often saw the same table ornaments and were served by the same waiters, while the fare was prepared by the same cook!

Van Buren saw to it that the food served at the White House table, prepared by his own London-trained chef, was unexcelled. The table itself was often a work of art. He took a fancy to Monroe's mirrored plateau, which Jackson had relegated to a storeroom, and had it gilded at a cost of seventy-five dollars. He used the matching Monroe candelabra and fruit *epergnes,* and added supplementary *compotiers* and *bonbonnières.* His flatware was gold plate; goblets, wine glasses, and water bottles were of finest cut glass. Guests dipped their fingers in emerald-green glass finger bowls and wiped them on the finest of linen napkins.

Van Buren's extravagance, his bold steps in practically eliminating the public from the Executive Mansion, and his ostentatious display of elegance in the trying times of the new nation's financial panic, cost him his reelection and led the way, in 1840, to the election of another soldier-hero, William Henry Harrison.

IX

President for a Month

William Henry and Anna Harrison

The day of William Henry Harrison's inauguration, March 4, 1841, dawned cold and cloudy. William Henry was the third son of Benjamin Harrison, one of the signers of the Declaration of Independence. His military genius at Tippecanoe and at the Battle of the Thames had brought him nation-wide fame, and he was swept into the Presidency on a wave of enthusiasm which roared, "Tippecanoe and Tyler too!"

The crowds waiting to cheer the inauguration of the new President shivered in the blasts of a chilly northeast wind sweeping through the streets of the capital city. Harrison, without an overcoat, refused the closed carriage, presented by the Whigs of Baltimore and drawn by four horses, which would have given him protection against the elements. Rather than disappoint the throngs waiting to see him, he insisted upon riding his splendid white charger up Pennsylvania Avenue to the Capitol.

"Tippecanoe" made a dashing figure indeed in his full-dress

uniform—skin-tight white breeches, highly polished black boots, and a cocked hat which he waved to the crowd with one hand while managing his spirited mount with the other. The crowds cheered the old hero lustily. At his right, slightly to the rear, rode Major Hurst, who had been his aide-de-camp at the Battle of the Thames. Colonel Todd, another aide-de-camp, rode in a similar position at the left.

The General, who delivered his inaugural address standing bareheaded, without overcoat or gloves, facing the cold northeast wind, spoke until two o'clock—one and a half hours. Only one thing marred the ceremonies: the new President had caught a slight cold. The cold might not have become serious had not the sixty-four-year-old Chief Executive insisted upon going through with the inaugural reception with the widowed Jane Finley Harrison, his charming daughter-in-law who acted as his official hostess. There were three inaugural balls that night, the price of admission suiting different pockets.

Mrs. Harrison, who was an invalid, had decided not to come to Washington for her husband's inauguration; she had previously lived in the capital city, when Harrison had served as Senator from Ohio, and had not been in favor of her husband's accepting the rigorous role of President of the United States.

Despite the heavy cold that persisted, the ninth President found his first two weeks in office busy ones. Ambitious and energetic, he insisted upon rising early and doing his own marketing. Invariably, he refused to wear an overcoat, although the weather that spring continued cold and stormy. One rainy morning, when he was out marketing as usual, he was caught in a sudden shower and came back to the White House sopping wet. On March 27 he was forced to take to his bed; the cold had turned into pneumonia.

He died eight days later, exactly one month from the day he was sworn in. At the time of his death he could not know

William Henry Harrison rode his white charger to the Capitol instead of taking the protection from the elements offered by a closed carriage. He felt he owed it to the crowds to let himself be seen. Right, the scene at his inaugural address.

Library of Congress

that his little grandson, Benjamin (Harrison was the father of ten children), was destined to become the twenty-third President of the United States.

The successor to William Henry Harrison, John Tyler, was the first Vice President to succeed to the Presidency through the death of the Chief Executive.

X

Southern Hospitality

The John Tylers

Mint juleps and eggnog were the order of the day when John Tyler, more beloved for his Southern hospitality than for his politics, moved into the White House as the tenth President of the United States. His wife, the former Letitia Christian of New Kent County, Virginia, whom he had married on his twenty-third birthday, had been an invalid for three years; the only time she appeared at a White House function as official hostess was when their third daughter, the beautiful blond Elizabeth, was married to William Waller in the East Room on January 31, 1842. Mrs. Robert Tyler, daughter-in-law of the President, wrote a description of the wedding:

> Lizzie had quite a grand wedding although the intention was that it should be quiet and private. This, under the circumstances though, was found impossible. The guests consisted of Mrs. Madison, Cabinet members, foreign ministers and some personal friends.
> Lizzie looked surprisingly lovely in her wedding dress and long

lace veil, her face literally covered with blushes and dimples. She be-
haved remarkably well, too. Any quantity of compliments were paid
her. I heard one of her bridesmaids express to Mr. Webster her
surprise at Lizzie consenting to give up her belleship, with all the de-
lights of Washington society and the advantage of her position, and
retire to a quiet Virginia home. "Ah!" said he,
>   "Love rules the court, the camp, and the grove.
>   And love is heaven and heaven is love."

The new First Lady had suffered a paralyzing stroke in
1839, from which she never fully recovered. According to her
daughter-in-law, however, she was still beautiful, with skin as
"smooth and soft as a baby's" and "sweet, loving black eyes."
She was, moreover, "gentle and graceful in her movements,
with an air of native refinement."

Mrs. Tyler had her own private quarters in the White
House, and spent her days quietly, seeing only her devoted
family and relatives who sometimes came to the capital city
to see her. She received few other visitors, and returned no
calls. Shortly after Lizzie's marriage Letitia suffered another
stroke. She died in the White House on September 10, and
though she was so little known, there were few dry eyes at
her funeral services on the afternoon of September 12, 1842.
Letitia Tyler was laid to rest in her family plot in Virginia.

During his wife's illness, President Tyler asked his sprightly
and charming daughter-in-law, Mrs. Robert Tyler, daughter
of Thomas A. Cooper and the former Miss Mary Fairlie of
Philadelphia—who was a belle in her own right and justly
celebrated for the sparkle of her wit—to act as his official
White House hostess. It is said that Mrs. Robert Tyler enjoyed her role in the Executive Mansion. She particularly enjoyed meeting celebrities who called at the White House,
among them the famous English author, Charles Dickens,
who was visiting America for the first time. Though she described Daniel Webster as "the almost awful-looking Mr.
Webster," she found him a witty conversationalist.

Something of her irresistible verve and charm is reflected in the following delightful letter which she wrote to her sister:

What wonderful changes take place, my dearest M—! Here am I, nee Priscilla Cooper (nez retroussé you will perhaps think), actually living in, and, what is more, presiding at—the White House! I look at myself, like the little old woman, and exclaim, "Can this be I?" I have not had one moment to myself since my arrival, and the most extraordinary thing is that I feel as if I had been used to living here always, and receive the cabinet Ministers, the Diplomatic Corps, the heads of the Army and Navy, etc., etc., with a facility which astonishes me.

"Some achieve greatness, some are born to it." I am plainly born to it. I really do possess a degree of modest assurance that surprises me more than it does any one else. I am complimented on every side; my hidden virtues are coming out. I am considered "charmante" by the Frenchmen, "lovely" by the Americans, and "Really quite nice, you know," by the English. . . . I have had some lovely dresses made, which fit me to perfection—one a pearl-colored silk that will set you crazy. . . . I occupy poor General Harrison's room. . . . The nice comfortable bedroom with its handsome furniture and curtains, its luxurious arm-chairs, and all its belongings, I enjoy, I believe, more than anything in the establishment.

The pleasantest part of my life is when I can shut myself up here with my precious baby. . . . The greatest trouble I anticipate is paying visits. There was a doubt at first whether I must visit in person or send cards; but I asked Mrs. Madison's advice upon the subject, and she says, return all my visits by all means. Mrs. Bache says so too. So three days in the week I am to spend three hours a day driving from one street to another in this city of magnificent distances. . . . I see so many great men and so constantly that I cannot appreciate the blessing! The fact is, when you meet them in everyday life, you forget they are great men at all, and just find them the most charming companions in the world, talking the most delightful nonsense, especially the almost awful-looking Mr. Webster, who entertains me with the most charming gossip.

Tyler's daughter, Letitia, who had remained at her mother's bedside in the first year and a half of the Tyler administration, was quite young when her mother died, but she assumed many of the duties of hostess. Here is Letitia Semple's description of the simpler side of White House life:

> We breakfasted at eight-thirty and dined at three o'clock, except on state occasions, of course, and had tea served after our daily drive, to escape from all the environments of political and social cares and duties, because my father's time was rarely his own. . . . "Now, sing, Letty," he would say when we found ourselves far from the mad crowd, enjoying the quiet of some country road. And then I would sing his favorite songs, the old Scotch ballads we both loved so well.

Tyler's household would sometimes gather in the Green Room for piano music and old-fashioned songs. John Tyler has the distinction of being, up to that time, the only President who composed music. He wooed Julia Gardiner with a serenade he wrote for her entitled, "Sweet Lady, Awake."

Miss Gardiner had come to Washington with her father to enjoy the social whirl of the capital after touring Europe. The Gardiners were impressed by their reception at the White House, where the "tall, slender President, with the noble Roman profile" greeted them most amiably. Julia recalled that he "welcomed us with an urbanity which made the deepest impression upon my father, and we could not help commenting . . . upon the silvery sweetness of his voice, that seemed in . . . tune with the incomparable grace of his bearing and the elegant ease of his conversation." The widowed President was almost instantly smitten with Julia's charms. He considered her "the most lovely of her sex . . . the most beautiful woman of the age, and . . . the most accomplished."

· Julia did not at first succumb to the President's romantic overtures, but tragedy hastened the courtship. Under the command of R. F. Stockton, who in February, 1844, had invited a large number of important people to make a trial run on the brand-new U.S.S. *Princeton,* this first screw-propeller steamship for the Navy sailed down the Potomac. The *National*

Among the four hundred persons aboard the U.S.S. Princeton on its trial run on February 28, 1844, were President Tyler and ex-State Senator Gardiner of New York. Tyler escaped injury but Gardiner was killed in the explosion of one of the big guns.

Intelligencer of February 29 gives this account of the trip:

> The day was most favorable, and the company was large and brilliant, of both sexes, around four hundred of them, including the President, heads of departments and their families. . . . Some distance below Fort Washington one of the large guns (known as the Peacemaker) was fired more than once, exhibiting the great power and capacity of that formidable weapon of war. The ladies had partaken of a sumptuous repast, the gentlemen had succeeded them at the table, and some of them had left it; the vessel was on her return up the river, opposite the Fort, where Captain Stockton consented to fire another shot from the same gun, around and near which to observe its effects many persons had gathered, though by no means so many as on similar discharges in the morning, the ladies who then thronged the deck, being on this fatal occasion almost all between decks and out of reach of harm.
>
> The gun was fired. It exploded and before the smoke cleared away, shrieks announced a dire calamity. The gun had burst at a point three or four feet from the breech and scattered death and desolation around. Mr. Upshur, Secretary of State; Mr. Gilmer, head of Navy; Commodore Kennon, an officer; Virgil Maxcy, diplomat at The Hague; Mr. Gardiner, ex-state senator of New York were among the slain; seventeen seamen were wounded.

Tyler himself escaped injury because he was detained by some toast drinking below deck. (He liked champagne).

Four months later, on June 26, 1844, John Tyler and Julia Gardiner were married in New York. The wedding remained a secret until the couple arrived at the White House. (Tyler had children older than his bride—he was fifty-four and she was twenty-four.)

President Tyler was happier in his married life than in his executive life. Shortly after he became Chief Executive he fell out of favor with the Whigs; they read him out of the party, and the Democrats refused to take him back. He became a "President without a party." He was so unpopular, in fact, that when a 'flu epidemic swept the country it was called the "Tyler Grippe."

Four months after the death of her father on the U.S.S. Princeton, *Julia Gardiner married President Tyler. This portrait by F. Anelli was done some twenty years later.*

John Tyler had fourteen children, seven by each of his wives—certainly the most prolific of all the nation's Presidents. His youngest child was born when Tyler was seventy years old.

The following, from an old newspaper clipping not identified by name or date, gives us an intimate glimpse into Tyler's times:

> "I've heard all the inaugurals from Polk's up to Grant's first," said Mr. Robins. . . . "My first winter in Washington was Mr. Tyler's last winter, in the winter of '44–'45, the winter that Mr. Tyler's beautiful and graceful second wife was the lady of the Executive Mansion. . . . I remember one little incident that occurred there at the time. The polka dance (introduced in Bohemia in 1830) had just been introduced into this country. A young married couple, named Bergh, who were friends of Mrs. Tyler's and who had just returned from Europe, consented, after a great deal of persuasion, to give the guests present at one of Mrs. Tyler's receptions an idea of the dance. They danced the polka in the center of the East Room."

During the Tyler administration, Christmas was the popular season. There was scarcely a house in Washington in which there was not a well-filled punch bowl. In some antique silver bowls was "Daniel Webster Punch," made of Medford rum, brandy, champagne, arrack menschino, strong green tea, lemon juice, and sugar. In less expensive bowls was found a cheaper concoction. But punch abounded everywhere, and the "bibulous found Washington a rosy place, where jocund mirth and joyful recklessness went arm in arm to flount vile melancholy, and kick, with ardent fervor, dull care out of the window," according to the inexhaustible *Reminiscences* of Perley.

Although assemblies were held once a week between Christmas Day and Ash Wednesday, members of the Cabinet and other high officials expected to give at least one evening party during each session of Congress. Edna Colman, in *Seventy-five Years of White House Gossip,* gives us this happy picture of the festivities:

*Mary Tyler, the President's eldest granddaughter, was given a birthday party
in the White House at which she was dressed as a fairy with a silver wand.
Among her guests were the daughter of the Mexican minister, Master Scher-
merhorn of New York, and Ada Cutts, Dolly Madison's grandniece.*

Guests assembled about eight o'clock, the younger portion devoting themselves to dancing, while the punch bowl attracted the older ones. A piano and two violins were considered a sufficient orchestra and one of the musicians called out the figures. At ten o'clock guests were invited to supper, which was often served on the back porches. Tables were always loaded with substantial good things, and the popular dainty reception menu of today would never have passed muster with either hostess or guests. Quantity and variety were the order in providing the refreshments. A roast ham was usually found at one end of the tables, with a saddle of venison or some other heavy roast at the other, roast wild ducks or poultry being placed about midway. Quantities of homebaked cakes and puddings, with plenty of punch and madeira wine, were always on hand. The diplomats served champagne. Eleven o'clock was the signal for a general scramble for hats and wraps.

The second Mrs. John Tyler took her new position as First Lady seriously. She is said to have received guests in "almost regal splendor," ostentatiously seated on no less than a dais. Washington society, intrigued and openly amused at "her large armchair on a slightly raised platform in front of the windows opening to the circular piazza looking on the river" . . . and at the "three feathers in the First Lady's hair, and her long-trained purple gown," raised its eyebrows and whispered. Because Julia Tyler "drove four horses—finer horses than those of the Russian Minister"—one Washington newspaper wrote an open satire about "the lovely lady Presidentess . . . attended on reception days by twelve maids of honor, six on either side, dressed all alike . . ." while "her serene loveliness received upon the raised platform, with a headdress formed of bugles and resembling a crown. . . ."

The President found to his discomfiture that his political opponents took advantage of his eager bride's lofty and somewhat pretentious attitude to ridicule him in public. Julia Tyler's heady triumph was cut short, however, by the end of her husband's single term in office. He was succeeded by James K. Polk, eleventh President of the United States.

XI

No Dancing, Cards, or Frivolities

James and Sarah Polk

Carriages had been barred from the Capitol grounds on the assumption that the day would be fair. Instead, it poured, and Washington officialdom and diplomats, their splendid uniforms ruined, their plumes wet and bedraggled, suffered along with the crowds hidden under umbrellas in the plaza below.

The inauguration of James Knox Polk, eleventh President of the United States, was a complete washout in more ways than one, as far as the public was concerned. The President-elect, who was certainly no orator, read his speech in a monotonous voice; few of the assembled people, listening in the dripping rain, could see or hear him.

That night, March 4, 1845, Washington celebrated with two inaugural balls for the new President—the price of tickets for one was ten dollars, for the other, two dollars. Both balls, however, lacked the gaiety and sparkle that usually characterized these fetes, for the new First Lady, whose Spanish-type beauty belied her strict Calvinistic upbringing, had a decided antipathy to alcohol, dancing, and other such frivolities.

The dancing, which had already begun, came to an abrupt halt when the strains of "Hail to the Chief," played by the Marine Band, announced the arrival of the President and his wife. Sarah Childress Polk was strikingly attractive in a gown of heavy white silk, which set off her dark charm. She swept proudly into the room with her husband, secure in his triumph. Four years ago he had been defeated in his campaign for election to the Vice Presidency; now, she felt, he was vindicated.

The new First Lady's ban on vain frivolities did not extend to the sartorial area; her usual style of dress was rich, even magnificent, and always expensive. She had come from a family of well-to-do merchants and was thus able to afford the elaborate materials she liked to fashion into her stunning wardrobe. The Presidential couple stayed at the inaugural ball about two hours—just long enough to greet the guests. After they left, dancing was resumed.

Sarah Polk, while she would not permit dancing or card playing at the White House, did everything else she could to make her husband's administration popular. At one of her receptions a gentleman is reported to have remarked: "Madame, you have a very genteel assemblage tonight." The First Lady, who presided over all functions with great dignity, replied with perfect good humor: "Sir, I have never seen it otherwise!"

Polk took his presidential duties seriously. Described as "a short man with a long program," he came into office when the country's relations with Mexico were strained. Two years later the United States and Mexico were at war. Until that time, however, the President felt that the taxpayers were entitled to as much of his time as he could give them. Every reception, every levee, meant longer hours, sometimes working far into the night to make up for lost time. Mrs. Polk, the first White House mistress to act as her husband's private sec-

In Polk's administration the White House was noted for its "genteel assemblages." According to this sketch from Perley's Reminiscences, *a livelier spirit prevailed at the Inaugural Ball held at the National Theater—tickets two dollars—on March 4, 1845.*

retary, frequently assisted him. Brilliant as well as beautiful, she was said to have a keener political sense than her industrious husband.

Nonetheless, she did not neglect her own official duties. She held two informal receptions every week—on Tuesday and Friday night—in what has been described as the "parlour." Guests usually numbered about fifty persons and included diplomats, Cabinet officers, and members of the House and Senate. Public levees were dull, guests having to content themselves with promenading up and down the East Room and chatting with friends. No food, not even punch, was served.

The one bright spot in the entertainment was the presence of the still irresistible Dolly Madison, now in her eighties. Her fortune gone, spent on a profligate son, she appeared in the same black dress and turban, and was treated with deference by both the President and his wife. She continued to take snuff, and still loved to play cards and to waltz. When a fire almost destroyed her husband's papers Congress suddenly awakened to the fact that they were of historical value and bought them for $25,000, which Dolly had been trying to make them do for years.

The money meant that Mrs. Madison could blossom forth in new finery, which she promptly did. When, on February 9, 1849, the President and Mrs. Polk gave a reception in her honor, Dolly was there in her customary décolletage and turban. According to eyewitnesses, her arms and shoulders were still beautiful at eighty-two. Resplendent in white satin, she received with the First Lady, seated on a dais. She left the reception on the President's arm shortly after midnight.

Polk's last year in office, 1848, was notable for three historic events: the United States acquired from Mexico the territory comprising California, Nevada, Utah, most of New Mexico, and parts of Arizona, Nevada, and Wyoming, as well as recognition of Texas as a possession; gold was discovered in California; and gas lighting was introduced into

*This dessert plate, representative of the china in use during the Polk admin-
istration, is in the collections of the U. S. National Museum. It is white, with
a mauve pink band.*

the White House. Mrs. Polk was, however, partial to the exquisite chandelier for candles in the reception hall, and refused to give them up.

Sarah Polk's last months in the White House were spent planning the purchase of a home in Nashville which she and the President named "Polk's Ease." Her husband had come into office at the age of forty-nine, the youngest President to date; his wife was eight years younger. Nevertheless, convinced there would be no second term, they had determined to retire after he went out of office.

On March 1, 1849, they gave a dinner party for the President-elect, General Zachary Taylor. Members of both political parties were invited, and the dinner is said to have been livelier than any of those preceding.

The Polks left the Executive Mansion on March 3, at sunset, Mrs. Polk leaving behind a reputation of goodness and stability that in a less comely woman would have been mere stuffiness.

Polk died at the age of fifty-three, worn out from overwork and excessive fatigue, three months after leaving office. The beloved Dolly Madison, one of the grand old ladies of the time and one of the greatest of White House hostesses, survived him by twenty-seven days.

XII

Grandma and Her Corncob Pipe

Zachary and Margaret Taylor

The inaugural ball of 1849 that heralded President Zachary Taylor—a sixty-four-year-old professional soldier known as "Old Rough and Ready" and a hero of the Mexican War—was described by Washington society reporters as one of the most brilliant affairs the capital city had ever witnessed.

Held in a specially-built structure located in Judiciary Square (where the old Pension Building now stands), it was a gathering of beautiful women magnificently gowned and jeweled, diplomats in foreign costume, and hundreds of others who gladly paid ten dollars (a large sum in those days!) for the privilege of being present.

The only blight on the festivities was the hot wax that dripped from the chandeliers onto the clothes of the dancers, though even this jarring note inspired one society reporter to write: "One man danced elegantly in such good time to Gungle's exquisite strains that the drops of candle grease falling on his coat looked like notes of music properly arranged!"

129

The new First Lady, Margaret Mackall Smith Taylor, a descendant of a fine old Maryland family, was a frail little woman who smoked a corncob pipe and preferred the quiet of her Baton Rouge home to the demands of social Washington. Worn out with the strain of moving from one military post to another while rearing a family, Margaret, who was sixty-three when her husband entered the White House (against her wishes), lost no time in relegating the role of official hostess to her pretty young daughter, affectionately called "Betty" by members of the family.

Betty was twenty-two, and the wife of Major W. W. S. Bliss, when she took over the reins as official hostess. She was an excellent housekeeper, and while the First Lady sat patiently in her room, busy with her knitting or smoking her corncob pipe, Betty ran the Executive Mansion; she secured new furniture and carpeting. Preeminently qualified for the position by a "certain quietude of manner, which foreigners say American women are deficient in"—according to *Society of Washington* (March 27, 1875)—Betty was beautiful and had "perfect taste in dress, but that was not her greatest charm. She had that *je ne sais quoi,* that knowledge of how to be just cordial enough, and not too cordial. Never has the White House had a gentler, sweeter mistress!"

In addition to her appearances at state dinners, weekly morning receptions, and large and frequent public entertainments, Betty presided over delightful little tea parties at which a succession of colored waiters carried trays heaped with varieties of homemade cakes and tarts. The beaux supplied the belles, according to one reporter, and were adroit at balancing a well-loaded plate on one knee while holding a cup and saucer on the other.

Betty's older sister, Sarah, who had married the influential Senator Jefferson Davis of Mississippi, had died of typhoid three months after her marriage. Both the President and his wife were very fond of their son-in-law, who was later to be-

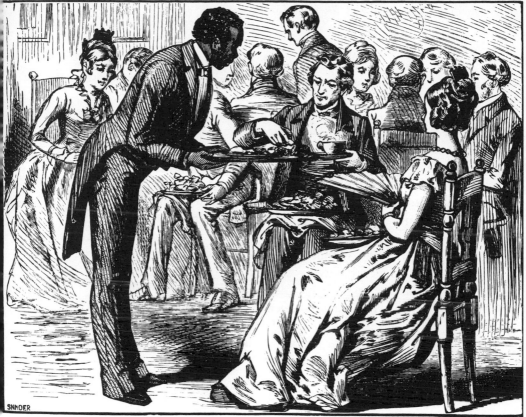

The original caption of this sketch, taken from Perley's Reminiscences, is simply, "Tea-party in Taylor's Time."

come President of the Confederate States of America, and when he married a second time, his wife was given a warm welcome as a member of the family. She attended many of the Taylors' small dinner parties (which the President preferred to larger ones) and, according to biographers, took an animated part in the conversation.

Zachary Taylor had spent his youth in the frontier wilderness of Kentucky and had little formal schooling or knowledge of White House protocol, so he sometimes found it difficult to accustom himself to the etiquette and the restraints of his new position. One day when the bachelor ex-Secretary of State called to present a number of fair Pennsylvania friends to the President, General Taylor is said to have remarked, "Ah! Mr. Buchanan, you always pick out the prettiest ladies!"

"Why, Mr. President," was the courtly reply, "I know that your taste and mine agree in that respect."

"Yes," said General Taylor, "but I've been so long among warriors that I hardly know how to behave myself, surrounded by so many lovely women!"

The bitter political discussions engendered by the threat of Civil War in the first six months of 1850 put a damper on Washington's social whirl; though the customary receptions at the White House and dances at hotels were given, there were few large parties. The President's first levee, however, created considerable interest when a delegation of six Osage Indians chose to attend in costume. Zachary Taylor's last public entertainments included the annual New Year's Day function of 1850 and a spectacular reception on March 4 of the same year to mark the anniversary of his inauguration.

For relaxation the President took morning walks through the streets of Washington, wearing a high black hat perched on the back of his head and a suit of black broadcloth much too large for him. The suit was made according to his orders —and he was a man who put comfort before style.

The First Lady, who, as we have remarked, preferred the

"President Taylor on the Street." From Perley's Reminiscences.

seclusion of her apartment and the comfort of her knitting and corncob pipe to public life, nevertheless saw to it that neither her husband nor her household was neglected, and often would listen, smilingly, as old "Rough and Ready" recounted the day's happenings to her over a cup of tea.

Zachary Taylor's last public appearance was on July 4, 1850, when he accepted an invitation to sit on the platform on what is now known as the Washington Monument grounds for the big Independence Day celebration. The July sun beat down on the monument, then in process of construction; its cornerstone had been laid two years before by James K. Polk. Overcome by heat, the President returned to the White House and, according to his biographers, ate cherries and drank "iced milk" against the advice of his physician. A vivid description of his last days is given by Perley in his *Reminiscences:*

> The old hero sat in the sun at the Washington Monument during a long spread-eagle address by Senator Foote, with a tedious supplementary harangue by Geo. Washington Parke Custis—exposed to heat nearly three hours. He had drunk freely of ice-water, and on his return to the White House had found a basket of cherries which he partook heartily, drinking at the same time several goblets of iced milk. After dinner, he still further feasted on cherries and iced milk against the protest of Dr. Witherspoon, who was his guest. When the time arrived to go to the Winthrop party, he felt ill and soon was seized with a violent attack of cholera morbus. This was on Thursday. On Sunday, he is reported to have said to his physician: "In two days I shall be a dead man."

Whether the iced milk and cherries had anything to do with President Taylor's illness is not established, but he was violently ill for five days before he died on the ninth of July.

Only sixteen months after Zachary Taylor took his oath, Vice President Millard Fillmore was sworn in—on July 10, 1850—as the thirteenth President of the United States. Mrs. Taylor and the nation were in mourning; she was to follow her husband in death two years later.

XIII

Regime of Conveniences

Millard and Abigail Fillmore

Millard Fillmore's administration (July, 1850–March, 1853) may well be called the "regime of conveniences," for he was the first President to have an iron cookstove, the first to have a bathtub with "centrally heated" running water, and the first to have a library in the White House.

"Fo' de Lawd's sake, Mistah Fillmo'!" protested his Negro chef, who had prepared state dinners for thirty-six persons in the big kitchen's open fireplace, "who cu'd cook on sich a contraptshun as dat?" The cook's sentiments were echoed by the public. One writer declared:

> The fireplace of a kitchen is a matter of great importance and I have never been so circumstanced as to witness the operations of many of the newly-invented steam kitchens and cooking apparatuses which the last twenty years have produced. . . . To say the truth, the inventors of cast iron stoves seem to me to have had every other object in view but the promoting of good cooking, and I am sure that meat cannot be roasted unless it is before a good fire.

135

But the President was adamant, although he himself had to engineer the drafts during the cooking of the first meal on the new "contraptshun."

The zinc-lined mahogany bathtub, supplied with running water from a new hot water heating furnace, was the "last word" in 1853, although Andrew Jackson is thought to have had the very first installed bathtub in the mansion. Water had been piped in from a spring in Franklin Park in 1833, supplying the President with "warm, cold and shower baths." Four years later, in Van Buren's administration, a reservoir was constructed in the basement and a pump supplied the kitchen, pantry, baths, and water closets with "fine, pure water." Before Jackson's time, portable tubs were used; the Madisons had a green tin tub (cost $30) in the basement.

President Fillmore was in the White House when the power of the temperance movement, already well under way in Europe, began to be felt in the United States. He himself was so "anti-alcohol" that he avoided hotels which served liquor. The Woman's Christian Temperance Union was not to be established for another twenty years, but already there were organizations of various kinds working all over the country. Fillmore was also anti-tobacco and anti-gambling. On Sundays the White House was closed to all visitors, and the family attended church, rested, and meditated.

There is no record of any protest when Congress gave Mrs. Fillmore an appropriation of five thousand dollars for installation of the first White House library in the second-floor Oval Room. The President's blue-eyed, auburn-haired wife, the daughter of the Reverend Lemuel Powers, a Baptist clergyman, was a talented musician—she played the piano, harp, and guitar—and had been a schoolteacher; she was shocked to find that the White House not only lacked a library but had neither a Bible nor a dictionary! Her distress was communicated to Congress, which gallantly supplied the necessary funds for correcting the deplorable situation.

Mrs. Millard Fillmore, in a photograph made at the White House.

Abigail Fillmore, who had not been present when her hus-band was sworn into office in July, 1850, had little heart for the duties her new position as First Lady demanded. Her health was delicate; also, a short time before the inaugura-tion, her sister, of whom she was extremely fond, had died. She soon managed to relegate many of her official duties to her daughter, Mary Abigail, named for her great-aunt, Abi-gail Adams.

Mary Abigail, just eighteen, was pretty and musical; she had her own piano and harp, which were kept in the Oval Room (the Fillmores used the Oval Room as a sitting room). She spoke fluent French, had youth's love of parties, and gladly took over from her mother such duties as calling and making public appearances.

Mrs. Fillmore, however, was no recluse. She was quite aware of the requirements of her position, and did her valiant best to meet them. Years before, she had permanently injured an ankle in a fall; this made standing for long hours painful. To enable herself to go through the strain of the receptions held every Tuesday morning and the drawing-rooms that took place every Friday evening when Congress was in session, she remained in bed several hours before each event. She man-aged to be present at many of the large dinner parties given Thursday evenings in the State Dining Room, and at the small dinners on Saturday in the private dining room, over which she presided with queenly grace.

Fillmore, an astute politician and a man who did what he believed to be right regardless of the consequences, soon sur-rounded himself with a competent Cabinet: he appointed John P. Kennedy Secretary of the Navy; Edward Everett Secretary of State; Charles M. Conrad Secretary of War; Thomas Corwin Secretary of the Treasury; Alexander H. H. Stuart Secretary of the Interior; Samuel D. Hubbard Post-master General; and John J. Crittenden Attorney General. The thirteenth President of the United States knew he had

Abigail Fillmore won an appropriation of five thousand dollars to install the first White House library. It was located in the second-floor Oval Room. (This photograph was made about 1902.)

little chance of reelection. He and his wife nonetheless made the White House a home.

They liked to have their friends around them, and shortly before Christmas, 1850, the President invited his former law partner, Solomon G. Haven of Buffalo, to spend the holidays at the Executive Mansion. "We have just one spare room in this temple of inconvenience," he wrote, "neatly fitted up— and just the thing for you and Mrs. H." The Havens accepted and Mrs. Haven, in a letter to a friend, remarked that "The President usually succeeded in leaving the Executive chamber at 10:30 at night and spending a pleasant hour in the library with his family."

Fillmore is said to have set a record in courtesy toward an incoming President. He invited the President-elect, Franklin Pierce, to accompany him to a lecture given by the noted English author, William Makepeace Thackeray. Later he took Pierce and Henry Irving on a trip down the Potomac on the *Vixen* for a look at the new steamship *Ericsson*. Still later, he and Mrs. Fillmore entertained both writers at dinner, followed by a reception.

Messrs. Thackeray and Irving also attended Pierce's inaugural ceremonies as guests of the Fillmores, and afterward helped the new President receive.

The day was bitterly cold and Abigail Fillmore developed pneumonia standing on the wind-swept portico of the Capitol. She and her husband had planned a trip abroad, but she was not to realize her dream. A month after leaving the White House she died in the same suite at Willard's Hotel as that used by the new President before entering the Executive Mansion.

XIV

Pall of Gloom

Franklin and Jane Pierce

A pall of gloom settled on the White House when Franklin and Jane Pierce entered it in March, 1853. Shortly after Pierce's election, the President-elect, Mrs. Pierce, and their only living child had entered a railway carriage at Boston, to go to Concord, New Hampshire. They intended to rest awhile at their Concord home before undertaking the trip to Washington. En route their train was derailed and rolled down an embankment. The boy was killed—the only fatality; his parents were slightly injured.

The tragic death of eleven-year-old Benjamin was the third such blow borne by the Pierce family. They had lost two other sons: the first had died in infancy and the second had succumbed to typhus at the age of four.

A brilliant orator, an able lawyer, and a natural leader, Pierce had permitted his wife, the former Jane Means Appleton, to stifle his political career for ten years before finally yielding to the demand that he run for President.

Even Mrs. Pierce, who hated Washington, to which she had come as the bride of Congressman Pierce nineteen years before, could not stop him this time. He had acceded to her request to give up politics for the practice of a circuit lawyer, but his great talents soon made him New Hampshire's leading citizen and chairman of the state temperance society. After his brilliant record in the Mexican War, when he rose to the rank of brigadier general, he was mentioned as possible vice-presidential timber. But he turned out to be the dark horse that rode into office over four seasoned campaigners, Lewis Cass, James Buchanan, William O. Butler, and Stephen A. Douglas.

Jane Pierce, whose father, the Reverend Jesse Appleton, had been president of Bowdoin College when Pierce was a student there, did not come to Washington until two months after her husband's inauguration. Her own frail health—she was suffering from tuberculosis—and the shock of Benjamin's death had kept her in bed. Even when she moved into the White House, she did not feel well enough to assume the role of official hostess, and appealed to her aunt-by-marriage, the charming and well-born Mrs. Abby Kent Means, in whose Amherst, Massachusetts, home she had married Pierce, to act in that capacity. She was fully cognizant, however, of the duties she owed to her husband's position and did appear at his side, frail and beautiful, at the annual New Year's Day reception in 1855. Later she presided at weekly state dinners and gave Friday receptions, at which she stood by her husband's side. But, writes one White House chronicler:

> Her woe-begone face, with its sunken dark eyes, and skin like yellowed ivory, banished all animation in others. She tried, but constantly broke down in her efforts to lift. Her life was over, in fact, from the time of that dreadful shock of her son's death.

Mrs. Means, however, continued to assist at formal White

During the time Congress was in session in Pierce's administration, a state dinner was given once a week for thirty-six guests. The table is set in the State Dining Room.

House functions, and with the help of the young and beautiful Mrs. Jefferson Davis, the pall of gloom that seemed to have settled over the Executive Mansion cleared somewhat.

Franklin Pierce's charm was such that he was able to get a bigger appropriation from Congress for that repairing and re-furnishing of the White House which each succeeding President seemed to feel was essential to his well-being. That august body gave him $25,000, which covered the cost of painting the mansion inside and out, buying a carpet for the East Room which is said to have weighed a ton, and installing a furnace and a hot-water heating system.

There is no record of any outstanding entertaining during Pierce's administration. During the sessions of Congress there was a state dinner once a week to which thirty-six guests were invited; on other weekdays a half-dozen or so might partake of the family dinner, at which no wine was served. There was also a morning and an evening reception every week in the season, at which Mrs. Pierce, dressed in deep mourning, received with the President. The evening receptions, which were the equivalent of the old drawing-rooms, were looked forward to with great interest by the young people of the day. Carriages and camellias were in demand; white kid gloves were kept on store counters, and Washington hairdressers were kept busy.

Pierce, like many of his predecessors and successors, had to face up to the temperance question. It was more difficult for him to abstain from the use of alcohol than it had been for Fillmore, who hated every form of stimulating beverage. Nevertheless, Franklin Pierce fought his craving for liquor— and apparently he won, because before he achieved the Presidency he had become a leader in the temperance movement.

Franklin Pierce was "gallant, handsome, true-hearted and genial," John Forney tells us in his *Anecdotes of Public Men.* "He was a soldier and gentleman, one of the most striking men that ever sat in a saddle, and one of the truest of friends.

The Pierces did little entertaining of an outstanding nature. In addition to the weekly state dinners, a morning and an evening reception were held each week. This drawing from Leslie's Illustrated Newspaper depicts the elegant evening reception held in the East Room on February 1, 1856.

Nothing in Pierce's character stands more to his credit than his devotion to his amiable, gentle and long-suffering wife during her painful invalid years. . . ."

President Pierce's gallant and genial friendliness was extended to James Buchanan, whom he had helped to win the Presidential nomination; although he remained in Washington for the inauguration, Pierce moved out of the White House so that it might be cleaned and made ready for his successor by Inauguration Day.

XV

Bachelor President

James Buchanan

Guests at the brilliant and elaborate Inaugural Ball of 1857
danced until four o'clock in the morning. Social Washington,
starved for the entertainment it had been denied during the
gloomy days of the Pierce administration, welcomed its new
bachelor President. The ban on dancing in the august halls of
the White House (initiated by the Polks) was still in effect,
but the five thousand revelers at the ball, held in a specially-
built structure, spent the night of March 4, 1857, in a whirl
of terpsichorean gaiety.

The feast provided included four hundred gallons of oysters, five hundred quarts of chicken salad, five hundred quarts
of jellies, sixty saddles of mutton and four of venison, eight
rounds of beef, seventy-five hams, one hundred and twenty-
five tongues, and three thousand dollars' worth of wine. In
addition, there were pâtés for every taste, and twelve hundred
gallons of ice cream in several flavors. The highlight of the
repast was a four-foot cake ornamented with a flag bearing

the insignia of each of the thirty-one states of the Union.

The new President gallantly remained until the end of the festivities. The belle of the ball was his pretty niece and official hostess, Harriet Lane. An exquisite blonde with violet eyes and a tall, willowy figure, Harriet was the youngest of four orphaned children left to Buchanan's guardianship when his sister, Jane, and her husband died. She had been trained, according to biographers, for the role of a princess—a part she had played, in previous years, with such grace (when her uncle was ambassador to the Court of St. James's) that she became a favorite of Queen Victoria. This young First Lady of the Land became the darling of Washington society during her uncle's term of office.

Buchanan, however, soon ran into a storm of criticism that threatened his popularity when he attempted to change the order of the New Year's Day reception. Striving to achieve some semblance of order at these heretofore chaotic affairs, in which the public customarily wandered and lounged at will, he staggered diplomats, Justices of the Supreme Court, high-ranking officers of the army, navy, and marine corps, government officials, and the public by putting police in charge to facilitate matters. When guests were requested by police to present themselves quickly and in the order in which they belonged, many became so enraged they left without even seeing the President. The President, however, persisted; during his next three years in office the New Year's Day receptions were organized according to his wishes.

James Buchanan had been in office almost four years when the first heir-apparent to the crown of Great Britain visited the capital of her lost colonies. When President Buchanan first learned that the Prince of Wales intended to visit Canada, he hastened to write Queen Victoria and extend to her son a cordial invitation to visit the United States.

Albert Edward, Prince of Wales, who later became King Edward VII, traveled unofficially under the name of "Baron

Renfrew." He was just nineteen, handsome and charming. Washington society was atwitter over this visit, and the White House bustled with activity. Even the President put himself out to accommodate Albert Edward. The young prince never knew that the Chief Executive had given up his own bedroom and moved to a cot in the anteroom to his office, in order that his royal visitor might have the ultimate comfort the mansion afforded.

Edward was already a model for diplomats, although correspondents described him as "a peachy-cheeked, beardless boy." When he noticed that the President wore no gloves at the reception, the Prince promptly removed his own and, following his host's example, shook hands "American fashion."

The highlights of the Prince's trip were the two banquets given in his honor by the President and Miss Lane: at 6:30 o'clock on Wednesday, October 3, and Thursday, October 4, 1860. On the first occasion the thirty-four guests included members of the President's family, the Prince's suite, the British legation, and the Cabinet; the diplomatic corps was invited for dinner the following evening. The Prince sat at the table to the right of Miss Lane at both dinner parties. The musicale that followed the first dinner is notable chiefly because it introduced to America the song, "Listen to the Mockingbird," dedicated by its author, Alice Hawthorne, to the lovely Harriet Lane.

On Thursday morning following, the Prince paid a visit to the Capitol and passed through the legislative halls of both Houses of Congress, the Supreme Court room, and the Library of Congress. The party then returned to the Executive Mansion, where members of the Cabinet and their wives had gathered. At twelve o'clock the doors of the mansion were opened for the President's reception in honor of his royal guest. The President and the Prince, with his suite, took their positions in the East Room, the Prince standing to the right of the President, with the Duke of Newcastle and Lord St.

Germains to the Prince's right. Lord Lyons, the British minister, stood to the left of the President. First the officers of the army, navy, and marine corps were successively introduced, and then the public—"of whom a very large portion were ladies," according to the *National Intelligencer*—whose pleasure at seeing and meeting the Prince was undisguised. With many of the ladies the Prince shook hands; to the sterner sex he courteously bowed.

That afternoon the Prince, with the Duke of Newcastle and Lord Lyons, was taken to the Department of the Interior. Later, the royal party, with Miss Lane and Mrs. Jacob Thompson (wife of the Secretary of the Interior), visited the Young Ladies' Institute of Mrs. Smith, where the Prince is said to have rolled several games of ninepins with the pupils.

The next day, Friday, the Prince of Wales, at his own request, made a visit to Mount Vernon. He was accompanied by the Duke of Newcastle, Lord St. Germains, Lord Lyons, and the rest of his retinue. As the party—which also included the President, Miss Lane, members of the Cabinet and their wives, the diplomatic corps and wives, leading army, navy, and civil service officers, and the mayor of the city—alighted from their carriages at the Seventh Street Wharf and approached the cutter *Harriet Lane,* which was to take them to Mount Vernon, they were surprised to see five barges crowded with people waiting alongside the wharf.

According to the *National Intelligencer,* which published the story on October 8, 1860, the patients in the local government hospital for the insane had become "inspired with the same desire to see the Prince which had animated all the rest, and in pursuance of the policy of embracing every proper opportunity of breaking the routine of a life which at best must have many moments of seclusion and monotony, the convalescent patients of both sexes, with their attendants to the number of fifty, had crossed the river in the five barges and taken position in full view of the ceremony." The medical

Albert Edward, Prince of Wales, visited the United States in October, 1860. The painting by Thomas Pritchard Rossiter shows the Prince visiting Washington's tomb at Mount Vernon, where he planted a tree near the grave. President Buchanan stands at the Prince's left. Harriet Lane is the lady with the parasol in the group at the left.

officer in charge of them, Dr. Stevens, was on the wharf, and as "Baron Renfrew" approached the cutter, accompanied by Miss Lane and under the escort of Major Ramsey, the doctor was introduced by the latter to "his Lordship," and presented him, in the name and behalf of the patients, with a handsome bouquet. The flowers were "politely received and kindly acknowledged by the approach of the Prince to the edge of the wharf, flowers in hand, and, with head uncovered, bowing to the delighted occupants of the boats. The patients were in no means behind the Prince in politeness, which the gentlemen to a man evinced by raising their hats and the ladies by waving their handkerchiefs. The band in attendance then struck up *God Save the Queen,* and Lord Renfrew and the President and their suites proceeded to embark for the mecca of American patriots."

Flying the flags of the United States and Great Britain, the cutter steamed majestically down the Potomac to Mount Vernon, where the party disembarked about noon. There the Prince, hat in hand, stood solemnly before the tomb of George Washington for a few moments; then the great-grandson of King George III planted a tree near the grave as a remembrance of his visit.

The return trip was much gayer. The Marine Band played the dance tunes popular at the time. His Royal Highness danced first with Miss Lane, whom he had known in London when her uncle was ambassador there, and then with the other young ladies. An elegant supper was served on board before the steamer returned to the city around sunset.

Soon after the return of the party to the Executive Mansion the Prince and his retinue repaired to the residence of Lord Lyons, the British minister, who was reputed to be one of Washington's most generous and expert hosts. They spent the night with Lord Lyons, and left for Richmond the next morning, October 6.

Another notable event that took place during Buchanan's

In May of 1860 the establishment of diplomatic relations between the United States and Japan was celebrated with a reception for the members of the first Japanese Embassy. Here, Buchanan presents to an ambassador an English copy of the first commercial treaty between the two nations.

administration was the reception given May 17 the same year (several months before the Prince of Wales' visit) to the members of the staff of the first Japanese Embassy in the United States. The Embassy's opening marked the official beginning of diplomatic relations between the two countries.

The Japanese Embassy, numbering seventy-one members, arrived in Washington on May 14, 1860. The principal mission of the Embassy was to get an English copy of the first commercial treaty between Japan and the United States, signed by the President, since the original—which had been concluded in 1854, was burned in the great fire at Yedo (Tokyo) in 1858. (The Japanese-language copy had been saved.)

The Japanese maintained their headquarters at Willard's Hotel (now known as The Willard), less than three blocks from the Executive Mansion. They made the short trip from the hotel to the White House in congressional carriages in a pageant that featured a military escort, martial music, and the guests' own native costumes magnificently embroidered in gold, crimson, and silver.

The public was not invited to the official reception, which took place in the East Room. Present were congressmen and their wives, foreign ministers, and high officials of the United States government. At a few minutes to twelve the great door to the East Room swung open and the President entered, flanked by the Secretary of State on his right and the Secretary of the Treasury on his left. The President's cortège advanced and took its position at the center of the room. The Secretary of State then retired from the room to accompany the entrance of the Embassy.

As the clock struck twelve, the great doors swung open again, and three Japanese ambassadors, with the Secretary of State on their right and an American and Japanese interpreter behind, silently approached the President through a double row of army and navy officers. When their slow, courtly, noiseless procession reached the President, the Japanese made three low bows in greeting the man they considered an emperor.

After their presentation to the President, they asked to meet Miss Lane and the wives of members of the President's Cabinet. In accordance with their wishes, the presentation was strictly private; as each lady was presented, the Japanese bowed deeply three times.

President Buchanan was too astute not to observe what was going on. "They take down notes of everything—nothing escapes them. They've got a long description of how I looked at the reception," he wrote. Later on during their visit they attended a Saturday band concert in front of the White House. The President saw a few of his friends among the group that had gathered, and walked down the steps to greet them. The Japanese were astonished that the Emperor of the United States would mingle and shake hands with the people; it was so unlike anything in their country! They themselves, the President learned, had specific instructions as to what they were to do and say. Everything had been written down for them in advance—the course they were to take, the number of bows they were to make. "They are very proud," Buchanan wrote. "They bow very low, but they won't do more than is prescribed for them in their instructions." The President entertained eight of the highest dignitaries at a dinner party.

As a token of appreciation for the United States Government's cordial treatment of the Embassy during its thirty-day visit to Washington, the Japanese Shogunate sent a total of twenty-eight boxes of gifts to Secretary of State Lewis Cass, among which was a "large water basin" for President Buchanan. The basin—blue with a crane-and-reed design, measuring thirty-eight inches in diameter—was used as a punch bowl at the White House.

President Buchanan frequently employed a French caterer, Gautier, to handle the food for the more elaborate receptions and dinners. Gautier excelled in satisfying both the eye and the palate. The oysters, lobster, terrapin, wild turkey, and partridge served under his instruction were said to be a gourmet's delight.

Entertaining had reached the point where the Presidential salary of $25,000 was not sufficient to pay for such elaborate affairs. It is known that Buchanan frequently dug down into his own pocket to meet the bills of butcher, baker, and candlestickmaker, since he enjoyed entertaining and was inclined to be liberal about it. At his last New Year's Day reception five thousand persons are said to have been entertained.

Washington society had grown increasingly competitive, and its leaders were rich men who thought nothing of spending $75,000 a year on entertainment alone. Fortunately for the President, his niece was as practical as she was pretty. For all her graciousness and charm as First Lady, Harriet Lane kept a stern eye on the food bills.

J. Buchanan Henry, the President's private secretary, was in charge of the expenditure of the library fund, payment of the steward and messengers, and of those household expenditures which came out of the President's own purse.

Miss Lane and Mr. Henry issued the state dinner invitations and assigned seats, in order of precedence, to those who accepted. It was Mr. Henry's duty, also, in the interval between the arrival of guests in the parlor and the procession into the dining room, to ascertain the name of each gentleman and tell him what lady he was to take in; in some cases this necessitated his introducing them to each other. "It was, he used to say, a very *mauvais quart d'heure* for him, as he was pretty sure to find at the last moment, when the President was leading the procession to the table, that some male guest, perhaps not accustomed to such matters, had strayed away from his intended partner, leaving the lady standing alone and much embarrassed! He had then to give them a fresh start," according to Perley in his *Reminiscences*.

Buchanan was always careful of his personal appearance and was, in some respects, a sort of male Miss Fribble, ac-

Harriet Lane, President Buchanan's niece, succeeded in having a conservatory built on the west end of the White House. In it were housed tropical plants, cacti, and vines, and an abundance of flowers of every description.

cording to John Forney, "addicted to spotless cravats and huge collars; rather proud of a rather small foot for a man of his large stature."

As a rule, he rose early, breakfasted and read the newspapers, and was in his office by eight o'clock. He usually set out for an hour's walk at five in the afternoon. Except during the summer months, when he resided at the Soldiers' Home and drove to the White House in the morning and back in the evening, he rarely used his carriage. (In those days the White House was "unfit to live in" during the summer because of nearby malarial swamps.) He dined at six, and held to the established etiquette of declining dinner invitations; he rarely attended outside parties or receptions, on the ground that acceptance of all such invitations would be impossible, and any discrimination would give offense. Once a week some of the members of the Cabinet, accompanied by their wives, dined at the White House *en famille*.

An excellent addition to the White House which was made in Buchanan's time was the Conservatory. This was the work of Miss Lane, who loved flowers and spent a good deal of time in the little retreat built on the west end of the White House. As soon as it was completed (actually, it represented an enlargement of a small conservatory built earlier), the Conservatory was opened to visitors on reception days. Entry was through a long entrance hall "hung with pictures and adorned with graceful statues." Leslie's *Illustrated Newspaper* carried a feature article on Miss Lane's Conservatory, which reads, in part:

> Here you may see orange and lemon trees loaded with fruit, rows of cactus plants of every size and shape, Camellia japonicas covered with bloom, Spirea, Ardisia, Poinsettia; running vines, including the celebrated South American pitcher plant whose tiny "pitchers," half-filled with water and covered with small green lids, hang among the leaves, attracting much curiosity and admiration. . . . It also affords a pleasant promenade and lounging-place for visitors on public days,

President James Buchanan's unhappy single term in office ended on March 4, 1861, with the inauguration of Abraham Lincoln. This sketch bears the caption, "Presidents Buchanan and Lincoln entering the Senate chamber before the inauguration."

and the universal opinion seems to be that the new Conservatory is a
most fitting and agreeable addition to the White House.

The interior of the White House was also renovated during
Buchanan's administration, and American-made furniture replaced many of the early French pieces.

President Buchanan, a man of such high personal integrity
that he made it a rule never to accept presents of any value
from friends or supporters, had the misfortune to be in office
when the rift between North and South opened beyond repair.
Unwanted as the nation's leader for another term, he stepped
aside, and Abraham Lincoln moved into the White House.

XVI

The Great Emancipator

Abraham and Mary Todd Lincoln

"I suppose I may take this as a compliment paid to me, and as such, please accept my thanks. I have reached this city of Washington under circumstances considerably differing from those under which any other man has reached it. I have reached it for the purpose of taking an official position amongst the people, almost all of whom were opposed to me, and are yet opposed to me, as I suppose."

President-elect Lincoln uttered these words in response to repeated calls from the crowd who gathered in front of Willard's Hotel on Friday evening, March 1, 1861, when he and Mrs. Lincoln were holding their first levee in Washington. A large number of men and women, including congressmen, army and navy officers, and members of the diplomatic corps, had been invited. At ten-thirty, as the strains of "Hail to the Chief," played by the Marine Band, were heard from the spacious parlors, the President-elect entered the front balcony with as many guests as could get on it; others clamored for window space. This levee probably would have been the beginning of the busiest entertainment program ever given in the Executive Mansion up to that time, had circumstances permitted. But circumstances, of course, did not.

South Carolina had seceded from the Union shortly after Lincoln's election, followed by Mississippi, Florida, Alabama, Georgia, Louisiana, and Texas. By the time Lincoln was inaugurated, the Confederate provisional government had been set up and its President, Jefferson Davis, had been inaugurated at Montgomery, Alabama. In little more than a month after Lincoln took the oath of office, the War Between the States would officially begin at Fort Sumter.

Abraham Lincoln arrived in Washington unannounced at six o'clock Saturday morning, February 23, 1861, and went directly and quietly to Willard's Hotel, where he and his family—who arrived in the evening—were to remain until after the inauguration. They occupied five of the most elegant rooms, in the southwest corner of the hotel, fronting Pennsylvania Avenue and overlooking the White House.

The President-elect, accompanied by Senator William H. Seward of New York, called at the White House at eleven in the morning to pay his respects to President Buchanan. The President, unaware of Lincoln's arrival in the city, was called from a Cabinet meeting. The surprised Buchanan received Lincoln cordially, and after a pleasant interview invited him in to meet his Cabinet. That evening at ten Buchanan's Cabinet called on the President-elect at Willard's.

After having dinner with Senator Seward, Lincoln returned to the hotel to find the long parlor hall thronged with men and women, young and old, who greeted him as "father and life." The President-elect's elation over his victory was reflected in his high spirits and broad grin. As he passed through the crowd, shaking hands to right and left as fast as he could and making humorous remarks to this or that person, he was so excited that he forgot to take off his hat. His breach of etiquette, however, was excused by one observer because the hat "was new and outshined the crowd."

The morning broke clear, calm, and beautiful, according to the press, but later clouds began hovering and enough rain fell to prevent the "usual heat of the past few days and the whirlwind of dust that otherwise could have rendered it excessively unpleasant."

At twelve-thirty President Buchanan, in his state carriage with liveried servants, alighted in front of Willard's and proceeded to Mr. Lincoln's room. After a brief conversation the two entered the carriage and, accompanied by Senators Baker and Pearce, rode in the procession to the Capitol. The carriage was so closely surrounded by marshals and cavalry as to hide it completely from view. The opportunity of seeing the President-elect was little better at the Capitol. Instead of walking in the open where the crowd could look at him, he was guided through a pineboard tunnel to the Senate chamber entrance; his egress was handled in the same way. All in all, the words "sorry sight" described the inaugural. Lincoln spoke clearly, but he "appeared pale and nervous, while Mr. Buchanan sat looking at his own boots, like a man disgusted . . . and anxious to quit and go home."

Martial law had taken over the city for the day, and that, combined with public indignation and despondency, gave the town an extremely dismal aspect. According to a New York news dispatch, "The very atmosphere of Washington is charged with sulphur, and war is surely before us if there be anything reliable in the usual signs of a gathering tornado."

Ex-President Buchanan escorted President Lincoln back to the Executive Mansion and, after a few courteous words of welcome and good-by, left him to enjoy his first White House dinner. The dinner was prepared by the ever-thoughtful Harriet Lane, Buchanan's niece, who had everything ready when the Lincolns arrived at the mansion after the inauguration ceremony. Their party of seventeen—which included the three

Lincoln boys, two sisters of Mrs. Lincoln, Mrs. Elizabeth Todd Grimsley, and other friends and relatives—sat down to the meal with grateful hearts. Mrs. Grimsley was a favorite cousin and a bridesmaid at Mary's wedding. She remained in the White House with the Lincolns for six months, and later wrote down an account of this visit.

At the Inaugural Ball held that night at the "Muslin Palace" (so called because the walls were trimmed in muslin), five thousand persons jammed the rooms for a glimpse of the new Chief Executive and his wife. The President, plainly uncomfortable in new boots and white kid gloves, led the grand march with one of the female guests on his arm. The new First Lady, the former Mary Todd, was radiant in white satin, her light brown hair ornamented with trailing jessamine and clustering violets. Her necklace, earrings, and bracelets were of pearl. She followed on the arm of her onetime beau, Stephen A. Douglas, with whom she danced a single quadrille. Guests who managed to reach the supper table around midnight found an elaborate buffet.

The Ball—called the "Union Ball" in defiance of those states that had already seceded—was a grand success. Mary Todd Lincoln, who had at long last realized her lifelong ambition to move into the White House, was now prepared to enjoy her new role to the utmost. Complications, however, soon arose.

Mary Lincoln felt that it was her prerogative as First Lady to hold the first levee, and that the William H. Sewards (he was now Secretary of State) were presumptuous in their proposal to precede her in holding this typically Washington affair. The President's wife won her point, and their first White House reception was given on Friday evening, March 8, 1861. When the day rolled around, however, it found the First Lady in tears; the new gown, ordered because she had spilled coffee on the one she originally intended wearing, had not yet arrived. As she walked the floor, wringing her hands, Elizabeth Keckley, the talented Negro seamstress who made the dress, was announced. She had, she explained, worked on it until the last minute.

"Now, don't you worry," she soothed, "I can dress you in time!" A short time later Mrs. Lincoln, resplendent in the new creation of magenta watered silk with a lace cape, her abundant brown hair tastefully bedecked with a wreath of a half-dozen red and white japonicas, triumphantly entered the East Room on her husband's arm. However, the belle of the evening turned out to be Mrs. Stephen A. Douglas. Mrs. Douglas, simply dressed in white, appeared in fine relief against the darker colors around her.

The reception was almost as much of a hodgepodge as Jackson's first reception. The White House driveway was blocked with carriages, and the entrances with those who had come on foot. Ladies who wore the enormous hoop skirts that were all the rage had difficulty getting out of—and later back into —their carriages. Their escorts were almost inundated by yards and yards of heavy silks and satins.

The East Room looked more like a political get-together than a presidential reception. Many of the guests were country folk from Lincoln's own state, Illinois; others were backwoodsmen from elsewhere. Many women, clad in hoopless woolen dresses, wore their sunbonnets, while many a wide-awake man, not finding a place for his hat and overcoat, carried the one aloft in his hand and the other on his back until exhaustion compelled him to retreat from the heaving current of people.

But Lincoln was glad to see them. Clad in the same suit he had worn at his inauguration, and with a fresh pair of white kid gloves, he, a head taller than the others, stood at the head of the receiving line for four hours, joking and shaking hands, using both right and left at the same time in order to hurry the line along. His wife, because of her enormous hoops, was forced to stand almost three feet away. Later, surrounded

by her relatives, she held her own court. Among those com-
plimenting her on her appearance was her half-sister, Mrs.
Clement White of Alabama, who made no secret of the fact
that she was in favor of secession; another was Mrs. Lincoln's cousin, Mrs. Elizabeth Todd Grimsley, to whom the
President also was deeply devoted. She was "tall, and so much
like the President she was at first taken to be his sister."

"It was gratifying," Mrs. Grimsley later wrote, "when the
Marine Band struck up Yankee Doodle, the signal for retiring. The President took me on his arm and we made the circuit of the East Room, a custom as old as the house itself, I
believe, and a silly one in that the wife of the President is
relegated to the escort of another gentleman."

The crowd had remained until long after midnight, and
when they left the confusion increased. Guests naive enough
to lay aside their wraps couldn't find them, for they were
either lost, stolen, or misappropriated. Ninety percent of the
men were forced to leave with covering other than their own,
and these were seen sulkily wending their way home; many
wrapped their heads in handkerchiefs against the March cold
rather than wear the greasy headgear that had been given
them.

And so ended the last reception at which the North and the
sparsely represented South were to mingle for many years.
But for all this it was noted as a "monstrous affair."

Mrs. Lincoln entertained the diplomatic corps at a reception the following day, but, according to Mrs. Grimsley, "the
Legations were not out in full force. Nor did they come together in a body, as was their custom. The French Minister,
Mercier, was absent. Lord Lyons was coldly dignified. Already the nations were looking at us askance."

Inasmuch as the Lincolns were unfamiliar with the rules of
official Washington, the State Department furnished a detailed
memorandum on what their conduct was to be at formal state
functions, the order of precedence, and the use of visiting

cards. The President and his wife were instructed not to address titled foreigners as "Sir"; they were told they might dine privately at six if they were hungry, but state dinners must take place at seven. There was also pointed advice on what a gentleman should, and should not, wear for specific occasions, including the broad hint that frock coats were not correct for evening functions.

Lincoln did his best. He "dutifully made smacking, violent bows" when the Chevalier Bertinatti, who had been appointed minister to Washington from the new Kingdom of Italy, paid his official call. He listened gravely to the long, flowering speech of the diplomat, who was decked out in silver lace, dress sword, and a cocked hat which he carried under his arm. The President, who was a man of short sentences as well as short speeches, then pulled a "little speech" from the pocket of his wrinkled black suit and read it.

In the meantime, Mrs. Lincoln was finding out that being First Lady of the Land was not as glamorous as it had seemed from afar. Determined to run the household as she saw fit, she had dispensed with the White House steward. The servants did not understand her swiftly changing moods: kindly and considerate one moment, irritable, unreasonable, and niggardly the next. Furthermore, with no steward to supervise the linen and silver, these articles began disappearing at an alarming rate.

On March 28, Lincoln gave his first state dinner at which he entertained Vice President and Mrs. Hannibal Hamlin along with members of the Cabinet. The dinner was "not gay," according to Mrs. Grimsley. Only a few of the Cabinet wives were there, and during dinner the President was called from the table for a hurried conference.

The next state dinner was given for the diplomatic corps on Tuesday evening, June 4, 1861. Of this dinner, Mrs. Grimsley wrote:

[It] passed off with the usual complimentary toasts, decanters passed, and with this, a new feature to me, was the exchange of civilities in the tendering of elaborate snuff boxes, not only among the diplomats, but all the ladies.

The New York *Herald* described the dinner the following day as "most *recherché* and elegant," saying that those who were fortunate enough to have been guests on such occasions at the White House for many years "pronounced it in every particular superior to anything they have ever before seen or participated in." There were thirty-five guests. Mme. Gerolt had the honor place at the right of the President, and her husband, Baron von Gerolt, sat at Mrs. Lincoln's right at the table.

Prince Napoleon Bonaparte—son of Jérôme Bonaparte, who had been entertained by Jefferson in the White House— was the next notable entertained at the Lincoln table. He had arrived in New York with his petite bride, Princess Clotilde, daughter of the King of Italy, to tour the western and northern portions of the country.

Secretary of State Seward made a special trip to New York to invite the Prince and Princess to visit at the White House, but the Princess was in mourning and remained in New York while her husband made the trip to Washington. The Prince, affectionately referred to as "Plon-Plon," chose to "lodge" at the French Embassy, but called on the President as soon as he arrived in Washington and had dinner at the White House Saturday evening, August 3, 1861.

The dinner was described as "elegant and *recherché*" but "quite *en famille*," as the Prince was traveling *incognito*. There were twenty-seven persons who sat down to the seven o'clock dinner, including Mrs. Lincoln and Mrs. Grimsley, the only ladies. Mrs. Lincoln's gown was white grenadine over white silk, with a long train. Mrs. Grimsley wore a salmon tulle dress with an "exquisite bouquet of flowers." The President, with Mrs. Grimsley on his right and General Scott on the left, was seated at the center of the table; opposite him was Mrs. Lincoln, with the Prince at her right and Secretary Chase on her left. General McClellan sat at the Prince's right. Others on the guest list included Robert Lincoln; Cabinet members; Lord Lyons, the British minister; Monsieur Mercier, the French minister; Senator Foot, president pro tempore of the Senate; Senator Sumner, chairman of the Senate Committee on Foreign Relations; and Messrs. Nicolay and Hay, the President's private secretaries.

According to the press, it had been the custom to have "state dinners prepared by some respectable restaurateur, but on this occasion Mrs. Lincoln determined to have the preparations made exclusively at home. To her exquisite taste alone, is to be attributed the beautiful arrangements for the occasion and the surpassing geniality of the dinner party. Mrs. Lincoln has upon the occasion shown her practical good sense to be equal to her graceful courtesy and charming manners."

Mary Lincoln's flair for mimicry and her ability to speak French added zest to the occasion; from time to time the President broke in with "and this reminds me . . ." and the Prince and General Scott—who sat directly across from him—were in excellent spirits. All in all, the party was such a success that the Prince gaily remarked: "Paris is not all the world!"

The First Lady gave two weekly receptions. The Saturday-afternoon receptions continued to be held in the White House through the social season, until the warm weather set in. Then the "mall" became a bright place for promenaders. The music of the Marine Band was a popular attraction. The Lincoln family sat on the south balcony ready to receive all who chose to join them there.

The Tuesday evening receptions continued into deep summer. As late as Tuesday, July 30, 1861, this notation appeared in the Washington *Star:* "There will be a public reception at the Executive Mansion this evening, between the hours of 8½ to 11 P.M." The following day the *Star* reported: "The levee at the Executive Mansion last evening was well attended

and largely by the military. The Navy was also fully represented, as well as both branches of Congress and the Cabinet."

Mrs. Lincoln left for the seashore in August and did not
return until November. The next reception was given on December 17, 1861, at the beginning of the social season.

Lincoln's first New Year's Day reception, January 1, 1862,
was reported by the New York *Times* as the greatest jam ever
witnessed on such an occasion. Between the hours of ten and
twelve, foreign ministers and their suites and government officials, having the right of private entries, made calls on the
President. At twelve the gates were thrown open to the waiting public, and the immense crowd made a rush for the reception room. Everybody wanted to be first, so everybody ran
and pushed and scrambled. A line of policemen was drawn up
on each side of the entrance from the carriageway to the
reception room.

After paying their respects to the President and Mrs. Lincoln, the dense and rapidly-moving crowd passed out through
one of the large windows in the hall and across a carpeted
platform to the sidewalk. The new carpets which adorned the
floors of the mansion had been neatly covered to protect them
from damage. According to the *Times:*

> The striking feature was the great number of uniforms visible—
> Generals, Colonels and Majors were plentiful as blackberries, while
> Captains and Lieutenants were multitudinous. If our soldiers prove
> as useful as they are ornamental, nothing more could be desired of
> them.

The whole city was gay and festive; war and politics seemed
for the time forgotten. The day was unusually beautiful, sky
clear and bright and the air soft and balmy, more like May
than January. By two o'clock the crowd had practically disap-
peared and gone to attend festivities elsewhere.

The one Tuesday reception which Mrs. Lincoln failed to
give was during the social season early in 1862. The New

On February 5, 1862, Mrs. Lincoln gave a lavish soirée which was widely criticized as being ill-timed. In this sketch from Leslie's Illustrated Newspaper, President Lincoln appears at the center and Mrs. Lincoln is the second lady to his left, her back turned.

York *Sunday Herald* reported, on the Sunday preceding: "The usual public reception at the White House is not to take place next week. The postponement is occasioned by the private party to be given by Mrs. Lincoln."

The country had been at war for ten months when the First Lady decided to give her own soirée, scheduled for Wednesday evening, February 5, 1862. The party was the exclusive topic in the *beau monde* of Washington, but the function, ill-timed, brought forth a storm of criticism from the public. Newspapers angrily accused Mrs. Lincoln of wanting to "show those Southerners who had closed their homes and refused all social engagements that she was as good as they." When she limited the invitations to five hundred and fifty favored guests (the number was later increased to over eight hundred), occasioning sore disappointment and chagrin to thousands who believed themselves entitled to an invitation, the New York *Herald* defended her for "trying to weed the Presidential Mansion of the long-haired, white-coated, tobacco-chewing and expectorant abolitionist politicians." Mrs. Lincoln is responsible to Congress for "the Presidential spoons," the editorial continued, "and it is not safe to trust an ice cream thus manipulated in the itching fingers of these sweet-smelling patriots."

Some abolitionists, however, did receive invitations, and among the few "regrets" were some from abolitionists. "Are the President and Mrs. Lincoln aware," wrote Ben Wade, well-known abolitionist, "that there is a Civil War? If they are not, Mr. and Mrs. Wade *are,* and for that reason decline to participate in feasting and dancing."

The guests consisted mostly of Cabinet members and their wives, Justices of the Supreme Court, diplomatic corps members, governors, senators, representatives, favorite members of the press, and special friends. Except for generals commanding divisions there were few army personnel. The most conspicuous, the center of observation wherever he moved, was young General McClellan, with his wife. Captain Charles Griffin, commander of the celebrated West Point battery, accompanied by his blooming bride, was the only uniformed guest mentioned in the social columns of the press.

The reception began at nine o'clock. As guests arrived they presented their invitations to a doorman at the entrance, passed on to the second floor to leave wraps, thence down to the Blue Room, and from there went to greet the President and Mrs. Lincoln, who had stationed themselves in the center of the East Room. The President's two secretaries, Nicolay and Hay, stood at his right and Marshal Lamon on his left.

Only a few of the men wore formal party costume. The President's attire was a plain suit of black with white gloves; he also wore his usual bland and pleased expression. He greeted all the guests with warmth, and chatted freely with those whom he recognized as friends.

Mrs. Lincoln was dressed in a gown of white satin, *en train* with hooped skirt flounced in black Chantilly lace and looped at intervals with bows of white ribbon edged with narrow black lace, a show of mourning in deference to the late Prince Consort of Queen Victoria, Albert Edward, who had died in December. Her headdress was a diadem of black with white flowers, and a bunch of crape myrtle drooping on the side. She also wore a corsage of crape myrtle. Her ornaments were pearls.

And there was no curb in the other ladies' toilette! The Adams Express was too slow for delivery, so they sent to Boston, New York, and Philadelphia for their costumes. "Such a display of elegance, taste and loveliness has perhaps never before been witnessed within the walls of the White House," one member of the press reported; another stated that the ladies were "dressed to the height of fashionable extravagance."

Among the tastefully dressed, according to Leslie's *Illustrated Newspaper,* were Mrs. McClellan, regal in a dress of white with bands of cherry velvet, and the young Mrs. Griffin, who was simply attired in corn-colored silk with a headdress of bright crimson flowers. She, according to Leslie's, "was the observed of all, as she leaned on the arm of the President." *La belle des belles* of the party was the violet-eyed and brilliant Miss Kate Chase, young daughter of the Secretary of the Treasury, Salmon P. Chase, who dared not hold her own court lest she arouse the animosity of the First Lady. She was dressed in mauve-colored silk and without ornament. A simple wreath of minute white flowers worn on her hair, which was arranged in a Grecian knot behind, was her only decoration.

Around eleven o'clock President Lincoln gave his arm to Miss Browning, daughter of Senator Browning of Illinois, and, with Mrs. Lincoln on the arm of Senator Browning following, headed a parade round and round through the beautifully lighted and profusely decorated rooms and long corridor as the Marine Band played operatic airs. The beautiful ten-gallon Japanese bowl (the gift to James Buchanan) was filled with champagne punch and placed on a table in the Green Room for the benefit of thirsty guests. Surrounding it were trays of sandwiches.

The supper, reputed by the New York *Tribune* to be "one of the finest displays of gastronomic art ever seen in this country," was set in the State Dining Room. The menu consisted of stewed and scalloped oysters, boned and truffle-stuffed turkey, *pâté de foie gras,* aspic of tongue, canvasback duck, partridge, fillet of beef, ham, venison, pheasant, terrapin, chicken salad, sandwiches, and jellies, cakes, ices, champagne punch, etc. It was prepared by Maillard, the famed New York caterer. Around twelve o'clock the dining room was thrown open for the guests to inspect the display before the food was disturbed.

The table, which extended practically the whole length of the room, and the small tables arranged along the walls, all were laden with dishes to tempt the appetite of an epicure. "The dazzling splendor of fruits, flowers, blazing lights, spar-

Mrs. McClellan.   Mrs. Lincoln.   Mrs. Senator Crittenden.

SOME OF THE PRINCIPAL COSTUMES WORN AT THE GRAND PRESIDENTIAL PARTY AT THE WHITE HOUSE, WEDNESDAY EVENING, FEBRUARY 5.

THE PRESIDENTIAL PARTY.

(Continued from page 210.)

But to return to the Presidential party. Early in the evening the windows of the White House were brilliant with lights, and by half-past nine the entrance was thronged with guests from a long line of carriages reaching to the avenue. The cards of invitation were received at the door, and the guests passed to the second story of the mansion, which had been thrown open for dressing-rooms. Thence they returned to the grand entrance, and were shown into the Blue Room, whence they passed to the grand saloon, or East Room, where they were received by Mr. and Mrs. Lincoln, with a gracious welcome and a kind word. Meanwhile the marine band " discoursed sweet music " from a side room. The saloon, when filled, presented the aspect no doubt contemplated and designed by Mrs. Lincoln, of a large select and elegant private party, with its animated conver-

Mrs. Vallette.   Mrs. E. G. Squier.   Mrs. Commodore Levy.   Mrs. O'Sullivan.   Mrs. Senator Weller.   Mrs. Senator Ames.   Mrs. Griffin.

A page in Leslie's Illustrated Newspaper of February 22, 1862, is devoted to "some of the principal costumes worn at the Grand Presidential Party at the White House, Wednesday evening, February 5."

kling crystal and inviting confections were everywhere!" Noted as prominent among the decorations and ornaments were:

> A representation of a U.S. steam frigate of forty guns, with all sails set and the flag of the Union flying at the main; a representation of the Hermitage; a warrior's helmet, supported by cupids; a Chinese pagoda; double cornucopias resting upon a shell supported by mermaids and surmounted by a crystal star; a rustic pavilion; the goddess of liberty, elevated above a simple but elegant shrine, within which was a life-like fountain of water; a fountain of four consecutive bowls, supported by water nymphs; an elegant composition of nougat Parisienne; a beautiful basket, laden with flowers and fruits, mounted upon a pedestal supported by swans; besides these were twenty or thirty ornaments and cake and candy, delicately conceived and exquisitely executed, and the designs of creams, jellies and ices were multiform and elegant.

The Monroe plateau, as usual, was the highlight of the decorations. A magnificent candelabrum surmounted a tall arrangement of flowers, and around the flowers were tropical fruits.

Promenading was resumed after supper, and it was not until three o'clock in the morning that the guests departed. The entertainment was pronounced a decided success, but it was compared to the ball given at Brussels by the Duchess of Richmond the night before Waterloo!

The abolitionists throughout the country were merciless in their criticism of the President and Mrs. Lincoln for giving this reception when the soldiers of the Union were in cheerless bivouacs or comfortless hospitals, and a Philadelphia poet wrote a scandalous ode on the occasion entitled, "The Queen Must Dance."

There was no dancing, contrary to popular opinion, nor was it generally known that after the invitations had been issued young Willie had suddenly taken cold and Mrs. Lincoln had been up for the two nights preceding the reception. Willie's fever worried his devoted parents, and they frequently slipped

The blue Japanese "punch bowl" used at the Lincolns' party of February 5 was a gift sent to President Buchanan after the first Japanese emissaries returned to Japan; it was designated as a "large water basin."

away from the party that evening to look in on him. His illness developed into pneumonia, and on February 20, 1862, Willie died.

The lad's death and the critical condition of the country, now in the throes of a full-scale war, put an end to all fashionable public receptions for two years. Mrs. Lincoln, whose grief was as violent as her temper, refused to be consoled. To those who suggested that she come out of her self-imposed seclusion, she snapped: "There is a war on!"

Historians have since described the Lincoln levees as "a curious mixture of fashion, elegance, and the crudity of everyday frontier life." Male guests appeared at the White House in hickory shirts, their trousers tucked into cowhide boots, and countrywomen filed past the receiving line in their Sunday best —shapeless garments devoid of style—while ladies of fashion, elaborately gowned and coiffed and magnificently bejeweled, dropped curtsies to the Presidential couple. One onlooker describes Mr. Lincoln as welcoming the sturdy farmer's wife and daughter in their cotton prints, Sunday mitts hiding their browned and toil-hardened hands, with as much courtesy as he did the grand ladies. In fact, he added, "His manner indicated they were actually more welcome."

When the tide of battle finally changed and a Union victory seemed assured, the receptions at the White House were resumed. It was about this time that Mrs. Lincoln insisted it was her prerogative, as First Lady, to lead the grand march on her husband's arm rather than follow on the arm of another gentleman. Her insistence that she was entitled to the same rank as her husband, and her jealousy when he so much as looked at an attractive woman, gradually alienated the public who, nonetheless, continued to worship the President. His wife's jealous outbreaks puzzled the Chief Executive, who was a devoted husband and father. On one occasion Presidential secretary John G. Nicolay, whose duty it was to arrange the seating for state dinners, noticed that a Cabinet member, his daughter, and her new husband had been excluded from the list. He knew why: Mrs. Lincoln hated the beautiful Mrs. Kate Chase Sprague, wife of Senator William Sprague of Rhode Island and daughter of Secretary of the Treasury Salmon P. Chase of Ohio. Nicolay ordered the names included. Afterward he remarked: "Having compelled Her Satanic Majesty to invite the Spragues, I was taboo."

Mrs. Lincoln decided to punish Nicolay by barring him from the dinner. Nicolay forced her to capitulate, however, simply by withholding his expert services

Lincoln himself was too great a man to understand his wife's pettiness. During these months, in spite of warnings that his life was in danger, he was often seen on the White House grounds after nightfall, walking about for exercise, deep in thought. Abraham Lincoln was a "character by himself, incomparable and unique," Forney tells us. He was among the "saddest of humanity," and yet his sense of the ridiculous was so keen that it bore him up through difficulties that would have broken down almost any other man. That he gave way to "uncontrollable fits of grief in the dark hours of war" is a fact beyond question. "Yet, he could lift himself out of his troubles and enjoy . . . the old quirks and quips of the clown in the circus, the broad innuendoes of the low comedian, the quiet sallies of the higher walks of the drama."

By this time the picturesque colonial life of America had begun to fade; the country was entering a new era. The names "Whig" and "Tory" gave way to "Democrat" and "Republican." Loyal chefs, anxious to honor their respective parties, invented such delicacies as "Democratic Potato Cake" and "Republican Cake."

Mrs. Lincoln had, without her husband's knowledge, spent so much money on clothes during the latter months of his first term in office that she was in morbid fear that he would not be reelected—in which case she would never be able to pay her debts. As soon as his victory was assured, however, she cheerfully bought an inaugural ball gown costing two thousand dollars.

The Inaugural Ball took place in the Patent Office, where supper was prepared for four thousand people. The spread included lamb, game, beef, poultry, seafood, pastries, jellies, confections, and various incidentals.

Mrs. Lincoln felt her triumph complete as she paraded about the ballroom in her two-thousand-dollar gown—a creation of shimmering white silk and lace. Her headdress was as elaborate as her gown, and she carried a fan trimmed with ermine. The cynosure of all eyes, she triumphed over the beauteous Mrs. Sprague. Her victory was short-lived, however. On April 14, 1865, six days after Robert E. Lee and his ragged Confederates surrendered to Grant at Appomattox Courthouse, Abraham Lincoln was shot as he sat in a box at Ford's Theater attending a performance of "Our American Cousin."

The Great Emancipator breathed his last the following morning. Edwin Stanton made the famous comment, "Now he belongs to the ages," and Vice President Andrew Johnson, a Tennessee Democrat, took the oath of office as the seventeenth President of the United States.

President Lincoln purchased this rosewood bed in December, 1864. Its dimensions are five and a half by eight feet; the carved headboard reaches a height of nine feet. The Lincoln bed is now in his second-floor study, used today as a guest room.

XVII

Plain People
from the Mountains

Andrew and Eliza Johnson

One of Andrew Johnson's first acts as President of the United States was to send word to the widowed Mrs. Lincoln, who "sat in the White House, half-demented, wringing her hands . . . ," inviting her to stay at the Executive Mansion as long as she wished.

In June, President Johnson was joined in the White House by his wife and family. The new First Lady had been an invalid for twenty years, and was not able to assume the heavy responsibilities and social duties incumbent upon a President's wife. Her only appearance in public during her husband's administration was at a party given by her grandchildren, at which she remained seated. As young guests were presented to her, she smiled and explained gently, "My dears, I am an invalid."

At seventeen, the former Eliza McCardle had married the nineteen-year-old Andy Johnson, who could neither write nor work arithmetic, and was able to read very little. In addition to caring for their home and children, she had taken her young husband under her tutorship, and helped him rise from gawky country tailor through the State Legislature to the Governorship of Tennessee; through both Houses of Congress to the Vice Presidency, and finally to the Presidency on the death of Lincoln.

Now fifty-eight, suffering from tuberculosis, Eliza selected for her own a small, quiet room in the southwest corner of the mansion overlooking the mall and the Potomac. Her room soon became the focal point around which the household revolved. Her time occupied by knitting, crocheting, or reading the books she loved, she was always waiting with a warm smile when the President and their grandchildren returned from a picnic or a stroll carrying wildflowers for her. Nobody, it seemed (and the nation agreed) was quite like Grandma, with her gentle ways, her simplicity, her patience and common sense. Though frail in body, she was strong in spirit and universally loved.

Mrs. Johnson never interfered in the management of the household. Such chores were turned over to Martha, her eldest daughter, but she did make periodical visits to the kitchen, wistfully eyeing pies and doughnuts in the making, but not quite daring to ask if she might help.

Martha, a handsome young woman of thirty-eight, soon assumed the responsibilities of hostess at White House social functions. The wife of David T. Patterson, who was elected Senator from Tennessee soon after Johnson became President, Martha had been educated at the Academy of the Visitation in Georgetown. During her father's term in the Senate she had remained at school, spending her weekly holidays with President Polk's family in the Executive Mansion, where she met Dolly Madison and the Blairs, Lees, and other old families of Washington, many of whom in later years gladly welcomed her return to the capital city. She had been early introduced into Washington social life, and the people who "imagined

The wartime restraints on White House social activities began to fall away toward the end of the year 1865. Receptions again took on a festive quality and attracted great crowds of visitors and onlookers. The drawing shows the East Gate on a grand reception day.

that Andrew Johnson's family were to prove a millstone about his neck forgot that Martha Patterson was his daughter." When some of the leaders of Washington society undertook to call at the White House and tender their patronage, Martha Patterson quietly remarked to them: "We are a plain people from the mountains of East Tennessee, called here for a short time by a national calamity, but we know our position and shall maintain it."

When the President's family joined him in Washington, the White House, "after the sad scenes enacted in it, was dirty and dilapidated." Martha Patterson faced the problem of making the place livable with the same fortitude with which she had faced the sorrows and privations of the Civil War; under her guidance it took on a note of cleanliness and cheer that caught the public's imagination.

As the war clouds began to lift, social functions once more took on a prewar tone. One contemporary wrote enthusiastically in January, 1866:

> Society in Washington has gone through a complete transformation during the past year. Never was a change in this respect so noticeable or so marked as here. It is seen at the receptions of the White House and all other social gatherings. The former are again resuming the brilliance of the palmy days of the Republic, and remind a person of the gay scenes at the White House when Miss Lane did the honors of the Executive Mansion. . . . Ladies arrayed in their rich silks, satins, tarletons and velvets, with their diamonds and jewels, now grace these gatherings. Gentlemen now consider it necessary to appear in their party attire. The general appearance of the rooms when the guests have all gathered there is that of a fancy dress ball. . . . Social life and society in Washington have never been more attractive or fascinating than this winter. It is daily increasing in interest, and bids fair to excel anything known here in the past.

In December, 1865, Congress appropriated $30,000 for renovation of the mansion. Workmen and decorators spent the greater part of the year 1866 putting the mansion into readi-

Thirty thousand dollars was spent on renovating the White House before the New Year's Day reception of 1867. The original caption on this drawing was, "The Promiscuous Company at the New Year's Reception."

ness for the reception to be held New Year's Day, January 1, 1867. After its completion, with the exception of the East Room, the social season did take on new brilliance. In addition to the New Year's Day reception, the President announced levees to be held on January 17, February 7, and February 22 from eight to eleven in the evening, and also that "Mrs. Patterson and Mrs. Stover would be at home on Monday afternoons."

The New Year's Day reception of 1867 was a great success. Perley describes the occasion in his *Reminiscences:*

> The East Room was not thrown open, but the suite of drawing-rooms, which had been redecorated and newly furnished, were much admired. The traditional colors of scarlet, blue, and green had been preserved, but the walls had been paneled with gilt moldings, and the furniture was far more elegant than that which it had replaced. There was a profusion of rare flowers from the conservatory.

Age and official perplexities had left their trace on Andrew Johnson's features, but he had lost none of his determined, defiant look. The President, noted for his meticulous dress, wore a plain black suit with straw-colored gloves, and received in the Blue Room, directly in front of the door connecting with the Red Room. The courteous Mr. Phillips, Assistant Marshal, introduced the visitors to him.

Mrs. Patterson and her blond sister, Marie, the wife of Colonel Daniel Stover, stood at the right of the President near the center of the room during the most ceremonious part of the reception. They were presented by Colonel B. B. French, Commissioner of Public Buildings. The two ladies were dressed "with exceptional taste and elegance and very nearly alike." Their gowns were fashioned of black corded silk, with tight-fitting basques. A vine of leaves was embroidered around the skirt a little below the waistline and descended in a double row down the front; near the bottom of the skirt the rows curved apart and formed a deep border. The only difference between the two dresses was that Mrs. Patterson's dress was embroidered in narrow white braid and Mrs. Stover's was embroidered in violet, with the leaves worked solid. Each of the women wore a narrow collar fastened with a brooch, and flowers in her hair—Mrs. Patterson a spray of mignonette and Mrs. Stover a white japonica.

As the weather was cold and rainy, Martha had prudently covered the new velvet carpets recently laid in the Red, Blue, and Green parlors to keep them from becoming soiled.

The diplomatic corps began arriving at eleven o'clock. Cabinet officers and their ladies entered next, then the Chief Justice, followed by Justices of the Supreme Court and the local judges, members of Congress, assistant secretaries, heads of bureaus, and chief clerks. As the band struck up "The Red, White and Blue," Admiral Radford entered with a large party of naval officers, all in full uniform; "Hail to the Chief" announced General Grant, who was attended by Adjutant-General Thomas and others. The reception, however, was marked by the absence of volunteer officers in uniform, who had, since the war, always been present in large numbers.

At twelve o'clock the officials took their leave and the waiting throngs were admitted to the White House. For two solid hours a living tide surged through the rooms, each man, woman, and child "being presented and shaking hands with the President as they passed him." There was "almost every conceivable variety of dress, and every part of the country, with many foreign lands, was represented," Perley tells us.

At the last levee of the season, held on February 22, the crowd was so massive it was impossible to enforce the customary regulations. Policemen stationed at the Red Room doors were swept on the tide to the Blue Room, where the receiving line stood.

A newspaper clipping of that time states:

> . . . The levees of President Johnson are especially brilliant, and frequenters of Washington society declare that under no former occu-

pant of the White House has such good order and system reigned, as under the present.

During Johnson's administration state dinners were held on Tuesday at seven o'clock. After dinner, around nine, guests repaired to the Blue Room for an hour of conversation.

The Johnson family dinner was a party in itself; the twelve members of the family, including five grandchildren, considered their dinnertime a kind of "social hour." Butter from the White House dairy was on the table. Martha Patterson established the reputation of having the "most up to date and cleanest dairy [the breed was Jersey] in Washington."

The President, who liked people and enjoyed meeting them, entertained Queen Emma of the Sandwich Islands (Hawaii), widow of King Kamehameha IV, when she stopped over in Washington on her way home from a trip around the world. The Queen arrived with her suite at half-past eight. She was received by Henry Stanbery, the attorney general, who escorted her to the Red Room where the President, Mrs. Johnson, Mrs. Patterson, Mrs. Stanbery, Secretary and Mrs. Gideon Welles, and other ladies and gentlemen were assembled. According to a newspaper account:

> The dusky Queen was dressed in a rich black silk with low neck, a broad mauve ribbon across her breast, a jet necklace and a diamond brooch. A jet tiara and white lace veil were worn upon her head. Contrary to custom, the doors of the White House were thrown open to as many as could be accommodated in the reception room so that all who pleased might witness the ceremony.

Leslie's *Illustrated Newspaper* provided some historical data about the Queen:

> Emma, dowager Queen of Hawaii, is a very pleasing person, and is partially of white extraction. Through her mother's side she belongs to the native Chieftains; her father was a grandson of John Young, one of Vancouver's companions. In 1856 she was married to Kame-

Her Majesty Emma, Queen Dowager of the Sandwich Islands, visited the White House during Johnson's administration. This drawing of her appeared in Leslie's Illustrated Newspaper.

hameha IV, who died in 1863. Their only son having died in 1862, the throne was occupied by the late King's brother, who now reigns under the title of Kamehameha V.

Andrew Johnson's four years in the White House may have been very successful on the domestic and social levels, but his official life was far from smooth. He was hated, insulted, and distrusted by both parties to the recently-concluded Civil War, and a lie everyone seemed to believe was that Johnson was a drunkard. In February, 1868, the House of Representatives passed a resolution of impeachment, the charge against him being that he had violated the law by dismissing his Secretary of War, Edwin Stanton. Johnson was acquitted by a single vote, and finished out his term. He did not attend the inauguration of his successor, Ulysses S. Grant.

Six years later, however, with Grant still in the White House, Andrew Johnson would win personal vindication. He would be returned to the Senate from Tennessee in 1875, and serve for a few months before his death on July 31.

XVIII

Breakers of Precedent

Ulysses and Julia Grant

Social Washington welcomed the change from the harrowing years of the Civil War, the deep gloom that had settled over the nation following Lincoln's assassination, and the first bitter years of the Reconstruction Period under Andrew Johnson. The brilliant Inaugural Ball held for Ulysses S. Grant on March 4, 1869, in the north wing of the new Treasury Department, then just completed, suited the spirit of the new era. Here, in part, is the description of the event which appeared in *Harper's Bazar:*

It has long been the custom to usher in each new administration by a complimentary entertainment which should give the people an opportunity of personally paying their respects to the new functionaries. This year the north wing of the new Treasury Building was chosen as the place of the reception, and was beautifully decorated for the occasion in the short space of two days. The massive columns of the portico were wreathed with flowers and foliage, and the entrance was surmounted with the welcome word PEACE in gas jets. Three magnificent rooms, on different floors, were fitted up for dancing; private apartments were allotted to the Presidential Party; and the basement was converted into supper rooms.

The new President and Vice President received the warmest congratulations from 6,000 persons that had assembled to do them honor. . . . Every kind of intoxicating liquor had been excluded, and all precaution taken to insure propriety: and in these respects the efforts of the managers were crowned with complete success. That people were jostled, dresses torn, wrappings lost and carriages missed here and there did not detract from the general good-humor, and the guests laughed instead of grumbled at these trifling mishaps, and only echoed the words of the great chief, "Let Us Have Peace."

In the succeeding months, capital society plunged into an orgy of entertaining and extravagance unheard of even in the lush days before the war. It was not unusual for eight receptions to be held in one block! (The Washington *Star* described the block on Eye Street, between Seventeenth and Eighteenth Streets on the afternoon of January 30, 1873, as the "liveliest looking portion of the city" that day. "Carriages blocked the street so completely there was scarcely room for the horses to make a turn.")

From the beginning, the new President let it be known that he refused to be handicapped by White House customs he considered useless and irksome. Both he and the new First Lady broke many of the old precedents that had chained former Chief Executives to the White House. Grant not only dined outside the mansion when it suited him, but returned calls.

Mrs. Grant, the former Julia Dent of St. Louis, wrote that the White House was a "garden spot of orchids." Her afternoon receptions, which the President often attended out of deference to his wife, were held between two and five P.M. and were open to the public, the only requirement being that guests leave their cards at the door. Levees, announced beforehand in the press and usually held between eight and ten P.M., with both the President and his Lady present, were open to the general public also.

Grant's first Inaugural Ball was held in the north wing of the new Treasury Department building. Thomas Nast's caricature of the supper scene (no liquor was served) appeared in Harper's Bazar.

General Grant carried with him into the White House his army habits of regularity. He arose at seven o'clock, read newspapers, and breakfasted with his family at eight-thirty on Spanish mackerel, steak or bacon and fried apples (the latter a favorite dish), rolls, pancakes, and coffee hot and strong. He usually took a short stroll afterward, walking slowly with his left hand behind him, sometimes holding a cigar in his right. Ten o'clock found him in his office. At three o'clock, the official business of the day ended, he almost invariably visited the White House stable. He was quite fond of his horses, including his bay charger; two carriage horses; a buggy horse; his son Jesse's ponies; his daughter Nellie's saddle horse, a natural pacer; a brood mare and three colts. Five vehicles stood in the carriage house: a landau, a barouche, a light road-wagon, a top-buggy, and a pony phaeton for the children.

Dinner was served promptly at five o'clock, and every member of the family was expected to be punctual. General Grant's favorite dishes were rare roast beef, boiled hominy, wheaten bread, and, for dessert, rice pudding, but he was not a heavy eater. The pleasant chatter of the four children—Fred, Ulysses junior, and Nellie, with Master Jesse as the humorist—enlivened the meals, while Grandpa Dent would "occasionally indulge in some conservative growls against the progress being made by the colored race," according to Perley. After coffee, the General would light another cigar and smoke while glancing over the New York papers. About nine o'clock a few chosen friends would often call, sometimes by appointment, but business matters were generally forbidden and official affairs were not to be mentioned.

Julia Grant enjoyed the whirl of entertainment as much as any of the ladies. Even the inclement weather—unusually cold for Washington—failed to dampen the gaiety, or the ladies' passion for silken and velvet gowns with exaggerated bustles and long trains and cobweb lace shawls. Fashion at that time decreed that dresses be cut very low at the neck; party frocks were extremely décolleté. Pearl powder had come into common use, and ladies young and old were using rouge and enamel.

The marriage of Nellie, the President's only daughter, to the young Englishman Algernon Sartoris was the first wedding in the White House in thirty years. General Grant had not approved the engagement of his daughter, then not yet nineteen, to a young Englishman who had enlisted her affection on the steamer while she was returning from abroad. But when he found her heart was set on it, he yielded.

Washington was at its loveliest when the ceremony took place in the spring, at eleven o'clock on the morning of May 21, 1874. So elaborate was the affair, so popular the Grants, and so socially prominent the groom, that society writers—including the female species which had so increased in numbers since the Anne Royall epoch—filled the newspapers here and abroad with full-page spreads on the event. The pastor of the Methodist Episcopal Church, Dr. Tiffany, officiated at the ceremony, which took place in the East Room before an altar banked by Easter lilies and other bridal flowers. The bride wore a white satin dress trimmed with point lace; her bridal veil, which completely enveloped her, was crowned with a wreath of white flowers and green leaves interspersed with orange blossoms.

According to Washington newspapers of the day, there were eight bridesmaids. They wore dresses of white corded silk, alike in every particular, with overdresses of white illusion and sashes of white silk arranged in a succession of loops from the waist down, forming a graceful drapery. Four bridesmaids wore blue flowers, and four pink.

Mrs. Grant's dress was black silk, with ruffles and puffs of black illusion, and lavender-colored ribbons, lilacs, and pansies. (She was in mourning at the time.)

After the ceremony the guests, including members of the diplomatic corps, resplendent in full dress, Cabinet officers,

Justices of the Supreme Court, and high-ranking officers of the army and navy—many of whom had served in military campaigns under Grant—proceeded to the State Dining Room for the elaborate wedding breakfast. They dined on such delicacies as soft crabs on toast, chicken croquettes with fresh peas, aspic of beef tongue, and decorated broiled spring chicken. The dessert was strawberries with cream. And of course there was a wedding cake, elaborately decorated with doves, roses, and wedding bells. Ice cream and ices of various flavors were served with small fancy cakes, punch, coffee, and chocolate. As the guests left, Thomas Pendel handed each a little box tied in white ribbon—wedding cake for "hopefuls" to dream on.

The fashion at the time was ornate floral decorations; favors had become the rage at dinner parties, a fad which continued until it became a display of the host's wealth rather than a memento of the pleasant occasion. Julia Grant adopted the custom wholeheartedly; the State Dining Room became a fairyland on official and special dinner occasions. The chandelier was festooned with ropes of roses and smilax; potted plants and flowers adorned the windows and alcoves; ten-foot-tall pink azaleas bloomed behind Mrs. Grant's chair.

When the Monroe plateau was used as the centerpiece it was decked with flowers. The spaces between the plateau and the ends of the table were used for smaller bowls of flowers, Monroe candelabra, and fruit *epergnes,* and were interspersed with garlands of smilax. From 1876 on, however, a silver ship was the Grants' favorite centerpiece. The ship was made and put on display at the Centennial Exposition in Philadelphia by the Mohawk Indians, who afterward presented it to President Grant. On occasion it was set on the mirrored plateau; the effect achieved was that the ship was afloat. The ship bears an appropriate inscription:

> "All alone went Hiawatha
> Through the clear, transparent water."

Nellie Grant, the President's only daughter, was married in the East Room on May 21, 1874. This was the first wedding ceremony performed in the White House since President Tyler married in 1844.

Usually a bouquet of flowers with streamers of satin ribbon lay at each lady's cover, which she either wore or carried in her hand after dinner. A boutonniere lay at each gentleman's place.

President and Mrs. Grant received their guests at seven o'clock in the Oval Room. They then proceeded to the State Dining Room, the President leading with the lady of highest rank on his arm and the First Lady following on the arm of that lady's husband.

The guests of President and Mrs. Grant partook of the most elaborate dinners ever to be served in the White House, sometimes consisting of twenty-nine courses and lasting for two or three hours. Six wine glasses stood at each cover. Roman punch or *sorbet,* dubbed "the life-saving station," was served at the end of the roast course as a refresher. A dinner for thirty-six guests might cost the President $700 to $1500, excluding beverages; the dinner given for Prince Arthur, third son of Queen Victoria, is said to have cost $2,000.

The New Year's Day reception of 1873 was a crowded affair. Julia Grant, splendid in a dress of pearl-gray silk, flounced and trimmed with silk of a darker hue and point lace, greeted the guests enthusiastically. The diplomatic corps, Supreme Court, army, and navy turned out in full force. Among those present, according to Perley, were:

> . . . nice people, questionable people and people who were not nice at all. Every state, every age, every social class, both sexes and all human colors were represented. There were wealthy bankers, and a poor, blind, black beggar led by a boy; men in broadcloth and in homespun; men with beards and men without beards. Members of the press and of the lobby; contractors and claim agents; office holders and office seekers; there were ladies from Paris in elegant attire and ladies from the interior in calico; ladies whose cheeks were tinged with rouge, and others whose faces were weather-bronzed by out-door work; ladies as lovely as Eve, and others as naughty as Mary Magdalene; ladies in diamonds, and others in dollar jewelry; chambermaids elbowed countesses, and all enjoyed themselves. . . .

President Grant's second inauguration on Tuesday, March 4, 1873, was shorn of its splendor by the bitterly cold weather. The wind blew in a shrill gale, sweeping away flags and other decorations. So intense was the cold that the breath of the musicians condensed in the valves of their instruments, making it impossible for them to play, and many of the cadets and soldiers had to leave the ranks, half-frozen. The customary crowds of civilians were completely routed by the cutting blasts.

At the Inauguration Ball, held in an immense temporary building which had no heating apparatus, the ladies were compelled to wear their wrappings, and the gentlemen kept on their overcoats and hats as they endeavored to keep warm by vigorous dancing.

Mrs. Grant, who wore a white silk dress trimmed with black chantilly lace, shivered as she stood beside her husband on the dais. The supper, prepared at great expense, was emphatically a cold repast. Ornamented molds of ice cream froze into solid chunks, and the plentiful champagne and punch were forsaken for hot coffee and chocolate, the only warm comforts in the building. The guests, each one of whom had paid twenty dollars for a ticket, were frozen out before midnight.

Grant entertained many important personages, including Prince Arthur of Connaught in January, 1870, King Kalakaua of the Sandwich Islands on December 22, 1874, and Dom Pedro II, Emperor of Brazil, on May 8, 1876.

Prince Arthur was royally entertained in the State Dining Room, which was decorated with evergreens and English and American flags. Covers were laid for thirty-six, and it was one of the most costly banquets given by President Grant. The First Lady, a favorite of members of the diplomatic corps for her wit and charm, was elaborately gowned in the bustle and long train then fashionable.

As King Kalakaua dined, his cup bearer and two other members of his entourage stood behind his chair. Their dress, which excited considerable comment, is briefly described as resembling "ladies' bertha capes." Every morsel of food that passed the royal lips was first scrutinized by the cup bearer.

Dom Pedro II had come to this country primarily to visit the Centennial Exposition at Philadelphia, and traveled incognito as "Mr. Alcantara," though he was accompanied by the Empress Theresa and his imperial retinue. Some days before his arrival the House Committee on Foreign Affairs, "in view of the repeatedly expressed desire of Dom Pedro II to travel through the United States as a private gentleman . . ." had reported adversely on a resolution proposing a public reception for the Emperor. Accordingly, Dom Pedro was met at the depot only by Señor Borges, the Brazilian minister.

President Grant must have been most pleased by this turn of events. A small item taken from the Washington *Star* of May 6, 1876—the day preceding the Emperor's descent upon the city—states simply:

> GONE A-FISHING: There was no official business transacted at the White House today, as the President spent the day with friends, at the Great Falls, fishing.

The Emperor was equally happy with the no-fuss-and-feathers arrangement. He spent a quiet Sunday afternoon visiting the Capitol, and enjoyed the evening at the National Observatory in company with the Brazilian minister and Professor Newcomb, the astronomer.

Dom Pedro's visit to the White House on Monday morning, May 8, was a purely social one. Accompanied by Señor Borges, the Brazilian minister, and his suite, he called at the Executive Mansion and was at once ushered into the Blue Room, to be greeted by the President and Secretary of State Hamilton Fish, who made the formal introduction. After the usual expressions of pleasure at meeting they proceeded to the Red Parlor, where Mrs. Grant, Mrs. Fish, and Mrs. Fred

The Centennial Exposition, held at Fairmount Park, Philadelphia, ran from May 10 to November 10, 1876. The Mohawk Indians displayed this hand-crafted silver ship, and presented it to President Grant for use at the White House when the Exposition closed.

Grant were waiting. Here the whole party "engaged in a very pleasant conversation, which lasted over half an hour, and after which, bidding adieu to the President and his family, the Imperial party entered their carriages and were driven to the Capitol."

When the Emperor, dressed in a black suit and wearing an old-fashioned plug hat, visited the diplomatic gallery of the House of Representatives, he rose to his feet when the chaplain began the prayer. If he felt any surprise on seeing that the members preferred to worship in a recumbent position with their heels on their desks, the Emperor gave no indication of it; he politely sat down again without a word.

President Grant, Mrs. Grant, Mrs. Fred Grant, and Cabinet members and their families were among the two hundred twenty-five persons who left on a special train on the morning of May 9 for the Philadelphia Centennial, which was to open the following morning. The Emperor had planned a trip to Mount Vernon that morning, but since the weather was inclement he decided to visit the Treasury Department before leaving for the Centennial at one o'clock that afternoon.

At the Centennial opening the following morning, the Emperor and his party were greeted by General Hawley and others of the commission. As General Hawley led the Emperor to his seat on the platform and the orchestra struck up the Brazilian National Anthem, Dom Pedro was loudly cheered. President Grant, escorted also by General Hawley, then advanced to the front of the platform, and as the orchestra played "Hail to the Chief," the President shook hands with the Emperor and other guests before making his speech opening the Centennial.

The Grants were a close-knit family, and in their time the Executive Mansion is said to have looked more like a private home than it did during any other administration. Mrs. Grant, besides being an excellent hostess, was a devoted wife and mother, cognizant of her family's culinary likes and dislikes.

In November, 1871, Grand Duke Alexis of Russia was a guest at the White House. The Russian envoy presented the Grand Duke to President Grant, who introduced his Cabinet. Grant then led his guest to the Red Room, and presented him to Mrs. Grant and the other ladies.

She took everything in stride—probably because of her training as a soldier's wife—and always arranged for six extra places to be set for the unexpected guests who were sure to drop in.

Although Grant insisted that members of his family be on time for meals, he was more lenient toward his friends. Once he waited half an hour for Senator Simon Cameron of Pennsylvania, who was late for a state dinner. When he did not appear, the President finally led the guests into the State Dining Room after issuing orders that the Senator be given a seat directly opposite him when he did arrive.

The company had been at dinner a full half hour when the legislator finally arrived, carrying a hickory walking stick. The President's secretary, who had been waiting for him, promptly escorted him (still carrying the stick), to the State Dining Room. Not the least bit apologetic over his tardiness, the guest took his seat and proceeded to do justice to the meal.

Though he served eight years and was extremely popular, President Grant never quite got over the difficulty of adhering to the White House code of etiquette. "I'd rather storm a fort!" he once told a guest after dutifully dancing with a lady at one of the many parties given during his administration.

Ulysses Grant, in addition to his presidential duties, turned his attention more and more toward the general improvement of the nation's capital, and Washington today owes much to his foresight and planning.

The Grants left the White House the day after giving a banquet which was designed to surpass any given heretofore in the Executive Mansion—that accorded the incoming President and Mrs. Rutherford B. Hayes on March 3, 1877.

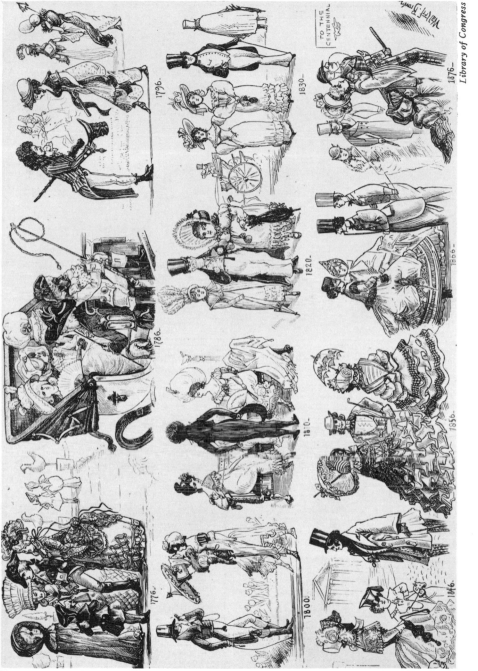

Harper's Bazar ran this "Centennial Review of the Fashions for the Past Hundred Years" in an 1876 issue.

XIX

Lemonade Lucy

Rutherford and Lucy Hayes

Washington society, after eight years of elaborate entertaining, frizzled hairdo's, bustles, and velvet trains, got the surprise of its life when the Rutherford B. Hayeses, with their quiet culture and conservative ways, moved into the White House.

Neither the President nor his wife cared for liquor, and lost no time in banning it from the White House table. The taboo created a furor of criticism among the élite of the social and official hierarchies of the capital city; Mrs. Hayes was sarcastically referred to as "Lemonade Lucy." The new First Lady had brought with her from her home what was known in those days as "the Ohio idea" of total abstinence from all intoxicating liquors, and Lucy Hayes enforced her ban although a story is told by Perley, in his *Reminiscences,* that a certain steward of the White House managed to get around the taboo and gratify the thirst of those who wished something stronger than lemonade.

The White House waiters, Perley tells us, "were kept busy replenishing salvers upon which tropical fruit [oranges] lay. Glances telegraphed to one another that . . . concealed within the oranges was a delicious frozen punch, a large ingredient of which was strong old Santa Croix rum. Thenceforth (without the knowledge of Mrs. Hayes, of course) Roman punch was served about the middle of each state dinner and was referred to by those in on the secret as 'the life-saving station.' " In his diary, however, President Hayes wrote that only rum flavoring was used, and that this was a joke "on the drinking people."

The people one met in the White House and at Washington social affairs during the Hayes administration were an improvement over those who had flocked to the capital city's social functions since the war. One of the evils attendant on the "gilded era" of the war and the flush times that followed, Perley says, was the universal desire of everyone to be a part of Washington "society":

> The maiden from New Hampshire who counted currency in the Treasury Department for $900 a year; the young student from Wisconsin who received $1200 per annum for his services as a copyist in the General Land office; the janitor of the Circumlocution Bureau, and the energetic correspondent of the Cranberry Centre Gazette, each and all thought they should dine at the foreign legations, sup with the members of the Cabinet, mingle in the mazes of the German, and with the families of the Senators. The discrepancy in income or education made no difference in their minds. . . . But while some of them, by their persistency, wriggled into society, the stern reality remained that their compensations did not increase, because their owners foolishly diminished them in what they called "maintaining their social position."

Hayes was sworn into office on March 3, 1877 (the fourth fell on Sunday). Had he waited until Monday, the United States would have been without a head for twenty-four hours, a condition which, in view of the critical times—the nation was torn by strikes and in the throes of a financial panic—was deemed unwise.

On this historic Saturday night, President Grant decided to honor his successor with a banquet. His party-loving wife, Julia, who determined to make the affair one of the most elaborate ever held in the Executive Mansion, saw to it that the decorations were overwhelming. Dining-room chandeliers were festooned with roses and smilax; potted plants filled the alcoves and windows, and flowers were massed behind Mrs. Grant's chair. The thirty-six guests found bouquets for the ladies and boutonnieres for the gentlemen at their places. Six wine glasses stood at each plate.

The guests had assembled when President Grant, President-elect Hayes, Secretary of State Hamilton Fish, and Chief Justice Morrison Waite slipped away unobtrusively to meet in the Red Room. There Rutherford Hayes, with raised hand in lieu of a Bible, took the oath of office as the nineteenth President of the United States. Then he and the Chief Justice signed the document (witnessed by General Grant and Secretary Fish), which was then entrusted to the Secretary of State for safe-keeping.

The following Monday Mr. Hayes was again sworn in—this time officially, at public ceremonies held at the Capitol—and took his oath on the Bible.

Lucy Hayes, with her plainly-arranged hair and high-necked black silk dress, exercised a greater influence over public affairs than any First Lady since Dolly Madison, according to one reporter. Here is a contemporary description of her:

> Tall, robust and with a dignified figure, the expression of her face, from the broad forehead which showed from her hair, worn in the old-fashion style, to the firm mouth and modest chin, bespoke the thoughtful, well-balanced, woman. She had a bright, animated face. . . . Her radiant smile . . . was the reflection of a sunny disposition and a nature at rest with itself. . . . She and husband never seemed fretted or flurried.

Mrs. Hayes was charmed with the White House, and lost no time in having the lumber rooms ransacked and old china and furniture brought out and renovated.

Instead of "frittering away the liberal appropriations of Congress for the domestic wants of the White House," she expended a large share of them in the purchase of a state dinner service of nearly a thousand pieces, illustrating the fauna and flora of the United States. The designs were executed by Theodore R. Davis of New Jersey, who, Perley tells us, had "fished in the rivers of the East and West, and in the sea, hunted fowl and wild game in the forests, the swamps and the mountains, shot buffalo on the plains and visited historic haunts of the Indians in the East, met the Indians in their wigwams and studied their habits on the prairies of the West." The designs, made in water colors, were bold and striking, but were difficult to produce perfectly upon porcelain with hard mineral colors. It was necessary to invent new methods and to have recourse to peculiar mechanical appliances, but the effort was successful and the set of Limoges faience which was produced became a rich legacy for future White House families.

Lucy Hayes had eight children, three of whom died in infancy. A devout Christian, she instituted morning prayers, to be said after the eight-thirty breakfast. At her Sunday-evening hymn sessions, in which Cabinet officers and Congressmen raised their voices together, singing such hymns as "Lead Kindly Light" and "Rock of Ages," her rich voice could be heard leading the songs of praise, while the deep, clear, bass tones of Vice President Wheeler rounded out the harmony. The First Lady was accomplished as an instrumentalist, and her husband, who was a devotee of folk songs according to the *Musical Observer,* once wrote her before their marriage: "With no musical taste or cultivation myself, I am yet so fond of simple airs that I have often thought I could never love a woman who did not sing them."

An evening in the private parlors of the Executive Mansion. On Sunday evenings Lucy Hayes held hymn-singing sessions at which Cabinet officers and congressmen raised their voices together.

Open house was held at the Executive Mansion between eight and ten o'clock Saturdays for Washingtonians and others who felt the impulse to drop in. Often fifty or more guests would appear at these impromptu affairs, which must have taxed the hospitality of Lucy and Rutherford Hayes. In fact, *Harper's Weekly* (July 2, 1892) states that the "world took . . . liberal advantage of [the Hayeses'] hospitality and worked . . . havoc to the Executive Mansion, and its own persons and garments."

According to one observer, Lucy Hayes never bowed to the tyranny of such fashions as "frizzled hair and . . . party-dresses cut so shamefully low in the neck as to generously display robust maturity or scraggy leanness." As soon as the First Lady emancipated herself, other Washington ladies followed suit. Actually, many of Lucy Hayes's evening gowns were elegant, made of rich material and carefully chosen colors. She had the good taste not to disfigure her beautifully shaped head with ridiculous coiffures, or to load herself with flashy jewelry.

State dinners under Hayes's administration, while not as elaborate as those enjoyed by his predecessor, were nonetheless delicious and tastefully served. Lucy Hayes's table "groaned with delicacies which called forth admiration," one eyewitness reported. Throughout the Hayes tenure of the historic mansion, there were neither champagne glasses nor alcohol-tainted punch bowls on the tables; the only exception to the taboo on liquor occurred at the banquet given on April 19, 1877, for Grand Duke Alexis Alexandrovitch of Russia, at which, thanks to the earnest pleading of Secretary of State Evarts, wine was served.

The popular custom of egg rolling on the White House lawns on Easter Monday is generally credited to President and Mrs. Hayes (although Dolly Madison is said to have introduced the idea in the first place). The children of Washington had for years enjoyed this sport on the grounds of the

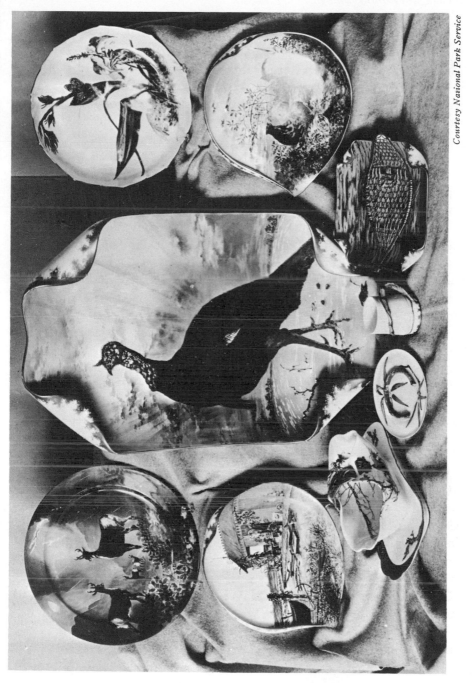

Lucy Hayes purchased a state dinner service of nearly a thousand pieces; the motif was flora and fauna of the United States, taken from original watercolors executed by Theodore R. Davis of New Jersey.

Capitol building, but when the guards chased the youngsters who gathered there on Easter Monday, 1878, President Hayes invited them to use the White House grounds—a gesture which endeared the Hayeses to parents and children throughout the nation and made the affair one of national significance.

The weekend party that heralded the close of the year 1877 turned out to be one of the most beautiful ever held in the White House, for the thirtieth of December was the Hayeses' silver wedding anniversary. This was the first celebration of its kind that had occurred at the Executive Mansion.

Friends who had attended the wedding ceremony, including the bridal party and the minister, Dr. L. D. McCabe of Delaware, Ohio, were invited to repeat their parts in a reenactment of the wedding service. The President himself had addressed these invitations, on which he had scribbled an intimate "I hope you will come."

In the East Room, at the doors and in the alcoves, tropical plants clustered in profusion. Mantels were banked with bright-colored cut flowers, and smilax was entwined in the huge crystal chandeliers. At the main entrance, just opposite the national coat-of-arms, two immense star-spangled flags, hanging from ceiling to floor, completely covered the large window. The Green, the Red, and the Blue parlors were similarly decorated with azaleas, hyacinths, and roses.

Members of the Cabinet and their families were the only official personages invited to this celebration. The guest list included: a delegation of the regiment (the Twenty-third Ohio Volunteer Infantry) which the President had commanded in the Civil War. Among the President's schoolmates present was a Mr. Deshla of Columbus, who said: "I knew him when we called him 'Rud'; when he was called 'Mr. Hayes,' then 'Colonel Hayes' and 'General Hayes'; then 'Governor Hayes' and now that he is President, we are equally good friends."

Precisely at nine o'clock on the thirty-first, the band struck up Mendelssohn's *Wedding March,* and President Hayes,

Rutherford and Lucy Hayes celebrated their twenty-fifth wedding anniversary on December 30, 1877. This was the first celebration of its kind held in the White House.

with his wife on his arm, came downstairs followed by members of the family and the special guests, two by two. The procession passed through the inner vestibule into the East Room, where the President and Mrs. Hayes stationed themselves, with their backs to the flag-draped window, and there remained until the invited guests had made their congratulations. Mrs. Mitchell—the daughter of the President's sister, Mrs. Platt—stood next to Mrs. Hayes and "clasped her hand, as she did when a little child, during the marriage ceremony twenty-five years back," Perley tells us.

Lucy Hayes wore a gown of white silk with draperies of white brocade, each with two rows of tasseled fringe along the top and a full plaiting at the sides and bottom of the front breadth; the heart-shaped neck was filled in with tulle, and the half-length sleeves had deep ruchings of lace. Her hair, in plain bands, was knotted at the back and fastened with a silver comb; long white kid gloves and white slippers completed her bridal array. (Perley tells us that on the day previous, which was the actual anniversary, Mrs. Hayes had worn her wedding dress, making "no alterations save in letting out the seams . . . of flowered satin, made when ten or twelve breadths of silk were put in a skirt, and there was no semblance of a train appended thereto.")

After receiving the congratulations of the company, the President and Mrs. Hayes led the way into the State Dining Room, which was elaborately decked with cut flowers and plants. The table was adorned with pyramids of confectionery, fancy French dishes, and ices in molds, the menu including every delicacy in the way of eatables but no beverage except coffee. At midnight, when the guns announced the New Year, congratulations and good wishes were exchanged, and then the company departed.

The following day was given over to the regular White House New Year's reception. The President and First Lady shook hands with those representing official Washington, and

This drawing by W. M. Rouzee, which appeared in Harper's Bazar, bears the caption, "President and Mrs. Hayes at divine worship in the Foundry M. E. Church, Washington, D. C."

later the general public was welcomed into the halls of the Executive Mansion. Lucy Hayes, in a stunning black velvet gown cut on princess lines with a train, the V-neck filled in with delicate Spanish lace, received her guests with a fresh, warm-hearted smile.

Before the end of the Hayes administration, Lucy, who very much enjoyed her role of First Lady, had become "the most idolized woman in America." Three great poets—Longfellow, Whittier, and Oliver Wendell Holmes—paid tribute to her in verse; she was acclaimed for her courage and Madonna-like beauty, and for the serenity and softness of her eyes and the gentleness of face. Her happiness and cheerfulness, according to Thomas Pendel, then doorkeeper, permeated the White House.

She was the first college graduate to rule as mistress of the White House, and the only presidential hostess to be memorialized for valor in a cause. The Woman's Christian Temperance Union presented a portrait of Lucy Hayes to the White House, where it hangs today. With the gift went a silken banner inscribed: "She hath done what she could."

XX

Tragedy in Washington

James and Lucretia Garfield

The little old lady leaned forward, listening intently to every word spoken by the eloquent orator on the platform erected over the lower flight of steps leading to the eastern portico of the Capitol. Overhead, bright streaks of light appeared in the sky, which had been leaden all morning. The snowstorm that had held Washington in its grip during the night had ceased; drying flags began to flutter in the breeze, and up Pennsylvania Avenue surged a wave of men, women, and children, shouting and cheering, toward the great event of the day—the inauguration of the new President, James Abram Garfield.

General Garfield, who a moment before had occupied the seat of honor with President Hayes on his right and Chief Justice Waite on his left, delivered his inaugural address in a loud, clear voice. Now the sun shone brightly, and the people who had pushed close to the platform could not help noticing the resemblance between their new President and an old woman listening delightedly to the ringing tones of his speech.

"Grandma" Garfield was the first woman to hear her son deliver an inaugural address. When he had finished his speech and taken the oath of office, Garfield, before receiving the congratulations of those around him, strode over to kiss the little old lady, amid the shouts and cheers of the crowd.

The capital city was seething with strangers from north, east, south, and west who had come by locomotive, steamboat, carriage, and on foot to attend the gala occasion. Washington hotels were filled to overflowing; late arrivals were happy to find cots in private homes. Many swarmed into concert halls, theaters, and even public buildings for the night.

The Inaugural Ball of March 4, 1881, was held in the new National Museum building, which had just been completed. The first thing that caught the guests' eyes in the central rotunda was a heroic-size statue of Lady Liberty, holding aloft a flaming torch. The high, arched ceiling of the room was almost hidden by a network of evergreens and flowers. Red-white-and-blue flags were displayed everywhere.

The new President and First Lady arrived at the ball at about nine o'clock. Lucretia Garfield wore a stunning dress of light heliotrope satin elaborately trimmed with point lace, a cluster of pansies at her neck, and no jewelry. Mrs. Hayes, who attended the ball with her, wore a cream-colored satin frock trimmed with ermine.

Supper was served in the "annex," a temporary construction, where preparations had been made for seating five hundred guests at a time. More than fifteen hundred pounds of turkey were provided by the caterer for the gargantuan feast that followed, which included a hundred gallons of oysters, fifty hams, two hundred gallons of chicken salad, seven hundred loaves of bread, two thousand biscuits, three hundred and fifty pounds of butter, fifty gallons of jelly, fifteen thousand cakes, a hundred and fifty gallons of ice cream, fifty gallons of water ices, two hundred and fifty gallons of coffee, and other delicacies in proportion.

General Garfield's mother was present at his inauguration on March 4, 1881.
Immediately after concluding his address, Garfield crossed the platform and
kissed his mother. Leslie's Illustrated Newspaper *shows Chief Justice Waite*
administering the oath of office, with Mrs. Garfield seated at his left.

The buoyant and jovial new President was as social-minded as his wife, Lucretia, was retiring. A former Major General in the Union Army during the Civil War, he had resigned from the army to take a seat in the House of Representatives. He served as Republican member until 1880, when he was elected to the Senate; shortly afterward, at the age of forty-nine, he became President.

Lucretia Garfield, familiarly called "Crete" by her husband, had a natural aversion to publicity, but made a zealous effort to carry out her social obligations at the White House until she became ill with typhoid fever. She won the commendation of Washington society, which considered her "lady-like, sweet-voiced, unruffled, well-informed, and always appropriately dressed."

Mrs. Garfield was a believer in good fare, and guests invariably found an abundance of wholesome, nutritious food at the White House table, as well as coffee, tea, and milk.

Flowers from the conservatory usually adorned the table at the family meals, at which "Mother" Garfield had an honored place at her son's right and was always waited on first, whoever else might be present. On the President's other side sat Jamie, who was his father's favorite. Harry, the oldest boy, sat next to his mother, and Molly, who was approaching womanhood, Irwin, and little nine-year-old Abram, named after his father, made up the rest of the intimate family group.

After dinner, President Garfield often enjoyed a game of billiards. The billiard table, banished during the Hayes administration since Lucy Hayes regarded billiards, along with cards and dancing, as vanities which had no place in the Executive Mansion, was happily restored to its former place. Garfield occasionally drank a glass of champagne, Rhine wine, or lager beer, but he was a temperate drinker. Now and then he indulged in a cigar.

Chief among the innovations of the Garfield administration was the practice of holding separate receptions for the different groups of the social and political *haut monde* of Washington. The Garfields' third reception, held on March 17, 1881, was given for members and officers of both Houses of Congress, and for the Justices of the Supreme Court.

On March 8, 1881, President Garfield accepted a portrait of Lucy Hayes from members of the National Woman's Christian Temperance Union, in recognition of her abolishment of intoxicating liquors from the White House table. There is a record that on one occasion he conferred the degrees at the college for deaf mutes at Kendall Green, just north of Washington.

Garfield showed at all times a deep, practical interest in educational matters. He had studied languages, science, literature, and the fine arts, and was president of a literary association. Occasionally he went to a concert or the theater. Perley, in his *Reminiscences,* tells us of the delight Garfield manifested when attending the readings of Charles Dickens. When Mr. Dickens, reading *A Christmas Carol,* came to the words, "Bless his heart: it's Fezziwig alive again!" a dog, stirred, perhaps, by some ghostly impulse, responded with a series of double-bass barks that not only brought down the house but threw Mr. Dickens himself into such convulsions of laughter that he could not proceed with his reading. "Bow! wow! wow!" was President Garfield's favorite greeting for months afterward when he met anyone whom he knew to have been at the lecture.

Garfield was a great lover of scrapbooks; his wife used to aid him in this hobby by cutting and sorting scraps which he marked in newspapers and pasting them into the books.

The nation was shocked and saddened by the tragedy which struck the White House only a few months after the jovial new President's inauguration. On July 2, 1881, James Abram Garfield, twentieth President of the United States, was assassinated by Charles Guiteau, and Vice President Chester Alan Arthur was sworn in as Chief Executive.

XXI

Twenty-four Wagonloads

Chester Alan Arthur

Twenty-four wagonloads of White House furniture—including everything from bedroom and parlor sets to mattresses and lace curtains which had graced the windows of the Executive Mansion—were being sold at auction. White House souvenirs were at a premium, and the bidding was spirited and high. The furnishings sold for over $6,000.

The death of President Garfield had sent his Vice President, the urbane and luxury-loving Chester Alan Arthur, into the Executive Mansion. After looking through the White House, Arthur flatly refused to move in until it had been redecorated. A widower, the fastidious Arthur, who had spent many years in New York, threatened to refurnish and redecorate the historic mansion at his own expense if Congress failed to appropriate the money. Fortunately, this wasn't necessary.

Although Arthur came into the Presidency in September, 1881, it was not until the following December that he agreed to move into the White House. (By then, the first elevator had been installed.) In the interim, during which the twenty-four wagonloads of furniture were sold at auction, Arthur lived in the mansion belonging to Senator John P. Jones of Nevada, where he set up temporary executive offices. He inspected the White House daily, making suggestions and giving orders to his close friend, Louis Tiffany—then the most famous decorator in New York—who was charged with the redecoration. Tiffany's efforts satisfied even the fastidious Arthur. In particular he admired the small dining room, which he preferred to the State Dining Room. The walls of this room were covered with heavy gold paper in large designs and enriched with pomegranate velvet drapes at the windows. Arthur added one of the splendid glass screens which survived through successive administrations until the Franklin Delano Roosevelts redecorated the mansion in 1933.

During Arthur's administration, old-fashioned formal etiquette was reestablished—there was no back slapping of guests, no familiar use of Christian names. Arthur did occasionally accept invitations to dinner.

He cherished the memory of his deceased wife, Ellen, a Southern beauty with a lovely singing voice who had died of pneumonia, and before whose picture in the White House a vase of fresh flowers was placed daily; and he was affectionately watchful over his son, Alan, a student at Princeton, and his daughter, Nellie.

The new President usually rose about nine-thirty, took a cup of coffee and a roll while dressing, and then went to his office. At noon, after a light repast—no meat, but oatmeal, fish, and fruit—he returned to his desk, where he remained until four o'clock. He then took a drive or a ride on horseback, sometimes accompanied by his daughter, Nellie. His dinner hour was six o'clock, and his favorite dish was a mutton chop with a glass of ale, or a slice of rare roast beef with a glass of claret, hot baked potatoes, and fruits. After dinner he returned to his desk, and often remained there until the

Chester Alan Arthur refused to move into the White House until it was completely redecorated. Louis Tiffany of New York was the decorator, and one of his contributions to the mansion's décor was a series of glass screens; illustrated are those separating the north portico entrance hall from the corridor.

early morning hours. He cheerily remarked that he was "a night bird," and his favorite enjoyment was to have two or three personal friends at a late supper, then chat with them into the "wee sma' hours," possibly on politics, for he is said to have been well versed in the subject, particularly state politics. He was a good listener and conversationalist.

Arthur was an ideal host to both his public and his private guests. Of "handsome presence, courteous, witty, tactful and possessing infinite *savoir faire,* he was the living refutation of the taunt which the Europeans sometimes level at us, to the effect that eminence in American politics is not attainable by one who is a gentleman at heart," wrote one observer.

The new President kept the domestic side of his ménage entirely apart from his official life. According to Thurston, in the *Bookman:*

> Coarse-minded, peeping correspondents, male and female, found scant material for vulgar paragraphs of kitchen gossip. His children were not photographed and paragraphed, or made the subject of a thousand flat and fabulous stories. Beyond the veil of self-respecting privacy which was drawn before the President's personal affairs few ever penetrated.

Arthur soon made his youngest sister, Mary, widow of the Reverend John E. McElroy, his official hostess. Mary McElroy's grace and charm made her universally popular. She introduced tea at her afternoon receptions, held between two and four o'clock, and served her delighted guests tiny sandwiches, cakes, punch, tea, coffee, and candies.

At official functions held in the State Dining Room, the President sat at the center of one side of the table in front of the centerpiece with the wife of the guest of honor at his right. Mary sat directly opposite him, with the gentleman guest of honor at her right.

Arthur's favorite centerpiece was one which he called "The Swinging Garden of Babylon," although it was more suggestive of a temple than a garden. Approximately four feet long and one and a half feet high, it consisted mainly of red and white carnations, honeysuckle, and roses, massed in their separate colors. Topping these were clusters of the rare and curious blossoms of the nun plant. The "garden" rested in the center of the Monroe plateau. Extending toward either end were containers of roses, mixed flowers, and lilies-of-the-valley. Each lady found a belt bouquet of roses at her place; for the gentlemen there were boutonnieres consisting of a single rosebud.

It has been said that the food served at Arthur's table rivaled that of any other President. The author is inclined to question this statement, in view of the feats of "Black Sam," the Melahs, and the Maillards, who had served his predecessors; also, Arthur reduced the number of courses at his table from twenty-nine, the number served at Grant's table, to fourteen. He did, however, continue to serve six different kinds of wine, and it is possible that his dinners were more formally served; also, Arthur often entertained larger numbers than had been usual at state dinners in the Executive Mansion. He sometimes had fifty to fifty-four, whereas thirty-four to thirty-six was the usual number of guests at dinners given by former Presidents.

An amusing and vivid eyewitness account of a reception held in the East Room for the public during the Arthur administration is given by Mrs. Pattie L. Collins, in the *Chautauquan* (July, 1884). She describes President Arthur as:

> . . . a tall gentleman, very grand and very dignified, quite like a gigantic icicle [who] glances at your card mechanically, takes you by the hand most indifferently, and in an inexpressible broad voice, without a single inflection, says, "It is a very pleasant day." You may say that you are charmed to have an opportunity to pay your respects to Mr. President . . . but it is not of the least consequence what you say, or whether you say anything at all! That is all, and you may salaam yourself out of the side door.

Mrs. Collins admired the East Room, recently done over by Tiffany, which she claimed had very much the appearance in general effect of the Gold Salon of the Grand Opera House in Paris. She was shocked, however, to notice the "windows in the East Room draped with lace curtains, from which here and there a figure had been *cut entirely out by a souvenir thief*."

When arranged in the form of a cross, the dining table in the State Dining Room, Mrs. Collins observed, would seat fifty-four people instead of the usual forty. She was interested to observe "a sideboard containing wine glasses of every shape, size and description." Someone laughingly explained this by saying: "You know when the little friends of the President's daughter come to see her, he likes for them to have a real good time, and they are for their dolls' tables. . . ." Apropos of the wine question, Mrs. Collins contributed the following:

> A colored employee, seeing a visitor take a copious draught of ice-water just within the vestibule, and return from his explorations through the East Room soon after, complaining of being sick, exclaimed in a triumphant voice: "Boss, I told you dat stuff wuz only fit to wash clothes in." Turning to me he added, "Dat's so, Missus, 'cept to cool your head when you got a ra'al bad headache, and can't git no cabbage leaves to wrap 'round it."

President Arthur's first New Year's Day reception was a brilliant affair. Mrs. F. T. Frelinghuysen, wife of the Secretary of State, accompanied the President into the Blue Room and stood next to his sister, Mrs. McElroy, at his right hand, with the wives of other Cabinet members. When his daughter and niece came in, he welcomed them with a happy smile and bent down and kissed them. Their simple white dresses and pretty ribbon sashes were in refreshing contrast with the gorgeous costumes of the diplomats.

The "observed of all observers," according to Perley, was Dr. Mary Walker, who came "tripping in with elastic step," shook hands with President Arthur, and was profusely poeti-

Dr. Mary Walker was the only woman surgeon to serve in the Federal army during the Civil War. She attended President Arthur's first New Year's Day reception wearing her customary male attire, a privilege granted her by an Act of Congress.

cal in wishing him the compliments of the season. She wore a black broadcloth frock coat and pantaloons, and carried a high black-silk hat in her left hand, while in her right she flourished a slender cane. After leaving the President, she passed along the line of ladies who received with him, giving to each a sweeping bow, and then went into the East Room, where she was carefully scrutinized by the ladies.

Dr. Mary Walker was the only woman in Washington at that time allowed to appear in male attire; she had been granted this doubtful privilege by no less a mandate than an Act of Congress, which also awarded her the medal of honor for her services to the Federal armies during the Civil War, in which she served as the only woman surgeon. Talented, distinguished, and eccentric, her masculine costume frequently got her into trouble; women hissed and made faces when she appeared, and it was said that once at the Capitol she created a sensation by punishing a man who had taken liberties with her hat by knocking him out according to the Marquis of Queensberry rules!

At President Arthur's dinner in honor of ex-President and Mrs. Grant shortly after their tour around the world, the parlors and East Room were profusely decorated with flowers; in the dining room palm trees and other exotics were massed in corners, and the mantels were banked with flowers. There were thirty-four plates on the long table, in the center of which was a plateau mirror on which were roses and lilies-of-the-valley. On either side of it were tall gilt candelabra bearing eleven wax lights each, and beyond these, large gilt *epergnes* overflowing with *Maréchal Niel* roses. At the end of the mirror were pairs of silver candelabra bearing shaded lights, and oval cushions of white camellias set with roses and orchids. At the extreme ends were round pieces of *Bon Silène* roses and lilies-of-the-valley. Around the elaborate center decoration were arranged crystal compotes and cut-glass decanters.

Large flat corsage bouquets of roses, tied with satin ribbon, were laid at each lady's plate, and small boutonnieres of rose-buds were provided for the gentlemen. The cards were of heavy gilt-edged board embossed with the national coat of arms in gold, below which the name of each guest was written. The Marine Band performed selections from popular operatic music.

The guests were received by President Arthur in the East Room. At eight o'clock dinner was announced, and the guests repaired to the dining room, each lady taking a seat at the right of the gentleman who escorted her. President Arthur escorted Mrs. Grant, who wore a low-necked white satin dress with a long train deeply flounced with lace, and a pro-fusion of diamonds. General Grant escorted Mrs. Freling-huysen, who wore a black velvet dress with flowing train, opening in front and showing a petticoat of plaited black satin.

Dinner was served in fourteen courses with eight varieties of wine, each having its appropriate glass. The guests sat at the table two hours.

Probably one of the smartest events of the Arthur admin-istration was the dinner given for Christine Nilsson, the Swedish soprano. At its close the Marine Band played as the President escorted the great singer back to the East Room. Later Mme. Nilsson sang "The Last Rose of Summer" and "Way Down Upon the Swanee River," to her own piano accompaniment.

Those who were active in fashionable life during President Arthur's incumbency regard that period as the smartest that Washington had ever seen. He averaged a dinner party a week (usually on Wednesday evening), at which the President min-gled freely with his friends. Instead of dinners supplied by a caterer at two dollars a plate, with cheap wines of doubtful origin, writes Perley:

> A gastronomic artist served the delicacies of the season, cooked the latest Parisian style, while the wines were of the rarest vintages. Never had epicures so enjoyed themselves at Washington, and they re-

joiced when they contrasted this dispensation with the barbaric reports of former years, when "hog and hominy" was the principal dish and tangle-fast whisky punch was the fashionable table beverage.

The final social event of his administration, according to the Washington *Republican,* was almost as hectic as Andrew Jackson's inaugural reception:

> Beginning at three o'clock, the doors had not been opened half an hour before the entrance hall, the corridor and anteroom were solidly packed. An hour after the opening people began climbing in the windows to lessen the jam on the Portico. Others sought entrance through the basement doors, and were met by those seeking egress that way from the crowded parlors. The Corridor, the conservatory, and all the apartments on the main floor were solidly packed. The musicians were swept away from their places in the Corridor, and three thousand women pushed, surged and struggled toward the Blue Parlor as their goal. An occasional man appeared here and there in the ocean of femininity.
>
> At four-thirty the President came part way down the private stairway and stood overlooking the surging crowd. Gathering courage, he made the start, and taking Mrs. Duke Gwinn, of California, on his arm, conquered his way slowly to the Blue Parlor. As he entered someone asked, "How did you ever get in through that crowd, Mr. President?" and his answer was a question as to how in the world he was going to get out of it again.

The paper goes on to describe Secretary of State Frelinghuysen struggling through the doorway, his face flushed with the heat and his hair "moistened around his forehead" after having run the gantlet.

General Sheridan was helped through a window by two policemen. His wife later told friends she remembered nothing until she was swept on into the presence of the President's sister, Mrs. McElroy. Senator Manderson and a party of ladies were taken upstairs, then down to the basement and out to the stairway onto the south front of the house, "by which they reached the portico and the windows of the Red Parlor."

Apparently the reporters were exhausted at this point, for there is no description of the food—if, indeed, any was served.

Perhaps one of the facts best remembered about Arthur's three and a half years in office is that lap dogs had come into vogue, and everybody who was anybody socially had one of these little creatures! The newspapers featured them, carrying pictures of them with costly rings on their paws and big bows of bright ribbon around their necks. Some dogs even had engraved visiting cards which their mistresses left along with their own. Whether or not they attended state dinners has never been established, but they did accompany their mistresses to teas and receptions.

Chester A. Arthur left the White House a more popular man than when he had entered it—though he served only a single term as President. The widower Arthur was succeeded by a Democrat and a bachelor, Grover Cleveland.

XXII

Wedding in the White House

Grover and Frances Cleveland

For twenty years the Republicans had been the party in power. With Grover Cleveland's inauguration on March 4, 1885, as the twenty-second President of the United States, executive power was restored to the Democrats.

Electric lights (electricity had recently been installed in the main business section of Washington) sparkled brightly over the nearly ten thousand guests present at the Inaugural Ball that evening, held in the interior courtyard of the unfinished Pension Building, which had been covered by a temporary roof. On the waxed dance floor, 360 feet long and 116 feet wide, enthusiastic citizens acclaimed the new President. Receipts from the sale of tickets to the ball amounted to around $40,000. Outside, hotels and boarding houses in the city were crammed to overflowing; half a million passengers had poured into Washington via the railroads during the past week, and steamboats had brought thousands more.

Cleveland's inaugural parade had been the largest the capital city had seen up to that date, and the shouting throngs, waving red-white-and-blue banners, were vociferous in their approval of the new administration.

Cleveland was forty-seven, and a bachelor, when he succeeded Chester A. Arthur in 1885. His sister, Rose Elizabeth, served as his official hostess; charming, gracious, and cultured, a teacher and writer who had had her own career, Rose Cleveland filled the White House role assigned her with dignity and intelligence.

Swans and eagles were the dinner-table motif at Cleveland's first state dinner, given for the Cabinet. The floral decorations were remarkably elegant: a profusion of palms, roses, India-rubber plants, azaleas, tulips, hyacinths, and growing orchids. At one end of the long table, white wax swans with outspread wings, under shelter of which rested a brood of snowy cygnets, upheld molds of jellied *pâté de foie gras*. At the opposite end figures of eagles held *pâté de foie gras* arranged on little horse-shoes. Arranged along the table were glass and silver stands of conserves, bonbons, and salted almonds.

The service used for the first course was that especially decorated for the White House during the Hayes administration. At each plate were set six Bohemian wine glasses, a cut-glass carafe, a tumbler, and a champagne glass. Saltcellars of cut glass with golden shovels, and silver pepper stands ornamented the table. On each plate, on top of a large folded damask napkin, rested a bouquet of roses and ferns tied with a broad white satin ribbon; on one end of the ribbon were painted the colors of the Union, and on the other end was an etching in black and white of the White House and surrounding shrubbery, with *Jan. 14, 1886* lettered in gilt underneath. Gilt bullet-headed pins for attaching the bouquets lay beside them. A large white card bore the name of the guest assigned to each seat; above the name, blazoned in gold, was the American eagle, above whose head, through a cluster of stars, appeared the motto, *E Pluribus Unum*.

At the plates laid for the gentlemen lay boutonnieres of green with a single *Bon Silène* rosebud. Rose Cleveland wore a corsage of pink roses on her gown of pink silk and white lace; Miss Bayard, daughter of the Secretary of State, occupied the seat to the right of the President; she wore *Péri du Jardin* roses. Mrs. Manning (wife of the Secretary of the Treasury), who sat at the left, wore lilies-of-the-valley and fern.

Guests assembled in the East Room, and when dinner was announced they passed down the corridor and entered the State Dining Room to the strains of selections from *The Mikado,* played by the Marine Band.

At Rose Cleveland's afternoon receptions and luncheon parties, her temperance principles were exemplified: no wine was served. At the first of the luncheons, the new President's sister received her guests in a morning dress of pink surah silk, with a high-necked bodice and panels of ruby velvet trimmed with white lace. Nearly all the ladies wore walking dresses and bonnets, although a few were dressed in evening attire that they would have worn to a dinner party, according to one observer.

Society was saddened early in the fashionable season of 1886 by the sudden death of Secretary Bayard's eldest daughter, a young lady whose "personal attractions, gifted intellect and quick wit endeared her to a large circle of devoted friends." A fortnight later, Perley tells us, the bereaved father suffered the loss of his wife, a "lady of gracious presence and refined disposition, who was the mother of twelve children, eight of whom survived her."

Grover Cleveland's administrations—he had two, 1885–89 and 1893–97—are interesting in that he was the only President to be married in the White House and the first whose wife held Saturday afternoon receptions so that employed women might have an opportunity to visit the mansion.

Cleveland and his lovely twenty-two-year-old ward, Frances

Folsom, daughter of his late law partner, were married in the White House on June 2, 1886, by the Reverend Dr. Byron Sunderland of the First Presbyterian Church, assisted by the Reverend William Cleveland, the President's brother.

Only relatives, intimate friends, and Cabinet members and their wives attended, though a large crowd assembled around the door of the White House. From here they could hear the music of the Marine Band as the ceremony began, and, when it ended, the Presidential salute fired from the Arsenal and all the church bells in the city ringing out.

At seven o'clock in the evening the Marine Band, stationed in the corridor—and led by John Philip Sousa—struck up Mendelssohn's *Wedding March*. The President, in full evening dress, with his bride on his arm, walked slowly down the western staircase through the corridor into the Blue Room. The room, graced with southern exposure, was solidly banked with tropical plants and flowers; glowing masses of scarlet begonias and Jacqueminot roses mingled with the bright tints of the frescoed walls and ceilings.

Frances Folsom was a lovely bride in ivory satin and a long veil; her train was four yards long. Attached to the left side of her gown was a scarf of soft white India silk, looped high, and forming an overskirt bordered on the edge with orange blossoms; full folds of mousseline, edged with orange blossoms, were draped across the bodice. Her bridal veil, of white silk tulle, five yards in length, was fastened to Frances' hair with orange blossoms, and trailed to the end of her magnificent train. She wore long gloves to meet the short sleeves of the elegant gown; her only jewelry was a diamond necklace, the President's wedding gift, and a sapphire-and-diamond engagement ring.

The couple turned to the right as they entered the Blue Room from the long hall, and faced the Reverend Dr. Sunderland, who immediately began the ceremony of the Presbyterian church. As Dr. Sunderland pronounced them man and wife,

On the second of June, 1886, Grover Cleveland and his young ward, Frances Folsom, were married in the Blue Room.
Cleveland is the only President to be married in the White House.

the Reverend William Cleveland stepped forward and concluded the brief ceremony with an invocation of blessing upon the pair.

As soon as the last congratulations were received, Sousa's band struck up the familiar wedding music from *Lohengrin,* and the President and his bride led the way through the East Room to the family dining room, where an informal wedding supper was served.

The centerpiece on the main table was a full-rigged three-masted ship composed of pinks, roses, and pansies displaying the word "Hymen." It rested on a mirror (the Monroe plateau), representing a lake, the shores of which were composed of selaginella and tiny pieces of coral. The surrounding "land" was represented by banks of Jacqueminot roses. The nation's colors hung from the main mast, and two small white flags with the monogram *C.F.* in gold hung from the other masts. At the ends of the table were vases of roses festooned in trailing vines and roses. Terrapin, breast of spring chicken, cold meats, salads, fish in a variety of shapes, *pâté de foie gras,* molds of ice cream, bonbons, and fruits were placed on the same table. The Hayes china was used and its prettiest dishes displayed. The guests sat at tables or slowly promenaded the room eating, chatting, and discussing the menu.

The four-tier cake, bearing the initials *C.F.* (which came from New York), held the center of the buffet table, where it rested in a double circle of roses and was flanked on either side by large cakes from Demonet's.

The young bride, with her husband at her side, cut the cake with a pearl-handled knife. Secretary of the Navy William C. Whitney proposed a toast to her health, which he drank in sparkling champagne—but Frances drank hers in Apollinaris (mineral) water!

Each guest received a small "Dream Cake," enclosed in a white satin box, to take home. The lid bore hand-painted flowers and the date, June 2, 1886. Under the narrow satin bow was a small card which the bride and groom had auto-graphed the previous afternoon.

At a quarter past eight, the President and his young wife left the supper room, and soon reappeared in traveling dress. He wore his usual black business suit; Frances wore a traveling dress of deep-gray silk and a large gray hat lined with velvet and crowned with ostrich feathers. A carriage was waiting for them at the south entrance of the White House; they left amid a shower of rice and old slippers, and were driven to the Baltimore and Ohio railroad station, where they took a private train to Deer Park in the Cumberland (Maryland) Mountains.

Since the day when the Adamses moved into the Executive Mansion there had been eight marriages within its walls, but Grover Cleveland was the only President who went through the experience himself!

The President, who was very eager to please his bride, had purchased new rugs and pictures for her apartment, which had also been repainted; he ordered fifty dozen articles of cut glass from the famous Corning Glass Works and a set of Wedgwood dishes. The Wedgwood was decorated with a bor-der of pink roses, a suggestion offered by the steward when President Cleveland's genius was being taxed to find the things which would be most pleasing to his Frances.

In previous administrations there was silver enough to serve only thirty-six guests; Cleveland had the old sterling melted and molded into a new set upon which he had *President's House* engraved.

A competent housekeeper was employed, so that the new First Lady might better enjoy her role as mistress of the White House. The young bride accepted her new role with vim and gaiety. Her charm and friendliness drew crowds at public receptions. So popular was she that people would slip into line a second time just to see her smile and shake her hand again.

Frances Cleveland particularly loved to entertain at luncheons such as the one given on February 22, 1887, described by Esther Singleton in her *White House* as the one at which the table was

> plentifully supplied with stands of candy, there being a dishful for about every two guests, besides saucers filled with almonds. . . . In most of the candy stands were sticks of chewing-gum done up in fancy papers. . . . The bouquets were alternate bunches of pink roses tied with heliotrope ribbon, and of heliotropes tied with pink ribbon. Thirteen courses were prepared. The two sisters-in-law, the mistress and the ex-mistress of the White House, agreed in the matter of serving no wines at their lunch parties. The guests were received in the East Room.

Frances Cleveland's personal convictions on the subject of wine were the same as those of Lucy Hayes. When President Cleveland served wine at his state dinners (at which for each cover there were eight glasses—seven for wine, one for water —and a carafe), Mrs. Cleveland's wine glasses were removed when dinner began.

An intimate pen portrait of the President is given by Perley in his *Reminiscences*. He found Cleveland

> an emphatically working man. . . . In conversing with strangers he generally stands with his hands clasped behind him, and when he thinks that he has heard enough from the person addressing him, he brings his hands forward. The President rises early, shaves himself, dresses without assistance, and reads newspapers until breakfast. From the breakfast table he goes to the library. . . . At one o'clock the President goes downstairs to lunch and on the way to the private dining room passes through the East Room to greet the people congregated there. The President wastes no time but goes along the line like an old-fashioned beau dancing the grand right and left figure in a cotillion and then goes to luncheon. After luncheon he returns to his desk and works steadily until five o'clock. Dinner is served at 7:00 and by 8:30 he is at work again, often remaining until midnight.

At the Cabinet dinner of January 20, 1887, the first state dinner given by the President and his bride, there were thirty

The custom of egg rolling on the White House lawn at Eastertime began in 1878. Before this time the children held this festival on the Capitol grounds. The sketch from Leslie's Illustrated Newspaper shows the contest of April, 1887, which Cleveland watched from his office window.

guests. The central table decoration consisted of a boat of red and white camellias, the sails trimmed with smilax, which was set in the center of the Monroe plateau and flanked on either side by stands of fruit and vases of roses. The plateau itself was bordered with rosebuds, tulips, and camellias. Beyond the plateau, toward the end of the table, were containers of orchids, yellow roses, tulips, and carnations.

A more novel floral decoration was used for the state dinner for the Justices of the Supreme Court on February 18. In the center of the table stood a great mountain of roses edged with smilax, on which were set two open books fashioned of white immortelles labeled *Book of the Law* in purple. Two swords of Justice, crossed, in red and white carnations stood at each end of the table. There were thirty-four guests at this dinner, which was served at seven-thirty. At each plate, except those of the President's wife and his sister Rose, stood nine wine glasses.

Cleveland's second Presidency (1893–1897), recaptured from Benjamin Harrison—by whom he had been defeated in 1888—was outstanding so far as entertainment was concerned, chiefly for the dinner on May 4, 1893, for the Infanta Eulalie of Spain. It was held in the East Room in order to accommodate the many guests who attended.

The press, in describing one of Cleveland's diplomatic dinners, says, in part:

> The company was unusually large, even for a dinner to the Diplomatic Corps. But the occurrence of particular interest was the presence of the wife of the Minister of China. It was the first time in the history of the Chinese Legation at Washington that the wife of a Minister had crossed the threshold of the White House. A week ago Mme. Yang Yu called privately on Mrs. Cleveland, to whom she was presented by Mrs. Gresham. This evening she made her debut, so to speak, in official society. To say that her personal appearance and bearing were something of a revelation would best express the interest and admiration which the fair young celestial excited in the other guests.

*Frances Cleveland and her youngest daughter, Esther, who was born during
Cleveland's second administration (1893–1897). Esther is to date the only
child of a President to be born in the White House. The picture appeared in
Harper's Bazar.*

Orchids were used to decorate the table when the diplomatic corps was entertained.

Mrs. Cleveland produced an innovation at her dinner parties; instead of following her husband and the ranking lady into the dining room, as was the custom, she waited until all the guests had left; then she and the ranking gentleman brought up the end of the line.

Around eleven o'clock on March 4, 1897, Mrs. Cleveland, in tears, bade adieu to the White House employees—who were also in tears. The few employees remaining from the earlier Cleveland administration made every effort to decorate the table just as she loved it; the State Dining Room table bore her favorite flowers, pansies and jonquils, and the red-bordered china she herself had selected.

She was not to return to the White House until January 11, 1913, as a dinner guest of the William Howard Tafts.

This illustration from Harper's Bazar is captioned simply, "Mrs. Cleveland's Room in the White House."

XXIII

A Devoted Family

Benjamin and Caroline Harrison

Family prayers were the order of the day when Benjamin Harrison, grandson of William Henry Harrison, and his wife moved into the White House—as the Grover Clevelands moved out—in March 1889.

The Harrisons were a devoted and happy family; their son, Russell, and daughter, Mrs. James R. McKee, and their families, and sometimes other close relatives, met every morning when possible in an upstairs room (or in the White House library when there were guests) for a session of family prayer and thanksgiving before going down to breakfast.

The new First Lady, the former Caroline Lavinia Scott, whom Harrison had married in 1853, was kind, motherly, talented, and, disdaining to engage a housekeeper, as her predecessor had done, kept a firm grip on management of the household. She dressed well and tastefully (as did the new President), and in addition to these many virtues, was also a musician, painter, and floriculturist.

253

The beautiful and witty Caroline had a great fancy for orchids, and it was she who filled the Executive Mansion's conservatories with the large and rare collection that became so famous. This tropical flower was used as a motif in the fabric design of one of her favorite frocks, in her paintings, and also on some china which she designed.

On October 1, 1890, while mistress of the White House, Mrs. Harrison became the first President-General of the Daughters of the American Revolution, and it was she who initiated the D.A.R. tradition of wearing orchid corsages.

Caroline Harrison's domestic flair led to the formation of the White House china collection of the Presidents which later was put into execution by Mrs. Theodore Roosevelt. Mrs. Harrison went through the mansion's closets during one of her expeditions into its many corners, and decided that the china of past Presidents should be arranged in order for posterity.

It was Caroline's passion for a well-run home that made her begin agitating for a new President's Mansion as soon as the Harrisons moved in, but a complete overhauling of the old one was as much as Congress would provide. Bedroom quarters were converted into suites, private bathrooms added —up to now there had been only one—and electricity installed to take the place of gas. Electric bells for summoning the servants were also installed.

Electricity was something new, and the Harrisons were afraid to touch the light switches. This made for a great deal of inconvenience and confusion. The bed chambers were "blacked out" until the Harrisons' fear of the mysterious power finally wore off. Electric lights in the halls and parlors, however, were turned on by the engineer in the evening and left burning until he returned the following morning. Nor was it easy to get used to the pushbuttons for calling the servants. Ike Hoover, chief usher at the White House, wrote that there was a family conference almost every time this had to be done.

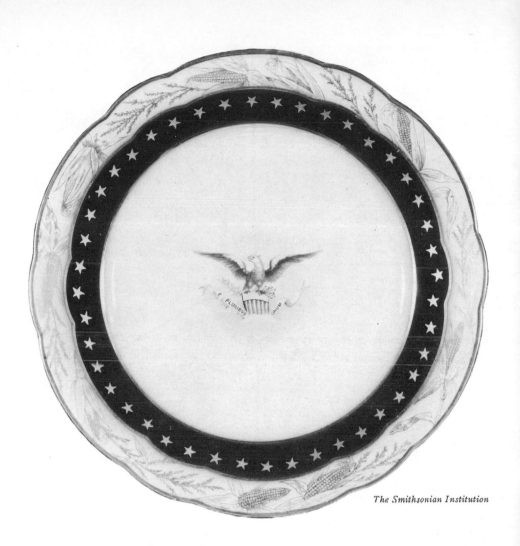

During the administration of Benjamin Harrison new state china was purchased. The Limoges dinner plate is shown here.

The photograph of the Blue Room made in Benjamin Harrison's time shows three of the interior exits: the left door leads to the Red Room and the right to the Green Room. Through the open door to the corridor is seen a portion of the glass screen separating the corridor from the north entrance hall.

Courtesy National Park Service

Compare the décor of the nineteenth-century Blue Room with that of the present Blue Room.

Benjamin Harrison, like Grover Cleveland, enjoyed good food, and made plans to carry on a full program of entertainment by employing the famous Hugo Ziemann as steward. The consensus, however, was that his administration lacked "style" compared to other administrations.

Hugo, the new steward, had catered for Prince Napoleon, and had worked at the Hotel Splendide in Paris as well as in New York and Chicago. He and Mrs. F. L. Gillette were co-authors of the "White House Cook Book" (originally published in 1887, its last edition is dated 1925), which had an enormous sale.

The menu for one of the outstanding dinners given by the Harrisons—that for Vice President Levi Morton and members of the Cabinet on January 7, 1890, included such gourmet-tempting dishes as green turtle soup, raw oysters, boiled salmon, fillet of beef *à la jardinière,* canvasback duck, and ices formed in the shapes of roses and chrysanthemums.

Four regular receptions were held each winter: for the diplomatic corps, the judiciary, the army and navy, and Congress. A vivid eyewitness account of these receptions is given in *Harper's Weekly* (July 2, 1892):

> The crowd is invariably enormous. The line of carriages of arriving guests reaches from the White House porch down the long circular driveway of the grounds, out of the gate, down Pennsylvania Avenue, past the Treasury, around the corner and down Fifteenth Street toward the Washington Monument. A late arrival will easily consume an hour in crawling from one end of the line to the porch. Then, when the door is reached and the wearied but expectant burdens of the carriage are discharged, they find themselves in a pack of human beings that is almost terrifying. It seems impossible that this good-natured crowd should be able to make its way through the single door into the White House. Sometimes the police make way for a belated distinguished guest; sometimes a window is open, and ladies are handed into receiving hands. The crowd inside the doors is as great as that outside and the progress from the porch, across the vestibule, up the stairway and down again, is slow.

*The family dining room of 1889 and that of the present day have one decora-
tive feature in common: the silver ship presented to Ulysses S. Grant by the
Mohawk Indians in 1876.*

In addition to these state receptions, according to George Granthan Bain, writing in the *Cosmopolitan* of April 1891:

> [The President stood] most every afternoon at one o'clock . . . for about ten minutes to receive and to shake hands with the indiscriminate crowd of visitors who assemble for the sole purpose of enjoying this pump-handle recreation with the first citizen of their common country. . . . Cranks and mothers who want their babies kissed by the President are the most serious annoyances known at the White House receptions. . . . President Harrison confines his caresses to Baby McKee, his gifted grandchild.

Tragedy cast its shadow over the White House shortly after President Harrison moved in. First, the wife and daughter of Secretary of the Navy Benjamin F. Tracy were burned to death in their home; their funeral services were held in the East Room of the White House. Later, Mrs. Harrison's father died. The deaths of the wives of Harrison's private secretary and his assistant followed. On October 25, 1892, just before the election, Caroline Harrison died.

President Harrison, sad and indifferent to social functions after the loss of his wife, welcomed the Grover Clevelands back to the White House when they arrived for the farewell and introductory dinner on March 3, 1893.

XXIV

Protocol Flare-up

William and Ida McKinley

The welcome-and-farewell dinner given by the Clevelands on the eve of William McKinley's inauguration was probably the smallest and simplest in the history of the White House. The incoming President had sent word that Mrs. McKinley's health would not permit elaborate entertaining. As it happened, the President-elect came alone, and he, the President, and Mrs. Cleveland dined by themselves.

Mrs. McKinley had been an invalid for several years and was unable to take on any active duty in the household, but she and the President did enjoy entertaining and did so extensively (particularly after August, 1898, when the Spanish-American War ended). She remained seated while receiving at receptions. On occasion the Cabinet wives received with her.

One of President McKinley's first acts was to reduce the size of the crowd at receptions. There were four official receptions: diplomatic, judiciary, congressional, and army and navy. Previously, one invitation had covered the four receptions of the season, but McKinley ruled that a separate invitation be sent for each function. Gate crashers had become a serious problem. This was solved by admitting only those with White House cards.

Another of McKinley's accomplishments was to settle once and for all that the Vice President outranked an ambassador.

British Ambassador and Lady Pauncefote's kettle boiled several afternoons after the McKinley-Hobart inauguration, waiting for Vice President and Mrs. Hobart to make the first call. Finally they decided something was wrong, and took the matter up with the Secretary of State, John Sherman. The ambassador was informed that the matter had been referred to Prime Minister Salisbury in London. Pauncefote then received a cable saying that the Vice President occupied the same relation to the President that the Prince of Wales bore to the British sovereign—that of heir apparent—and he was commanded to visit Mr. Hobart. This decision also carried over to placing the Cabinet dinner ahead of the diplomatic dinner on the calendar of White House events.

The highlight of McKinley entertainment was the dinner party. He brought new zest to this traditional function by adding interesting young people and distinguished oldsters to the regular guest list. Instead of thirty-six, or even fifty—the highest number the State Dining Room would accommodate— he would have anywhere from sixty-two to eighty-two guests, necessitating makeshifts in the corridor. Occasionally the table extended the entire length of the corridor, from the East Room to the State Dining Room.

On January 9, 1899, the President gave a dinner for the Paris Peace Conference commissioners, who had recently negotiated the treaty with Spain under which she relinquished Cuba and ceded to the United States Puerto Rico, Guam, and the Philippines. The table, set for seventy-two guests, was in the corridor, and was decorated with orchids.

Clergymen attending the annual Methodist Conference were

President McKinley's first state function at the White House was a reception for the diplomatic corps. The caption on this sketch reads: "There Was No Rush and Scramble as at Receptions of Previous Administrations." The President is in the center, Mrs. McKinley on the right, and Secretary of State John Sherman third from the left.

entertained at dinner by the McKinleys on November sixteenth of that year. This, too, was an impressive affair, with members of the President's Cabinet and high-ranking officers of the army and navy present.

The President and Mrs. McKinley gave their first state dinner in honor of the diplomatic corps on January 26, 1898. Covers were laid for sixty-two, and the table was set in the corridor. The Marine Band played in the conservatory. The floral decorations were pink roses, and pink shades on the candles added to the rosiness of the scene. Bouquets of roses and lilies-of-the-valley for the ladies, and boutonnieres for the gentlemen, completed the table décor.

Had McKinley lacked personal forcefulness and will power, he would probably have been overwhelmed by the many protocol flare-ups which erupted during his administration. One followed after another.

Probably the most embarrassing concerned the seating arrangement at one of the diplomatic dinners. Manuel de Aspiroz, the Mexican ambassador to the United States, was given the name of Madame Hengelmuller, wife of the Austrian minister, in his escort envelope. It was, however, a rule of diplomacy that no Austrian envoy call upon or speak to Ambassador Aspiroz. Some thirty years earlier he, as an army lieutenant and a crack rifleman, had been commanded to execute Maximilian, an Austrian whose short reign as Emperor of Mexico came to an end when Napoleon III withdrew his troops from the puppet emperor's support. Austria had informed every foreign office of the estrangement, but somehow a slip was made on this occasion. Dinner was ready and the guests were there. State Department officials were in a quandary! What could be done—quickly? Ambassador Aspiroz settled it himself by asking that Senator Allison be allowed to accompany Madame Hengelmuller; he would take Allison's chair at the foot of the table.

The question as to whether the Chief Justice of the Supreme Court was more important than an ambassador arose during McKinley's administration, when the White House unwittingly gave a foreign minister the seat of honor. Chief Justice Fuller was so furious that when the company retired he left without coffee, cordial, or smoke, remarking that in future he would demand a plan of the table before accepting a dinner invitation anywhere.

The Supreme Court had long kept a jealous watch over its prerogatives. On one occasion the Justices, learning that the diplomatic corps would be received first, declined to attend their own party.

There was another social tempest in a teapot at a memorial ceremony which took place in the Senate wing of the Capitol. Somebody made the mistake of seating the Court behind the diplomats. Ever since then, on such occasions, the Court has sat in the front row on one side of the chamber, the diplomats on the other side. Eventually this led to separate state dinners for the Justices and the diplomats.

One of the most brilliant of the state banquets given during McKinley's administration was that honoring Admiral George Dewey, hero of Manila, on October 3, 1899. The eighty guests included representatives of the Supreme Court, the Cabinet, Congress, army and navy, and the governors of nine states, the presidents of three universities, some personal friends of the President, and the brother and the son of the Admiral. They were received in the East Room, where the guests were introduced to the President and Admiral Dewey by Colonel Bingham and Rear Admiral Crowninshield.

At the close of this short ceremony President McKinley offered his arm to the Admiral and led the way to dinner. The long table, because of the large number of guests, was placed in the main corridor. It was profusely decorated in warm-toned blossoms ranging from pink begonias to deep-red or silver shades. At the center of the board was a mound of delicate green ferns, out of which emerged tall branches of roses. Palms, ferns, and rubber plants lined the corridor.

The new President's flag was the chief wall decoration. Flags of the Secretary of War and Secretary of the Navy, each half the size of the President's flag, and the blue flag of the Admiral with its four white stars, also added appropriate color to the occasion.

Usually Mrs. McKinley, because of her frailness, sat at the right of her husband, but on this occasion Dewey had that place of honor. After dinner, coffee and cigars were served in the State Dining Room, which was also decorated in red-white-and-blue flags and greenery. Here the President sat on the south side of the room, with Admiral Dewey on his right and the Secretary of War on his left.

The following autumn when President and Mrs. McKinley gave their regular Cabinet dinner, they invited the Admiral and his wife—the former Mildred McLean, daughter of the wealthy and socially prominent Washington McLeans and widow of General Hazen. A tiny woman who made up in determination what she lacked in size, Mrs. Dewey was displeased with the seating arrangements, and showed it by dragging her Admiral home as soon as the guests arose from the table.

McKinley was fond of singing hymns. One of the White House employees is quoted by the *Musical Observer* as saying that on Sabbath evenings during McKinley's administration there would often be a gathering of a few friends in the Blue Parlor after dinner. Hymnals would be brought out and everyone would join in the singing, accompanied by the piano. McKinley's favorite was "Lead, Kindly Light." (He is said to have whispered the words of "Nearer, My God, to Thee" to his wife as he lay on his deathbed.)

The President loved carnations, particularly red ones. He felt defenseless without one in the lapel of his coat, calling it his "good-luck charm," and he kept a vase of them on his desk. His interest in the carnation had begun in 1876 when he

The seating arrangement shown here is that used at President McKinley's state banquet in honor of Admiral George Dewey.

Library of Congress

South

North

Mr. Pruden	Asst. Secy. Adee
Mr. Charles Dewey	Asst. Secy. Allen
Asst. Secy. Meiklejohn	Commissioner Wright
Commissioner Ross	Asst. Secy. Hill
Provost Harrison	Representative Livingston
Gov. Rollins	Representative Grout
Judge Goff	Hon. J. G. Schurman
Senator Daniel	Gov. Lowndes
Capt. Lamberton	Senator Beveridge
Senator Lindsay	Senator Martin
Gov. Smith	Senator Tillman
Senator Depew	Senator Proctor
Senator Hanna	Rear Admiral Schley
Admiral Sampson	Senator Aldrich
Genl. Miles	Senator Davis
Senator Sewell	Mr. Justice Gray
Atty. Genl. Griggs	Secretary Long
Mr. Justice Brown	Admiral Dewey
Secretary Hay	The President
Mr. Justice Harlan	Secretary Root
Secretary Hitchcock	Mr. Justice White
Rear Admiral Sicard	Postmaster Genl. Smith
a	Senator Platt
Senator Foraker	Gov. Wolcott
Gov. Roosevelt	Senator Chandler
Senator Thurston	Senator Elkins
Ex-Secretary Bliss	Senator McComas
Senator Penrose	Ex-Secy. Alger
Representative Boutelle	Genl. Merritt
Ex-Secretary Herbert	Hon. Seth Low
Rear Admiral Crowninshield	Captain Mahan
Gov. Tyler	Gov. Powers
Ex-Postmaster Genl. Gary	Mr. George G. Dewey
Gov. Pingree	Gov. Atkinson
Representative Foss	Asst. Postmaster Genl. Heath
Colonel Herrick	Surgeon Genl. Sternberg
Genl. Corbin	Mr. Cortelyou

The Red Room as it appeared before the 1902 renovation of the White House. Traditionally, the First Lady receives guests in the Red Room, which also serves for private and semi-official functions.

Courtesy National Park Service

The Green Room, locale of informal receptions, as it appeared before the 1902 renovation.

campaigned against Dr. Levi Lambord, a Democrat, for a seat in the House of Representatives. Dr. Lambord, a flori-culturist, always appeared with a carnation in his lapel. On one occasion Major McKinley expressed interest in the flower and asked what it was. From that time until the contest closed Dr. Lambord took an extra carnation for the Major's lapel whenever they were to meet on the platform. On receiving the first one from the Doctor, Major McKinley had remarked: "Perhaps it will bring me luck." Major McKinley won the election, and the carnation won a place in his heart.

On September 6, 1901, when he was standing in the receiv-ing line at the Pan American Exhibition in Buffalo, a small girl asked the President if he would give her something she could show to her friends to prove that she had shaken hands with him. He pulled the red carnation from his lapel and handed it to her. Seconds later he was shot twice by Leon Czolgosz, the second person in line following the child.

Even as he fell, President McKinley's first thought was of his wife. To his secretary he said, "My wife—be careful how you tell her—oh, be careful!"

The frail Mrs. McKinley, who had accompanied her hus-band to Buffalo and was sleeping in their hotel suite when the shooting took place, surprised everybody. For the eight days the President survived she remained by his side. She stood by staunchly during the funeral services, and accompanied his body to Canton, where he was buried.

After McKinley's death people throughout the nation paid him tribute, but perhaps none was more sincere than that of the happy old Irish lady known as "Star Mary" (whose real name was Mrs. Nicholson and who had lived in Washington since the Civil War), a news vendor at the northeast corner of Fifteenth and F Street, and as much a fixture in Washing-ton life as the lamppost she stood under. "Star Mary," in her ancient shawls and her battered old hat, which was as "dis-tinctive in its style as the latest importation from Paris," according to a story in the Washington *Star* (December 28, 1901), is reported to have said of McKinley:

> Sure . . . and I misses President McKinley very much, indade I do. He was that good soul. He used to come by my corner in the afternoon and stop his carriage. "Mary," says he, "come here and let me have the latest news." "God bless ye, Mr. President," says I, and handed him the pa-aper. Sometimes he would give me half a dollar and sometimes a quarter, just as he happened to have the change about him. He was a good soul, was Mr. McKinley.

Vice President Theodore Roosevelt took the oath of office, and became President, on the day of McKinley's death. On October 29, 1901, Leon Czolgosz was electrocuted at Auburn, New York.

XXV

Rough Rider

Theodore and Edith Roosevelt

The tragic news that President McKinley had been assassinated reached the nation's Vice President, Theodore Roosevelt, while he was vacationing in the Adirondacks. "Teddy" took the oath of office as the twenty-sixth President of the United States on the day McKinley died, Septemeber 14, 1901.

A man of tremendous force and vigor, Roosevelt was just forty-two when he entered the White House—the youngest President the country had known. Both he and his wife, the former Edith Kermit Carow, whom he had married in London in 1886, felt that the White House was more than just a temporary residence for the President—it was, rather, a nation's "home," and they set themselves the task of making it an impressive one. The first major renovation of the mansion since 1815 was undertaken by Theodore Roosevelt.

Congress appropriated more than half a million dollars for the task of renovation and refurnishing. There was no question that extensive work was needed, since a series of piecemeal changes had resulted in a mixture of unrelated styles of decoration and furnishing. Also, the business of government had grown to the point where much of the family living space on the second floor had been taken over for Cabinet meetings and other official purposes. Enormous crowds of guests and sightseers put a constant strain on both structure and equipment, to the degree that dishes rattled on the sideboards when the waiters walked across the floor of the State Dining Room.

The dining room itself was far too small to accommodate the large numbers of guests invited on many occasions. Its capacity was a comfortable fifty—or a crowded seventy—and for this reason it had become commonplace to resort to setting a table in the corridor, or even in the East Room, when necessary. In order to enlarge the State Dining Room, the main stairway was removed from the west end of the corridor to the east of the entrance lobby.

The renovation was undertaken by the firm of McKim, Meade, and White of New York; they began work in June of 1902 and were just about finished by the end of the year. The result of their labors was a completely overhauled and redecorated main floor, with a State Dining Room that could comfortably seat one hundred and four persons. The walls were attractively paneled in English oak, and a silver chandelier, hanging from the elaborately decorated ceiling, matched the silver girandoles on the walls. Edith Roosevelt chose Wedgwood ware featuring the Great Seal of the United States. (This Seal is protected by patent and copyright for the exclusive use of the Executive Mansion.)

An office building was erected at the end of the west terrace, the east terrace (which Andrew Johnson had removed) was reconstructed, a few attic rooms were added, and the second floor—now reclaimed by the President's family—was repaired and modernized.

Although the mansion's rehabilitation was costly, and although the Roosevelts themselves were accustomed to social

Before the 1902 renovation, the State Dining Room could accommodate only fifty comfortably. It had frequently been necessary to resort to the corridor for state dinners.

position and affluence, the administration of Theodore Roosevelt was not nearly as extravagant as Grant's had been. It was, in fact, a point of pride with the Roosevelts that they were able to manage well without unnecessary expenditure. When a magazine article referred to him as a "gourmet," the President promptly replied:

"When anyone desires to make a widespread impression that the President and family sit down to a four or five-course breakfast, a six or seven-course lunch, and a ten-course dinner, the President feels that a denial is not inappropriate."

He went on to say that the regular White House breakfast consisted simply of hard-boiled eggs, rolls, and coffee. When he lunched alone, "Teddy" contented himself with a bowl of milk. If Mrs. Roosevelt and the children were present, the lunch consisted of cold meat (if there were any leftovers), tea, cantaloupe in season, and bread. Instead of a ten-course dinner, the Roosevelts' evening meal usually consisted of three courses—and often only two!

Guests, however, were not subjected to a Spartan diet. One guest who attended luncheon at the White House wrote enthusiastically of the bouillon, salt fish, chicken in rice, rolls, and baked beans served; he added that the President enjoyed his first helping of baked beans so much that he took a second helping, and appeared to relish the dessert—Bavarian cream served with preserves and cake. As a rule there was only one kind of wine served at dinner. The President drank alcoholic beverages sparingly.

Simple as the Roosevelts' tastes might be when dining *en famille,* lavish plans could be made when the occasion warranted. One such occasion was the visit of Prince Henry of Prussia. The Prince had come to the United States to sail the yacht *Meteor,* which had been under construction in New Jersey, home to Germany. On the afternoon of his arrival, the Prince, accompanied by the German ambassador, made an official call on the President. The visitors were shown into the

One hundred and four persons could be accommodated in the State Dining Room after its enlargement.

Green Room, where the ambassador remained while the Prince, alone—the ambassador did not rank high enough to make the presentation—entered the Blue Room to present himself to the President, Mrs. Roosevelt, and their daughter, Alice. ("We all liked him," Alice Roosevelt Longworth wrote many years later in her book, *Crowded Hours*.)

That evening the Prince, accompanied by Admiral Evans, drove to the White House for an elaborate stag dinner. The Executive Mansion was gay with hundreds of flags—American and German. The horseshoe table had been set up in the East Room, since the new State Dining Room was not yet complete, and the decorators had outdone themselves to make a brilliant display of this historic room. Thousands of red, white, and blue lights, arranged to form anchors, stars, and ropes, gleamed in the overhead canopy of green. Festoons with pendant balls of light stretched from chandeliers to side walls, and over windows, doorways, and arches; mantels were banked high with pink and white flowers, and the open space between the vacant wall and the inner side of the crescent-shaped table was broken by a semicircle of primroses and azaleas. The triple east window was curtained with German and American flags, and the centerpiece on the table was (as usual) the historic Monroe plateau.

The menu had been selected by Edith Roosevelt, and she gave special attention to the dessert: ice cream molded and colored to resemble fruit, and served in candy sea shells. One side of the shell bore the German eagle, and the other the American coat of arms, on which sugar flags of both countries waved. Punch, served in small boats flying the *Meteor*'s flag, was distributed. The President toasted the Emperor and the German nation in champagne. "We admire their great past and great present," he said, "and we wish them all possible success in the future. May the bonds of friendship between the two peoples ever grow stronger!"

The Prince, who had won the hearts of all who met him,

When Prince Henry of Prussia visited the White House in February, 1902, the horseshoe table was set up in the East Room. In this illustration from Harper's Weekly, the Prince is second from the left, the President third.

responded gallantly: "The President and the people of the United States," adding the usual expressions of good will.

After the banquet the President and Mrs. Roosevelt and their daughter, Alice, who was to christen the ship, accompanied by members of the Cabinet and high-ranking officers of the army and navy, left by special train with the Prince and his party for Jersey City, where the *Meteor* awaited the launching.

The next morning Miss Roosevelt smashed a bottle of champagne on the vessel's gleaming white hull and said, "In the name of His Majesty, the German Emperor, I christen this yacht *Meteor*." Then she cut the last rope, and the yacht slid down the ways.

No story on Theodore Roosevelt would be complete without an account of the debut, and, later, the marriage, of his daughter—a spirited girl whom the ladies of the press glamorized as "Princess Alice." Her debut took place in 1902 during the Christmas holidays. It was, to Alice's regret, a comparatively sedate affair, for though she considered herself quite a young lady, to her parents she was still a child. She wanted champagne and a cotillion; she got, instead, punch (non-alcoholic) and a dance.

Her marriage, on February 17, 1906, to Congressman Nicholas Longworth of Ohio was sophisticated enough, however, to satisfy even Miss Roosevelt. The decorations and presents are said to have been worth a king's ransom; the guests came from far and wide, filling the White House and the Washington hotels to overflowing.

"Nick's" bachelor dinner, given at the Alibi Club the night before to the Harvard Alumni, was decorous enough until the President left. Things then livened up considerably; one usher woke up the next morning dreaming of icebergs and found himself in the bathtub, in water that had thoroughly cooled.

The wedding took place at eleven-thirty the next morning in the East Room, before a window draped in cloth-of-gold

A hand-painted cover and red, white, and blue ribbons adorned the menu for the dinner in honor of Prince Henry.

Courtesy Mr. and Mrs. Wilbur B. Montgomery

MENU

Marcobruner, '93	Huîtres sur Coquille
	Croûtes panachées
Sherry Amontillado	Potage Consommé Brunoise
	Olives Celeri frisé Amandes salées
Moët & Chandon Brut Imperial	Terrapin à la Baltimore
Chateau d'Arsac Grand vin le Monteil 1893	Filet de Boeuf Hambourgeoise
	Chapon à l'Ambassadriee
	Petits pois Sauce Suprême
Moët & Chandon White Seal	Asperges, Sauce Mousseline
	PUNCH
	Sorbet Imperial
	Canard Canvasback Rôti
	Hominy Salade de Saison
	Glace
Apollinaris Liqueurs	Petits Fours Cerises Fondantes
	Marrons glacés
	Café

Dinner given by the

President of the United States

at the

White House, Washington D.C.

February 24th 1902.

and ornamented with ropes of smilax and Easter lilies. The officiating clergyman was the first Bishop of Washington, Henry Yates Satterlee, one of the founders of the Washington Cathedral. An improvised altar was set on a dais covered with a priceless Oriental rug. The President "gave the bride away."

After the ceremony, President and Mrs. Roosevelt and the bridegroom's parents moved to the Blue Room to receive the guests, among which were Cabinet officers, Justices of the Supreme Court, diplomats, senators, congressmen, and high-ranking officers of the army and navy, as well as many of the socially prominent, and, of course, many friends. In all, one thousand persons attended the wedding party.

The "wedding breakfast" was served at about twelve-thirty. The small private dining room was given over to the bridal party, the State Dining Room to the other guests.

The menu included croquettes, patés, salads, assorted sandwiches, ice cream hearts, wedding bells, and wedding rings, petits fours, champagne, claret punch, lemonade, coffee and tea, and the Bride's Cake. There were several three-tiered cakes, elaborately decorated in orange blossoms and doves. The bride cut the cake with Charlie McCauley's sword (Major McCauley was a White House aide). So great was the crowd of well-wishers that neither she nor the groom had a chance to eat.

When Theodore Roosevelt became President there were only three state dinners given each season: one each for the Cabinet, the Justices of the Supreme Court, and the diplomatic corps. Roosevelt added a fourth, out of deference to "Uncle Joe" Cannon, Speaker of the House of Representatives, when "Uncle Joe" flatly refused to attend any of the other dinners because he felt he was not given the precedence his position warranted.

A minor highlight of the Theodore Roosevelt administration was the acquisition of the golden goblet. This masterpiece of the goldsmith's art was twelve inches high, and shaped like

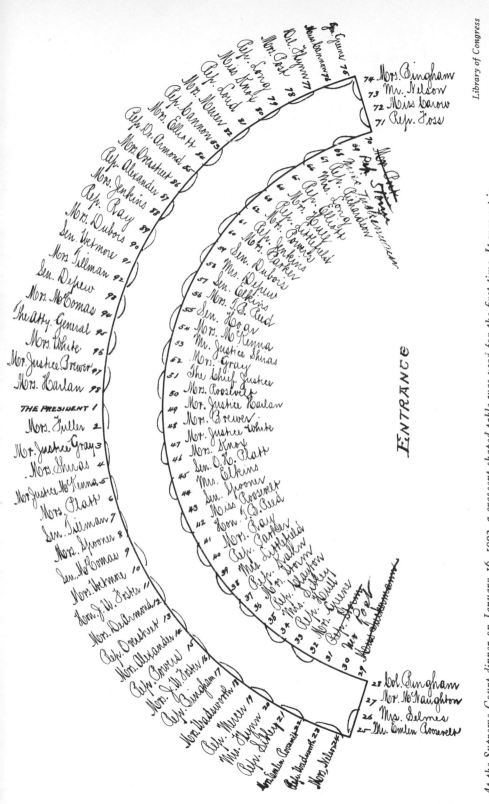

At the Supreme Court dinner on January 16, 1902, a crescent-shaped table was used for the first time. It was set in the East Room. Here is the seating arrangement.

74 Mrs. Bingham
73 Mr. Nelson
72 Miss Carow
71 Rep. Foss

76 Rep. Emery
75 Miss Sanners
76 Col. Flynn
77 Rep. Flynn
78 Mrs. Bosh
79 Rep. Long
80 Miss Knox
81 Rep. Loud
82 Mrs. Mercer
83 Rep. Cannon
84 Mrs. Elliott
85 Rep. Dr. Armond
86 Mrs. Crosthiser
87 Rep. Alexander
88 Mrs. Jenkins
89 Rep. Ray
90 Mrs. Dubois
91 Sen. Wetmore
92 Mrs. Tillman
93 Sen. Depew
94 Mrs. McComas
95 The Atty. General
96 Mrs. White
97 Mr. Justice Brewer
98 Mrs. Harlan

THE PRESIDENT 1
Mrs. Fuller 2
Mr. Justice Gray 3
Mrs. Shiras 4
Mr. Justice McKenna 5
Mrs. Platt 6
Sen. Tillman 7
Mrs. Spooner 8
Sen. McComas 9
Mrs. Wetmore 10
Hon. J. W. Foster 11
Mrs. DeArmond 12
Rep. Dreskert 13
Rep. Alexander 14
Mrs. Powers 15
Mrs. J. W. Foster 16
Rep. Bingham 17
Hon. Wadsworth 18
Rep. Mercer 19
Mrs. Flynn 20
Rep. Sibley 21
Mrs. Wadsworth 22
Hon. Franklin Roosevelt 23
Mrs. Nelson 24

70 Mrs. Bosh
69 Rep. Stryer
68 Mrs. Richardson
67 Rep. Richardson
66 Rep. Long
65 Mrs. Elliott
64 Rep. Hull
63 Mrs. Littlefield
62 Rep. Jenkins
61 Rep. Powers
60 Mrs. Parker
59 Mrs. Dubois
58 Sen. Depew
57 Sen. Elkins
56 Mrs. T. B. Reed
55 Sen. Hoar
54 Mrs. McKenna
53 Mr. Justice Shiras
52 Mrs. Gray
51 The Chief Justice
50 Mrs. Roosevelt
49 Mr. Justice Harlan
48 Mrs. Brewer
47 Mr. Justice White
46 Mrs. Knox
45 Sen. O. H. Platt
44 Mrs. Elkins
43 Sen. Spooner
42 Miss Roosevelt
41 Hon. T. B. Reed
40 Mrs. Ray
39 Rep. Parker
38 Mrs. Littlefield
37 Rep. Hahn
36 Mrs. Storm
35 Rep. Clayton
34 Mrs. Sibley
33 Rep. Hull
32 Mrs. Greene
31 Rep. Storm
30 Mrs. Roosevelt
29 Hon. Roosevelt

28 Col. Bingham
27 Mr. McNaughton
26 Mrs. Selmes
25 Mr. Emlen Roosevelt

ENTRANCE

a champagne glass. It had been presented to the President by the San Francisco Chamber of Commerce when he visited that city in 1904. From that time on it was always beside the President's plate during dinner.

During Roosevelt's administration the Peace Conference between Russia and Japan was held at Portsmouth, New Hampshire, in August, 1905, and Roosevelt was awarded the Nobel prize for his work in arranging this conference.

The President's last luncheon before leaving the White House was that given his "Tennis Cabinet" of thirty men who met at the White House on March 1, 1909, three days before his successor, William Howard Taft, came into office. Roosevelt is said to have seated his guests according to his affection for them, regardless of precedence. On one side of him was the French ambassador, and on the other a man described as "a Wild West character."

According to Major Archibald Butt, White House master of ceremonies and a graduate of the city rooms of several Southern newspapers, there wasn't a dry eye in the crowd as they all bade "Teddy" good-by.

XXVI

Four Years of Strife

William Howard and Helen Taft

"Four years of strife" was the phrase used by Ike Hoover, chief usher at the White House, to describe William Howard Taft's administration. There seemed to be a continuous mixup. First, a feud developed between President Roosevelt and President-elect Taft. On the morning of the inauguration precedent was thrown to the winds when Mrs. Taft insisted on riding back to the White House with her husband after he had taken the oath of office. Ex-President Roosevelt went directly to Union Station to take the train for New York.

The weather that day—March 4, 1909—Alice Roosevelt Longworth gleefully noted, was foul. A deep snow had fallen the night before and the late morning sun turned it into slush.

Alice was among those to whom inaugural luncheon invitations had been sent by Mrs. Taft, but she begged off to accompany her father to the station. The new First Lady then informed Mrs. Longworth that she would send her a ticket to enable her to enter the White House in case she changed her mind. This was too much for Alice! She wrote in her *Crowded Hours:* "I flew shouting to friends and relatives with the news that I was going to be allowed to have a ticket to permit me to enter the White House! I—a very large CAPITAL I— who had wandered in and out for eight happy winters!"

That evening the President dined with his Yale Class of '78 before picking up Mrs. Taft for the Inaugural Ball. She wore a gown fashioned of white chiffon over satin, heavily embroidered in silver.

The new First Lady lost no time in taking over her duties as mistress of the White House. She had visited the mansion a few days before and was graciously shown around by Edith Roosevelt. At one point Mrs. Taft whispered to her companion, "I would have put that table over here." Mrs. Roosevelt's only thought was that in another twenty-four hours Mrs. Taft could move the table anywhere she wished, without saying a word about it.

Mrs. Taft began her revolution of the White House by reducing the number of employees and replacing the steward with a housekeeper. She wrote:

> I wanted a woman who could relieve me of the supervision of such details as no man, expert steward though he be, would ever recognize. The White House requires such ordinary attention as is given by a good housekeeper to any home, except, perhaps, that it has to be more vigilantly watched. Dust accumulates in corners, mirrors get dim with dampness; curtains sag and lose their crispness; floors, their gloss; rugs turn up at the corners, or fray at the ends, and chair cushions get crushed and untidy. . . . Pantry boys get careless; maids forget to be immaculate and the linen is not properly handled.

None of this was imaginative. Mrs. Taft had been deeply shocked to discover that the precious White House silver, when not in use, was kept in haphazard fashion in chests and boxes in a storeroom. The linen was sadly depleted (guests thought nothing of making off with a napkin or two as a sou-

Mrs. William Howard Taft was the first First Lady to ride in the presidential carriage as the inaugural parade rode from the Capitol to the White House. Previously, it had been traditional that the outgoing President accompany his successor on this momentous trip.

venir), and dinner sets, subject to breakage, were inadequate for large functions. Unlike many of her predecessors who preferred to select their own china pattern, Mrs. Taft was satisfied with that chosen by Mrs. Roosevelt, and replaced enough to make a service for one hundred persons.

Helen Taft appreciated the historic plates and platters used by Presidents long gone, and used them at small luncheons and dinners. "I found them valuable inspiration to lively conversation among my guests," she said. There were enough plates remaining from the Lincoln service for one course for a party of thirty. "The butler and waiters," she wrote, "handled them with a caution bordering on reverence."

Another innovation of Mrs. Taft's was to substitute colored footmen in livery for the police guard which had been stationed at the main entrance for a century. She felt that the police guard was in no way distinguishable from the rest of the citizenry, and many strangers who wandered up to the door looked in vain for someone to whom it seemed right and proper to address a question or hand a visiting card.

White House servants were paid by the government. At that time they received from twenty-five to fifty dollars a month. The only private servant was the President's Filipino valet who had been with him several years.

The morning after the inauguration the clock had not yet struck ten when Mrs. Taft had discussed with the housekeeper, Mrs. Elizabeth Jaffray, the subject of menus, including luncheon, dinner for that day, and the first of her large teas, scheduled to be given within a few days. The luncheon menu included bouillon, smelts with tartar sauce, lamb chops, green peas, and Bermuda potatoes. Dessert included raspberry jelly with whipped cream, coffee, salted almonds, and bonbons.

Mrs. Taft had, in her earlier roles as wife of the Governor of the Philippines, and, later, Secretary of War, acquired a good deal of skill in official entertaining, and had long since become philosophical about her husband's happy-go-lucky attitude where extra guests were concerned. The addition of a few more, usually at the last moment and without notice, didn't bother her—although it upset the staff, which was accustomed to the military punctuality of the Theodore Roosevelts.

"How many for luncheon, Madam?" the cook would ask.

"I haven't any idea," the First Lady would reply.

Nor had she. That first spring, when Congress was in extra session revising the tariff and the President was continually in conference, he would invite members of both Houses for lunch or dinner, and frequently for breakfast, usually at the last minute. Even if no guests were expected, Mrs. Taft made certain the larder was full—just in case. She then sent her plans for the day to the executive social officer. At eleven o'clock the house telephone would ring, or she would receive a note to the effect that So-and-so would lunch with the President and Mrs. Taft. So the table would be laid while the kitchen staff stood by awaiting final orders. A half-hour later a second guest, or a group of guests, might be announced. The butler would rearrange the table. The cook never considered it safe to start preparations until half an hour before the meal. Even then, the President was likely to be thirty minutes to an hour late and, when he did appear, bring several unannounced guests. Breakfasts and dinners were not quite so uncertain as luncheons.

The President was a big man (six feet, two inches tall) and a big eater (he weighed over three hundred pounds). A larger bathtub had to be installed for him, for every time he took a bath in the old one he got stuck and had to be pulled out. His breakfast usually consisted of two oranges, a twelve-ounce steak, toast, guava jelly, and coffee. When he reached three hundred and thirty-two pounds, the amount of steak was reduced, by doctor's orders, to eight ounces.

Taft was a teetotaler, although he served champagne punch at receptions. Ike Hoover, in his *Forty-two Years in The White House,* said it was good, too! "One quart bottle of champagne for every two bottles of charged water. With a little lemon and sugar and ice floating on the top, it was the pride of the household and the pleasure of the guests." The First Lady would take a cocktail, but only one, before dinner.

The Tafts' first official entertainment was the diplomatic tea given on March 12, 1909, eight days after he came into office and almost, as Mrs. Taft plaintively remarked to friends, before she had time to get settled. The menu consisted of lobster à la Newburg, chicken patés, salad, assorted sandwiches, rolls, cakes, ice cream, candies, coffee, and punch.

On this occasion President and Mrs. Taft again threw precedent to the winds. It was customary for the President and First Lady to retire after their guests had been presented to them. The Tafts, however, remained. This bewildered the guests. What was expected of them? When and how should they take leave? Finally, Mrs. Taft had to instruct an aide to announce to the most noted of them that nothing was expected and that they should retire when they wished, without adieus.

The First Lady was "at home" informally three afternoons a week. Callers included her personal friends and women who had written expressing a desire a meet her. She always received in the Red Room. "I made it almost cozy despite its size," she said, "by having the fire going and the candles lighted."

The President thrived on White House social life. He was good company and always enjoyed social festivities, particularly dinner parties; and he was a ladies' man. Mrs. Taft's first afternoon reception for the congressional wives started out as a purely feminine occasion, but at Mrs. Taft's invitation the President received with her, and was lionized by four hundred women who hadn't expected to meet him.

The first state dinner given was for Vice President and Mrs. James S. Sherman. Customarily guests entered the dining room in order of precedence: the President and the lady guest of honor leading, followed by the First Lady and the ranking gentleman, and so on. This rule did not appeal to Mrs. Taft's sense of hospitality, and to prove her "claim to a natural tendency toward simple and every-day methods," she reverted to Mrs. Grover Cleveland's more cordial method of waiting for all the guests to pass, then, with her escort, taking her place at the end of the line. "There were humorous aspects to our position," she wrote, "but it was difficult to get used to living in so much grandeur. . . ."

Mrs. Taft used pink Killarney roses on the famous Monroe plateau as the centerpiece for the Vice President's dinner. She loved flowers and never ceased to marvel at the beauty and profusion of those grown in the mansion greenhouses, particularly the orchids for which it was noted. These were used to decorate the table for the diplomatic dinners.

As the cool spring weather gave way to hot weather, the First Lady had the terraces set up with tables, chairs, flowers, and shrubs for elaborate entertaining. But this idea was not a success—bugs and dampness outweighed the discomforts of the heat inside.

Two months after the inauguration Mrs. Taft suffered an illness which left her with a speech affliction and other handicaps. After that she was not able to handle her full share of duties as mistress of the White House, and was assisted by her sisters. Her daughter, Helen, before her debut, presided in her place at a dinner given for Prince and Princess Fushimi of Japan.

Ten months later Helen made her debut at a tea to which twelve hundred guests had been invited. On December thirtieth of that same year, her parents gave a ball for her at which the guests, all friends of the debutante, numbered three hundred. The ball was held in the East Room, and the guests danced to the music of the scarlet-coated Marine Band, for whom a special room was built on the east terrace. This room faced the triple windows, from which the panes and sashes had been temporarily removed.

The most brilliant of all the entertainments held in the White House during the Taft administration was the dinner and dance given in June, 1911, by the President and his "Nellie" in celebration of their silver wedding anniversary. Invitations reading "1886–1911" were sent to approximately eight thousand persons. (The newspapers next day estimated that fifteen thousand stood outside the fence looking in.)

A splendid garden party was planned, but the day started off badly. Mrs. Taft's father was seriously ill in Cincinnati, and Professor Willis L. Moore, Chief of the Weather Bureau, called at the White House personally that morning to give the President the weather forecast. "Conditions are most unfavorable," he said. "There will probably be showers this afternoon and tonight. It is raining almost everywhere, even in the British Isles and Scandinavia."

Not a drop of rain fell, and, of course, Professor Moore was the butt of many a joke that evening. Even the newspapers carried the story of his unfortunate forecast the next morning. Better still, a telegram arrived shortly before the party got under way, announcing that Mr. Herron, Helen Taft's father, had improved.

Helen Taft had only recently suffered a stroke, and it was remarkable to everyone present that she managed the ceremony—and much of its preparation—so well. She wore a white satin gown profusely embroidered with silver roses and carnations, and a long train, also embroidered. On her hair, which she had piled high on her head, was the diamond tiara her husband had given her as an anniversary present.

At eight o'clock the Presidential procession started from the south portico; a carpet was run out to indicate the line of march. In the lead were Colonel Spencer Cosby, U.S.A., and Lieutenant Commander Leigh C. Palmer, U.S.N., followed by Major Archibald W. Butt and Captain Graham L. Johnson. The procession took a circular course, coming finally to a halt at an illuminated arch where the receiving line stood. First

The diplomatic dinner of January 16, 1912, was held in the State Dining Room. Table decorations were five hundred orchids and fern, and the Monroe gilt table set was used. Dinner was delayed twenty minutes for the Russian ambassador, Baron Bahkmeteff.

to be received was the diplomatic corps, then members of the family, and then the long, long line of guests. As the guests were introduced, they moved off to join the throngs milling about the grounds or sitting on the benches and chairs scattered about. A little before eleven o'clock the band left the south portico and began to play waltzes in the East Room, which attracted a great crowd of dancers.

At eleven o'clock the State Dining Room was thrown open and a buffet supper was served. For those who wished to have supper out-of-doors, in view of the magnificently illuminated grounds and fountain, tables were set out on the west terrace with four or six chairs at each. Champagne was served, and great bowls of Rhine wine punch were plentiful.

There was a mammoth wedding cake, baked by one of New York's leading caterers and requiring the services of a corps of expressmen to insure its safe delivery from Union Station. Here is a description of it, as given in a newspaper account of the anniversary celebration:

> [Its frosting] was circled with twenty-five crystal hearts imbedded in scrolls at regular intervals. Out of the top were seen dainty cherubs whom the froth of a frosted sea seems to have cast up against a great cornucopia filled with reproductions of a rare exotic of the gardener's art, with clinging angels clamoring for them. Around the great circle of confectionery, and alternating with the hearts, were twenty-five miniature silken reproductions of Stars and Stripes and the President's flag. At the base were roses, cut from their stems and flung against the towering sides. Fluttering on the edge of the cake were turtle doves in their customary attitude as the poet sees them.

The President and Mrs. Taft repaired to the south portico after the ceremonies were over, to receive intimate friends and relatives at their leisure.

At one o'clock more than half the guests still remained within the White House grounds. It was after two when the music ceased and the last light was extinguished.

On Tuesday evening, January 16, 1912, the Tafts gave a

President Taft was the last President to have a White House cow. Her name was Pauline.

diplomatic dinner at which one of the diplomats had a rather embarrassing experience. It was an unusually brilliant occasion; the thermometer outside read zero, and fires were lighted in the East Room's four great fireplaces. Major Archibald W. Butt, chief White House aide, and his assistants received the guests in the East Room, and directed members of the diplomatic corps and other special guests to the Blue Room.

By eight o'clock all the guests had arrived except the Russian ambassador, and when he entered a moment later he suddenly turned and fled down the staircase. An usher then brought a message to Major Butt: the Russian ambassador had returned to his hotel to put on his uniform. He had come in civilian dress, and the entire diplomatic corps was decked out in ceremonial splendor! The unfortunate ambassador had, of course, been seen, and the rest of the corps found his predicament delightfully humorous.

Major Butt reported the diplomat's delay to the President and Mrs. Taft, and asked whether they would wait dinner for his return. The President answered, "By all means. Delay the dinner."

President Taft had many advantages over his predecessors. He was the first President to receive a salary of $75,000 a year; and his was the first administration in which the government assumed the servants' payroll. He was the first to have an automobile and the last to have a White House cow.

The brown-haired, gray-eyed Helen Herron Taft, who had been one of the most promising graduates of the Cincinnati College of Music and a founder of the Cincinnati Orchestra, was the only woman in American history to have the distinction of being the wife of a President and of a Chief Justice of the Supreme Court of the United States—Taft filled this office from 1921 until his death in 1930. She thoroughly enjoyed her role as First Lady, even though afflicted, and bitterly regretted her husband's defeat, in 1912, by Woodrow Wilson, Governor of New Jersey.

XXVII

No Politics at the
Dinner Table

The Woodrow Wilsons

One of the first acts of Woodrow Wilson after he took the oath of office on March 4, 1913, was to rule that politics were not to be discussed at the White House dinner table. Mealtimes, during the eight years of the Wilson administration, were social get-togethers, and, according to David Lawrence, during this entire period no one was ever invited to luncheon or dinner for political purposes. The new President intensely disliked the idea of being pleasant for policy's sake.

Washington society soon learned that social standing and the intricacies of protocol were of no importance to Woodrow Wilson. On a previous occasion, when, as president of Princeton University, he had played host to President Theodore Roosevelt at a luncheon, he had openly revolted against the ruling that the President had to precede the ladies. Now that he was President, he flatly refused to subscribe to such nonsense, claiming that "a man who is a gentleman before becoming President should remain one afterwards."

Furthermore, the new President and First Lady had requested that there be no Inaugural Ball—a festivity dear to the hearts of Washington's social élite—since they both considered the custom somewhat frivolous in the face of the solemn responsibility assumed in taking office as President.

President Wilson, who had perhaps the most scholarly background of any President, had attended Davidson College, North Carolina, the University of Virginia, Princeton University, and Johns Hopkins University, where he received his Doctor of Philosophy degree on his thesis, *Congressional Government* (his first published book). Both President and Mrs. Wilson were Presbyterians; his father was the Reverend Joseph Ruggles Wilson, a stalwart of the Southern Presbyterian Church and hers was the Reverend S. E. Axson of Rome, Georgia.

The Wilsons had three daughters—Margaret, Eleanor, and Jessie. The family's taste in entertainment ran to music, art, literature, the theater, billiards (which the President taught the girls to play), golf for himself, and dancing for his daughters. Margaret and Eleanor loved to dance, and on occasion "forgot" they were honor guests who were supposed to leave the party early so that others could go before the small hours of the morning!

The Wilsons were a close-knit family and loved having relatives and intimate friends about; often members of both families visited them for long periods at a time. They were fun-loving, witty, and gay, the President often leading in the banter. An impersonator, he told tales to perfection, including dialect and Negro folk stories, which he loved. He sang tenor, having been a member of the Princeton Glee Club in his student days, and he, Margaret, and Eleanor formed their own singing trio. He was interested in the gowns ordered by Mrs. Wilson, and often asked her to put on a new frock so he could see how it looked; occasionally he even made suggestions as to what would improve it!

The President's cousin, Helen Bones, who acted as Mrs. Wilson's private secretary and lived in the White House as a member of the family, was as popular in Washington society as she was with the Wilsons. In the evening her room was often the assembling place of the entire family—a typical scene was Mrs. Wilson seated on the sofa, the President standing before the fire with a cup of tea, and the jolly Belle Hagner, social secretary, in deep laughter while the girls reminisced on the day's happenings.

The President's close friends included women as well as men. Charming and brilliant women who could tell a good story and converse amusingly stimulated him. He liked all good company, male and female, and took both as a matter of course. His daughter, Eleanor Wilson McAdoo, wrote in *The Wilson Family* that her mother, who was inclined to be grave, shared in these friendships, and that she "never saw her show any trace of jealousy."

Mrs. Wilson (*née* Ellen Louisa Axson) had been educated at Shorter College in Rome, Georgia, and had studied at the Art Students League of New York. A few of her landscapes had won praise from prominent critics. Ellen Lou, a dreamy and impractical girl before her marriage, caused friends to predict that Woodrow would have a poorly run household. But no sooner had Wilson joined the faculty at Bryn Mawr (and they found themselves settled after their marriage) than Ellen Lou started a home economics course in Philadelphia. She soon became quite expert at household management, cooking, and training servants.

Ellen Lou Wilson adapted herself to the White House surroundings with ease, and within weeks after the inauguration she was deep in philanthropic work. The Washington slum area distressed her, and she lent her influence to improving the situation, giving tirelessly of her time and supplying money and food. She visited the trash-filled alleys and dilapidated homes to see and talk with the inhabitants, and soon interested Congressmen in the matter. She finally succeeded to the extent of seeing a bill put before Congress for the project. Often, after spending the greater part of the day in the slums, she would receive callers in the afternoons; and she managed to attend two or three teas a week.

The White House was not forgotten. When she received an appropriation from Congress to restore the flower gardens on either side of the south portico, she insisted on laying out one side herself and having the other done by a landscape architect. Ellen Lou was close to her husband, and took great interest in the development of his program, helping in every way possible. At the same time, she carried on the usual official entertainments—receptions, musicals, teas, and dinners, such as that given for the diplomatic corps on January 2, 1914. The menu on this occasion included "caviar in ice, turtle soup with cheese straws, mousse of halibut with lobster sauce, artichokes with mushrooms, fillet of beef, stuffed tomatoes, string beans, new potatoes, asparagus with Hollandaise sauce, mallard duck, mixed salad, ice cream, cake, marrons, caramels, mints, and coffee. The dinner wines included claret, hock, sherry, and champagne. The liqueurs were cognac and *crème de menthe*."

Jessie and Eleanor Wilson were married within six months of each other in the White House: Jessie to Francis B. Sayre on November 25, 1913, and Eleanor to Secretary of the Treasury William Gibbs McAdoo on May 7, 1914.

Jessie's was a pretentious wedding attended by all the government dignitaries and their wives, diplomats, army and navy officers in full dress, and many friends. The Marine Band played in the foyer as the wedding procession marched from the State Dining Room through the long main corridor into the East Room, where they assembled on a white vicuña rug—a wedding gift—in front of a small, satin-covered *prie-dieu* flanked by tall white-tapered candelabra. The couple faced the big east window, which was banked with flowers and fern.

Margaret, the eldest sister, was maid of honor; Eleanor and six of the bride's friends were the bridesmaids.

Eleanor's wedding was small. Her mother had had a fall in January from which she had not recovered, and to save her exertion it was decided (although Mrs. Wilson protested) that only Cabinet members and wives and a few relatives and close friends would be invited. Jessie and Margaret were her matron and maid of honor, and the rest of the bridal party consisted of two little flower girls—Secretary of the Interior Lane's daughter and the daughter of the groom by a former marriage—and Dr. Cary Grayson, the best man. The Marine Band played in the foyer as the wedding procession, the bride on her father's arm, came slowly down the stairs, through the corridor, and into the Blue Room. There they stood, among masses of lilies and apple blossoms, on the same white rug and in front of the same little *prie-dieu* that Mr. and Mrs. Sayre had recently used. The bridal supper, consisting of bouillon, chicken-liver paste, boned capon and peas, Virginia Ham with salad, strawberry ice cream, cake, coffee, and champagne, was served in the State Dining Room. The bride cut the cake with the sword of a White House aide.

Mrs. Wilson's health continued to grow worse, and by the time Secretary and Mrs. McAdoo returned from their honeymoon she had given up all activities. The slum-clearance bill so dear to her had been speeded up, and just before her death on the sixth of August—seventeen months after Wilson's inauguration—the President was able to tell her that the bill had been passed.

Without the support of his beloved Ellen Lou, the President fell into despair. Mrs. Wilson had been his mainstay and confidante, and, in her quiet way, an influential factor in his success. Now Jessie and Eleanor were married and had their own homes; Margaret was away much of the time on concert tours. The President and Helen Bones were often alone, and the White House had lost its sparkle. In the following months Dr. Cary T. Grayson, the President's physician, became greatly concerned over his patient's melancholy attitude, and urged that social activities in moderation be renewed.

Then one day Miss Bones and Mrs. Edith Bolling Galt, who had become friends after being introduced by Dr. Grayson, stepped off the elevator with their shoes muddy after a walk through the park. Unexpectedly, the President and Dr. Grayson, who had been golfing, came around the corner also wearing muddy shoes. The President and Mrs. Galt (the widow of a Washington jeweler) had never met, but all burst out laughing! The ice was broken; romance bloomed; and on December 18, 1915, Woodrow Wilson and Edith Galt were married in the bride's small home. They had no attendants, and only members of the families and close friends were present. The bride's mother gave her away. After a buffet supper the bride and groom took a honeymoon trip to Hot Springs, Virginia.

The new Mrs. Wilson, in a white gown brocaded in silver, with "angel sleeves," made her first appearance as hostess at the diplomatic reception in January, 1916, when she greeted over thirty-three hundred guests. She described the event in her *Memoir:*

> It was thrilling to greet all the Cabinet in the Oval Room upstairs and then with the President precede them down the long stairway, with the naval and military aides forming an escort, the Marine Band playing "Hail to the Chief," and the waiting mass of guests bowing a welcome as they passed into the Blue Room.

When ambassadors and ministers and their wives called at the White House, Mrs. Wilson invited them separately, rather than in groups, to tea before the fire in the Red Room, which was served at half-hour intervals. Having received as much background information about them as was possible, she was able to talk about affairs of mutual interest.

In May informal lawn parties began. Almost always there

President Wilson's second wife was the former Mrs. Edith Bolling Galt.
They were married in 1915.

was good weather—known as "regular Wilson weather"—for these occasions. The President and Mrs. Wilson (who received under a large tree), were introduced by Colonel Harts, military aide, and Captain Berry, naval aide, and guests found refreshments served under a large colored marquee.

The menace of war and the approach of the 1916 presidential campaign made it necessary for President and Mrs. Wilson to change their breakfast hour from eight o'clock to five, for the days were just too short to accomplish the things that had to be done.

Wilson was reelected in 1916, and the United States declared war on Germany on April 6, 1917. Mrs. Wilson put her whole heart into the war effort. She and the Cabinet wives pledged themselves to reduce their mode of living to the simplest possible form, and to forgo luxuries that had until now been taken for granted. No gloves were to be worn at any time. Before the end of the month Mrs. Wilson had the trees, flower beds, and shrubbery protected, and put eight sheep to work on the White House lawn—to save manpower, the lawn was to be grazed, not mowed. The sheep increased in number; in addition to keeping the grass and weeds down, they served as a popular attraction and their wool was auctioned off to raise funds for the Red Cross. This organization sent two pounds to each state in the Union and to the four possessions —Alaska, Puerto Rico, Hawaii, and the Philippine Islands— to be sold at auction as "White House wool." The total realized was $52,828; the two pounds sent to Alaska brought $5,881.70, excelling any of the other receipts.

In the meantime, Margaret Wilson embarked on a concert tour and returned in June with $10,000 for the Red Cross. A Red Cross sewing unit was established in the White House, using the sewing machine that Mrs. Wilson had brought from her home as a bride.

Despite the fact that official entertaining had been reduced to a minimum, Mrs. Wilson wrote that the White House was

During the First World War sheep grazed the White House lawn, saving manpower for the war effort. Their wool was sold at auction in each state and the four possessions for the benefit of the Red Cross.

a "veritable kaleidoscope of arrivals and departures." Included among the visitors from the Allied nations was Arthur
Balfour of Great Britain, whom the Wilsons entertained at a
dinner at which Edith Wilson and Helen Bones were the only
ladies to sit with the fifty male guests. Others entertained at
the White House were M. René Viviani and Marshal Joseph
Joffre of France; also Italians, Belgians, Russians, Japanese,
and many others.

After the Armistice was signed, and while the President
was laboring to achieve lasting peace, he and Mrs. Wilson
gave a lawn party on August 22, 1919, for the wounded boys
in Walter Reed and naval hospitals. At the party the President himself served ice cream and cake to the boys.

About a year after the signing of the Armistice, the President invited the King and Queen of the Belgians to visit this
country as his official guests, and planned a ceremonial tour
of the nation for them. Unfortunately, illness struck Woodrow
Wilson while the royal pair were still en route, and many gala
plans were of necessity canceled.

When the President had recovered somewhat from his
illness Albert and Elizabeth came to Washington, where,
through the State Department, Mr. and Mrs. Breckinridge
Long placed their home at the disposal of the royal visitors.

On the day of their arrival the President and Mrs. Wilson
had flowers sent with a note of welcome, and Mrs. Wilson
went immediately to call upon Her Majesty. As a welcoming
gift, she brought Elizabeth a fan with shell sticks with her
name imprinted on it in gold.

King Albert and Queen Elizabeth came to the White House
the following afternoon, Thursday, October thirtieth, accompanied by their young son, Prince Leopold, and two aides.
Tea was served in the Red Room; when it was over Mrs.
Wilson asked his Majesty if she could take him upstairs where
the convalescent President was waiting to receive him. Then,
Mrs. Wilson tells us in her *Memoir,* Queen Elizabeth, with

"all the naiveté of a girl," cried: "Oh, but Albert mustn't go yet! We have a present for the President, and we must wait here until it arrives so we can present it ourselves." After some delay two men brought in a "beautifully made box of polished wood, about three feet long and two feet wide, with mounted brass handles and raised metal lettering." The inscription read:

> *Souvenir du Roi et de la Reine*
> *des Belges a Son Excellence*
> *Monsieur Wilson Président des*
> *États-Unis d'Amérique*

When the box was opened with a key, it revealed a case lined with crimson velvet which contained three trays holding eighteen exquisite plates. On each plate was a "hand-painted representation of an historic place in Belgium, each framed in an identical border of rich black and gold." The back of each plate bore the same inscription as that on the handsome case. It was a royal gift, and one that gave the Wilsons lasting pleasure. Mrs. Wilson's *Memoir* continues:

> After this, Her Majesty handed me a small case of grey suede which held a fan of Belgian lace mounted on amber sticks. On the supporting large stick . . . a garter of small diamonds enclosed two letter "E's" in sapphires. She explained that the initials were for her name and mine, Elizabeth and Edith, "in a circle of friendship." The lace was specially woven, and very beautiful. The main motif represents the angels of peace chasing the dragons of war, and in the background stand, as a sort of guard of honour, the national emblems of all the Allied countries—the American Eagle, the English Lion, the French Cock, the Russian Bear, etc.

President Wilson was not too ill at this time to enjoy a little joke. The Washington *Star* (October 28, 1919) carried this story:

Secretary Tumulty, upon leaving the President's room, remarked
that he was going to see the King of Belgium.

"The King of the Belgians," corrected the President.

"I accept the amendment," said Mr. Tumulty.

"It is not an amendment; it is an interpretation," retorted the President, probably having in mind some distinction regarding the covenant
of the League of Nations.

It was after World War I that Congress appropriated
money for the purchase of White House china. A few earlier
Presidents had tried to secure American ware, but could find
none of suitable quality. For this reason they had imported
china specially decorated to their taste—flora and fauna, for
example, or patriotic designs such as the American Eagle and
the United States coat of arms. Wilson, though ill at that
time, was determined to acquire American china to replace
the imported ware. The quality of domestic ware had greatly
improved; furthermore, Wilson desired the use of the President's seal as the motif, because this would be most appropriate for "the President's home."

Seventeen hundred pieces of the finest quality vitrified
ivory-tone translucent china, service for one hundred and
twenty, was purchased from the Lenox Pottery in Trenton,
New Jersey. Designed by the firm's chief artist, it is tinted
cream-white, with a deep ivory border. The flat pieces are
bordered with the Stars and Stripes etched in gold, and at
the center of each piece is the President's seal.

The only color in the set is in the rim of the service plates,
which is a rich, lustrous blue edged in gold; the seal decorates
the center of the service plates, which measure eleven inches
instead of the usual ten and a half, to enable the beauty of
the decoration to be seen even when the entree or soup plate
has been placed on it.

The administration of Woodrow Wilson ended in 1921,
and he died in 1924. His failure to win Congress over to the
League of Nations was a bitter disappointment to him, and

President Wilson was the first to purchase American ware for the White House state service. The President's seal was used as the motif, also for the first time. Shown are the dinner plate and service plate of the 1700-piece set of Lenox china.

on September 26, 1919, he suffered a breakdown during an extensive speaking tour designed to bring this cause before the people of the nation. He never completely recovered, and he finished out his second term a very ill and disillusioned man.

In the election of 1920, Warren G. Harding was elected twenty-ninth President of the United States.

XXVIII

Garden Parties

Warren and Florence Harding

Plans to revive the Inaugural Ball, a custom discontinued during the Wilson administration, were in the offing when Warren Gamaliel Harding, Senator from Ohio and the Republican party's "dark horse" came into office on March 4, 1921. The country, however, was talking economy, and Congress set up such a howl at the thought of so unnecessary an expenditure that the idea was hastily dropped. Instead the Edward Beale McLeans gave a dance at their enormous town house. Visiting statesmen, newly appointed Cabinet officers, and other government officials attended in full force. Guests danced until dawn; all in all, the affair was a great success.

Harding came into office in an era that recognized the President as a human being, not a virtual prisoner who never stepped outside the White House except on formal occasions. His wife, the former Florence Kling, loved dogs, horses, and outdoor life, and she and the President were frequently seen at horse shows and similar public gatherings. They also enjoyed cruises on the Presidential yacht, *Mayflower*—and brought the White House chef along.

The President—big, handsome, and a companionable sort of person—had been persuaded to run for the Presidency against his own better judgment. He never believed himself suited to the office, and he definitely did not want it.

Warren Harding disliked protocol as much as his predecessor had. The tradition that the President, like the King, comes first was distasteful to him. The rule that he had to walk ahead of his wife, except on formal occasions—when he gave her his arm—or to have her trail behind in passing through a door bothered him; also, he found it difficult to accustom himself to being served before his wife and the other ladies at the dinner table. When the President and Mrs. Harding went for a drive, he would step back and assist her into the limousine, then enter and sit—again according to protocol—on her right.

The musically-talented, petite, blue-eyed First Lady, known by friends as "The Duchess," responded graciously to the limelight. She was the daughter of a banker, the wealthiest man in Marion, Ohio. Both she and the President were hospitable folk who enjoyed entertaining and being entertained.

During the summer following the inauguration, Mrs. Harding gave a series of garden parties which turned out to be a huge success. The weather was always favorable, and the gay frocks and picture hats of the ladies contrasted effectively with the green lawn and the scarlet uniforms of the United States Marine Band. Everybody had such a wonderful time on one occasion that the band played "The End of a Perfect Day" several times before guests took the hint!

At these garden parties, the First Lady succeeded in carrying out a pet theory of hers—that the way to get through a difficult situation successfully is to keep up fresh enthusiasm and never get over having "thrills." According to one society reporter in the Washington *Post* (May 29, 1921):

Mrs. Harding with Evalyn Walsh McLean (right), the social leader in Washington, D. C., until her death on April 26, 1947.

> Mrs. Harding . . . has literally shaken hands with tens of thousands of persons, in a steady streaming line through the White House gates. . . . The Garden Party, second of a series this week, furnished twelve hundred more hands for Mrs. Harding to shake and she, standing under the old oak on the lawn of the White House with the President, outwardly at least displayed the same freshness and verve for the occasion that marked her prominence after the nomination. . . . No President's wife in the memory of the Capital has displayed such endurance.

The First Lady's musical talent was encouraged by her husband's interest in music. Warren G. Harding was one of the most enthusiastic sponsors of music to occupy the White House—an enthusiasm fostered, no doubt, by his early experiences with the town band. As he put it: "I played every instrument but the slide trombone and the E-flat clarinet." At one time, when Harding felt the urge to have his own band, he organized the Citizens' Cornet Band of Marion, Ohio, which played with bipartisan gusto for both Republican and Democratic rallies.

The President and Mrs. Harding carried out a full schedule of official entertainments, and a small dinner was given practically every night. They seldom dined alone.

The President's favorite parties were the famous stag dinners of twelve to fifteen guests. Cocktails whetted their appetites for sauerkraut and wienerwurst. After dinner, bridge or poker was played in a smoke-filled room, the men drinking beer or Scotch-and-soda, blissfully unmindful of the fact that prohibition was in effect. However, no wine ever appeared on the dinner table, formal or informal.

The stag breakfast was another of Harding's innovations. Mrs. Harding usually slept late and breakfasted in her room. The President either ate alone in the small dining room or had several friends in for a good hearty breakfast—grapefruit, cereal, bacon and eggs, wheat cakes, maple syrup, corn muffins, toast, coffee—and toothpicks.

Housekeeper Elizabeth Jaffray, in her *Secrets of the White House,* wrote that she could hardly believe her ears when, shortly after he entered the White House, Mr. Harding sent the butler for toothpicks.

"Surely you are mistaken!" the housekeeper exclaimed. "No, Ma'am!" the servant replied, "he asked me plain as anything for toothpicks."

"Well, we'll just forget it," Mrs. Jaffray said firmly.

But it wasn't that simple. Later the butler was back.

"The President asked real forceful-like for those toothpicks."

That afternoon Mrs. Jaffray went shopping for toothpicks.

In the first year of Harding's administration he called the Washington Conference to limit naval armaments. Since the conference was attended by Great Britain, France, Italy, the Netherlands, Belgium, Portugal, China, and Japan—as well as the United States—official luncheons and dinners for foreign delegates entailed some elaborate preparations.

The visit of Marshal and Mme. Joffre to Washington in April, 1922, was one of the highlights of the Harding administration. The hero of the Marne and his wife were lionized at a state reception to which officers of the army and navy who had served under Joffre and General John J. "Black Jack" Pershing were invited. The reception was unusual in that only a few of the guests were not in military service.

The appearance of the French war hero was as dramatic as it was colorful. The function opened when a marine in dress blues appeared at the foot of the state stairway bearing the flag of France. Another marine, carrying the Stars and Stripes, stood on the opposite side of the corridor. Then Marshal and Mme. Joffre, escorted by a White House aide, appeared. The spontaneous burst of applause brought a smile to the face of the gruff old soldier who had saved his country by recruiting hundreds of Paris taxicabs to carry every available soldier to the battlefront.

Then the President, the Marshal, Mme. Joffre, and Mrs. Harding walked toward the Blue Room, the doors of which were flanked by marines bearing the Stars and Stripes and the President's flag. They entered amid a fanfare of trumpets and the familiar strains of "Hail to the Chief." Then, while all stood at attention, the Marine Band played *The Star-Spangled Banner*. This was followed by France's national anthem, the *Marseillaise*.

The first to greet the President, Mrs. Harding, the Marshal, and Mme. Joffre in the receiving line was the former French ambassador and Mme. Jean Jules Jusserand. Then followed the members of the French Embassy, the Marshal's military aides, Vice President and Mrs. Coolidge, the President's Cabinet, the Justices of the Supreme Court, members of both Houses of Congress, and other high government officials.

Mrs. Harding kept a well-trained eye on the kitchen, although she seldom interfered with the housekeeper. Her favorite activity was traveling with her husband (whom she always referred to as "Warren Harding") on his many trips around the country.

It was on just such a trip that Warren G. Harding died suddenly on August 2, 1923, in a San Francisco hotel with his wife at his bedside. Vice President Calvin Coolidge thus became the thirtieth President of the United States.

XXIX

Economy Enters the Mansion

Calvin and Grace Coolidge

President Coolidge settled the precedence problem at the White House. It had been a burning one since Washington's administration, but was not solved until 1927, when the Belgian ambassador's wife flatly refused to sit by "that barbarian"—the German ambassador, director of the Krupp Armaments Works during World War I—at a state dinner.

The aides hastily switched place cards, but as a result of this *contretemps* the President ordered the State Department to appoint a director of White House ceremonies. Today this post is filled by the Office of Protocol, employing twenty-four career men who specialize in "ceremonials," "decorations," and "courtesies and privileges." Rules of protocol play an important role in the nation's capital; State Department experts now plan every detail of the programs of visiting kings, queens, and other foreign dignitaries, but until Coolidge took action there was no policy for such planning.

Coolidge, whose six years in the White House were probably the most expensive the government had paid the bills for up to that time, was the only President to go out of office with a nice little nest egg. This was attributed partly to his own prudence, and partly to the fact that in Harding's administration a law was passed whereby the government defrayed the President's expenses for official entertaining.

Calvin Coolidge took a personal interest in domestic details, unlike his predecessors, who left such things to the distaff side of the family. The cost of food became a matter of presidential concern. He not only kept a sharp eye on household expenses, but checked the menus and gave an occasional peek into the kitchen to see what was going on.

At the request of Mrs. Coolidge, Mrs. Elizabeth Jaffray, White House housekeeper, went to the First Lady's bedroom to see a new gown especially purchased for a state dinner. While there she encountered the President. Just to have something to say to him, she asked:

"Did you look in at the dining room, Mr. President?"

"Yes."

"Didn't you think it was beautiful?" the housekeeper persisted.

"Yes, it's all right."

"Did you step downstairs into the kitchens?"

"Yes, and I don't see why we have to have six hams for one dinner. It seems an awful lot of ham to me."

"But, Mr. President, there will be sixty people here. Virginia hams are small, and we cannot possibly serve more than ten people with one ham and be sure of having enough."

"Well, six hams look an awful lot to me!" the President repeated.

Coolidge's second administration started off with a *faux pas* that has since made history. It was customary for the incoming President to serve a brief but adequate luncheon to members of his party who were to share the reviewing stand in front of the White House on Inauguration Day. But when President

Library of Congress

President Coolidge was accompanied by two Secret Service men on his horse-back-riding expeditions. Here, one of the men signals a driver not to approach any closer.

Coolidge returned to the White House after taking the oath of office, he, his wife, and Vice President and Mrs. Charles G. Dawes proceeded to the second floor, where they lunched on sandwiches and coffee.

The rest of the party, including Cabinet members and their wives, remained on the first floor, foodless. Colonel Sherrill, the President's military aide, saw the situation and solved the problem by inviting them to share the luncheon that had been provided for the White House aides. They accepted, and the entire party trooped over to the War and Navy Building.

Shortly afterward the Coolidges and the Daweses returned to the first floor to find everybody gone, and were forced to proceed to the reviewing stand unescorted. The rest of their party straggled into the reviewing stand later, smiling and quite pleased with themselves and their meal.

The taciturn Coolidge seldom bothered to explain his actions. However, he was often casual and friendly with White House servants, who adored him. Probably the most graphic description of his vivaciousness is that given in the June 1933 issue of *American* Magazine by Ava Long, housekeeper during the Hoover administration, who said that the story was told her by servants who had come down from the Coolidge administration:

> Almost everyone was given a nickname by him. Frank, the house-man on the second floor, became "The Frog." He called the front doorman "Front door Jack" and the back doorman (who took care of the dogs) "Back Door Jack." Maggie, the chambermaid, who had taken care of the presidential suite for twenty-three years, was "That Person." It amused Mr. Coolidge to pretend that he thought Maggie, who was one of the neatest persons in the world, careless in her personal appearance. "Mummy," he would say to Mrs. Coolidge in Maggie's presence, "can't you speak to That Person and get her to try to look a little tidy? Look at her apron strings. They're untied this minute!" Poor Maggie would bridle and grab for her apron strings, which were always tied as primly as if they were set in cement. But she loved Mr. Coolidge's teasing and he knew it.

Mr. Coolidge never rang a bell for a servant unless there was nobody within sound of his voice. When he came in from his morning exercise, instead of going upstairs and having his valet ring for his breakfast, he usually stuck his head inside the pantry door and said to Carnacion—the Porto Rican pantry man, whom he called "Carnation": "Carnation, I want my supper." It was a little joke between Carnacion and the President that Mr. Coolidge always asked for his supper when he wanted his breakfast.

One morning when he came in through the back door and stopped to speak to Carnacion, the pantry was empty. Mr. Coolidge went over to the dumb-waiter, put his thumb on the bell, and kept it there until somebody answered his signal from below. Hannah, the pretty second cook, thought Carnacion was getting fresh ringing the bell so long, so she yelled up the dumb-waiter, "Hey, take your finger off that bell! Who do you think you are, the President of the United States?"

"That was my impression," said a voice distinctly not Carnacion's.

Hannah says she spilled a platter of sausages on the floor when she looked up to see Mr. Coolidge's face smiling dryly down at her.

The President often joked with the cooks, too, who took great pride in their cooking and did their best to please him. But try as they might, they failed to bake the corn muffins and custard pie to his liking, and he complained to his wife.

Many recipes were tried and found wanting. Mrs. Coolidge solved the dilemma by writing the proprietor of a Massachusetts inn where she and the President had frequently dined. Mrs. Jaffray's book, *Secrets of the White House,* gives the recipes that finally succeeded in delighting the presidential palate:

CORN MUFFINS

2 cups cornmeal
1 cup flour
1 cup sweet milk
2 eggs, well beaten
½ cup sugar
2 tablespoons baking powder

CUSTARD PIE

¾ cup sugar
1 rounding tablespoon of flour
Mix sugar and flour, add a pinch of salt
2 eggs, beaten
2½ cups milk
Pour into pie plate lined with thin layer of pie crust not previously baked. Bake in oven until custard is set. Sprinkle a little grated nutmeg on top when removed from the oven.

President Coolidge's dry humor was in evidence in the matter of the stag breakfasts he substituted for the formal luncheons he considered expensive and unnecessary. Whether the breakfasts were introduced for diversion, for some obscure political purpose, or as a means of getting some free meals remained a mystery. Both Democrats and Republicans were invited, which enabled the President to charge the bill to official entertaining. Undoubtedly it was irritating to be telephoned sometimes as late as midnight and politely "invited" to breakfast with the President at eight the next morning.

Coolidge would greet his guests in the Red Room and then lead the way to the small dining room. The fruit course was eaten in silence, everyone waiting for "Silent Cal" to start the conversational ball rolling. He would say nothing. By the time the rest of the meal, consisting of bacon and eggs, buckwheat cakes, sausage, corn muffins, toast, and coffee, had been served, everyone would be making conversation with his nearest neighbor in an attempt to cover the general embarrassment. The dour Vermonter would open his mouth only to put food into it. The meal over in half an hour, the President would solemnly bid each adieu without explaining the object of the meeting.

On one occasion he solemnly poured his coffee into a saucer while his breakfast guests stared in amazement. Some followed suit. The President then added sugar and cream, and,

In this Herbert French photo, Mrs. Coolidge exhibits her pet raccoon, named Rebecca, to a crowd of children gathered on the White House lawn for the annual Easter egg-rolling contest.

Library of Congress

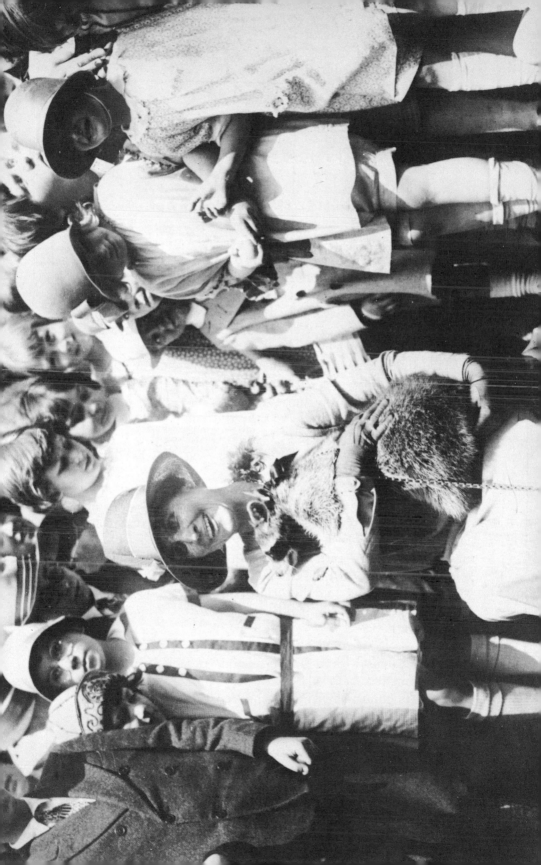

while everyone waited uncomfortably for him to drink it, he carefully lifted the saucer from the table and set it on the floor for his dog. (The person responsible for this story is the late Representative Ira G. Hersey of Maine, who was present when the incident occurred.)

Coolidge was a stickler for the formalities of office, and Mrs. Coolidge and their son, John (Calvin Junior had died at the age of sixteen, shortly after his father entered the White House) were expected to come to the dinner table in full evening dress. On one occasion John mentioned that he might be late, and asked if it would be all right if he came in to dinner dressed as he was. His father replied: "I should like to advise you that you will be dining with the President of the United States, and you will present yourself in the proper attire."

Will Rogers was a dinner guest of the Coolidges one evening. As he removed his coat and hat he was informed by the usher that the President and First Lady had gone in to dinner and that he would not have time to change his attire. The next morning, in referring to his late arrival and not having had time to dress for dinner, Rogers told the ushers he'd never owned a dinner coat in his life.

Charming, gracious, and smiling Grace Coolidge was often credited with being "ninety percent" of the Coolidge administration. She and the President entertained Charles Lindbergh after his flight to Paris in the *Spirit of St. Louis,* and many other guests, such as Marshal Foch, the dynamic and handsome "Black Jack" Pershing, Marshal Joffre, Queen Marie of Rumania and her children, Prince Nicholas and Princess Ileana, and Edward, Prince of Wales (now the Duke of Windsor).

When the Prince of Wales was invited to a luncheon which, according to his wishes, was informal, even the President's austerity melted before His Royal Highness's undeniable charm. The golden-haired, pink-cheeked Edward, just twenty-five, won the hearts of all those who met him. All in all, the luncheon—which consisted of broiled chicken, peas, Bermuda potatoes, mixed salad, cheese biscuits, strawberry ice cream, cakes, coffee, and salted almonds—proved a great success.

Social events reached a brilliant peak in the state dinner given at the White House for Queen Marie of Rumania. The Queen arrived at the White House promptly at eight o'clock, accompanied by seventeen-year-old Princess Ileana and Prince Nicholas, and went at once to the Red Room, where the Rumanian national anthem was played. The royal visitors were then taken to the Blue Room, where about fifty invited guests were assembled in a circle. Captain Wilson Brown, the President's naval aide, escorted the Queen around the circle and introduced the guests. The Queen then took her station at the right of the doorway, and as the Marine Band played *The Star-Spangled Banner* the President and Mrs. Coolidge joined their distinguished guests, first meeting the Queen, then the Prince and Princess, and then circling the room to welcome the other guests.

The Queen's robe, a Patou model in heavy white crepe covered with a design of brilliants and tiny white beads, was sleeveless, and cut low in back. Sweeping wing draperies covered her arms and extended to the edge of her skirt, which was designed with three deep scallops in front and back. She wore her favorite tiara, of diamonds and pearls, and three strands of perfectly matched pearls were fastened about her throat. The rest of her jewelry consisted of rings and bracelets of diamonds, and her decorations were a blue ribbon (the highest Rumanian decoration) and several American Red Cross medals.

Grace Coolidge looked as regal as her guest in a gown of heavy cream satin with a square neckline, brocaded with velvet nosegays about the size of a saucer in pastel shades—rose, blue, green, cream, and pale pink. A train in two long panels, lined with blue chiffon to match the blue of the nosegays, fell from her shoulders, giving the effect of two trains. Mrs.

Coolidge also wore two long strands of pearls and matching earrings. She carried a round bouquet, in the center of which were blue flowers in a circle of violets and pink and white rose-buds, edged with blue flowers, similar to that carried by the Queen.

The young Princess Ileana, slender and pale, wore a girlish gown of blue georgette embroidered in cut steel and crystals, with bands of the trimming falling from the round neck of the bodice to the bottom of the skirt, parting below a large ornament to show an underdress of plaited chiffon. Her jewelry consisted of a bandeau around her forehead, two strands of pearls, and a bracelet. She also wore a ribbon with a Rumanian cross attached.

The company went at once to the State Dining Room. The complete gold service was used for the table, the long mirror with its railing of gold reflecting pink roses and blue delphiniums in gold vases. The heavy candelabra held tall, gold-colored candles. Four compotes of gold, two at either end of the oblong table, held dark purple Belgian grapes. Other attractions of the scene were the new cut-glass service on the table and Lazlo's portrait of President Coolidge on the wall.

The President escorted the Queen to the dining room, where she was seated at his right; Mrs. Coolidge entered on the arm of Prince Nicholas, who sat at *her* right. Next came Princess Ileana with Secretary of the Treasury Andrew Mellon.

After dinner the President and Prince Nicholas led the way to the second-floor library, where the men smoked and chatted, and Mrs. Coolidge brought the Queen and ladies to the Blue Room for conversation.

In the Blue Room pale pink roses decorated the mantel; on low stands alternating with the palms in the circular window were huge bowls of pink cosmos. The great Sèvres vases in the East Room, presented to President Garfield by the President of France, held white cosmos blossoms, and on the four mantels of rare marble, fern and pink dahlias were arranged.

On August 27, 1923, Mrs. Coolidge was "snapped" on Pennsylvania Avenue while walking with Colonel Charles Hitchcock Sherrill.

Pink roses decorated the Green Room, and in the main corridor red cosmos and dahlias mingled with ferns and palms.
A large bowl of scarlet carnations adorned a table near the
stately grandfather's clock bought in President Arthur's time.

Queen Marie was perhaps the most "modern" queen in
Europe at that time, and probably more up-to-date in her
tastes and sympathies than any European king. She was the
granddaughter of Queen Victoria, and always spoke English
to her children.

In New York, she had told two hundred reporters that she
was especially interested in the position of women in America,
and in "what they had been doing in the cause of peace. . . .
Women have done so much for peace. Some day women will
end war; that is, if they don't start fighting among themselves. . . ." When asked by the reporters, "Do you like American cooking?" the charming Queen was emphatic in her reply: "Oh, *don't* I!"

Her shingled, permanent-waved locks were another sign of
the Queen's modern femininity, and, as one Washington reporter noted, she "smoked American cigarettes and liked
them," and, furthermore, saw no harm "in the use of lipstick
to enhance her royal good looks."

Washington reporters found Queen Marie to be:

> . . . a thoroughly charming, human woman, and devoted mother, and
> thereby a doubly charming Queen, who throws no regal barriers
> about herself and family, and wins through graciousness and sim-
> plicity the dignified position which a less attractive monarch might
> attempt to achieve through pomp and ceremony!

The story is told that, while visiting the old garden at Mount
Vernon, the Queen stopped in front of a rosebush which Su-
perintendent Harrison H. Dodge explained had been planted
by General Washington and named the Nellie Custis rose; it
was, he said, "a wishing rose." The Queen said delightedly,

Bob Hoke's drawing for the Star *bears the caption, "Calvin Coolidge was the first President to have a radio set in the White House. President Truman was the first to have a television set."*

"Nicky, make a wish! Nicky! Nicky! Nicky!" and to the Princess she said: "Maybe you'd like to make a wish also, dear." So the young Prince and Princess both laid their hands on the rosebush and made a wish. But when Nicky was asked what he had wished, he bashfully refused to reply, saying, "Oh, now, I really couldn't say, you know."

At Mount Vernon, the Queen, the Prince, and the Princess stood inside the enclosure of the tomb, the young Prince with bared head, while the Queen laid a wreath on the tomb. It is said that on the way to Mount Vernon the Queen stopped the car twice, first to put on a heavy wrap, as it was getting cold, and again to look at the scenery.

A sign in front of a roadside restaurant said, "Queen Marie, get your waffles here."

Though during his entire administration Coolidge's watchword had been "economy," he allowed himself one extravagant purchase (perhaps a key to his inner self)—the eight beautiful Sheffield candlesticks that his successor was to use to such good advantage, for Calvin Coolidge—whose "I do not choose to run" kept his backers and the nation on the political fence—was not renominated. His successor was another Republican, Herbert Clark Hoover, who became the thirty-first President of the United States.

XXX

The Medicine-Ball Cabinet

Herbert and Lou Hoover

The Herbert Hoovers switched from the rigid economy of the Coolidge regime to entertainment on so extensive a scale that there was company, company, and more company! Guests arrived for breakfast, luncheon, and dinner at the White House, and spent weekends at the Hoovers' Rapidan retreat in the Shenandoah Valley. Often teas were in progress in different rooms at the same time in one afternoon, Mrs. Hoover moving from one to the other. Sometimes she gave two large teas at different hours on the same afternoon and a dinner in the evening. This First Lady loved to entertain, and was adept at turning a mere delegation greeting into a full-fledged social tea.

During their first three years in the White House the President and Mrs. Hoover are said to have dined alone only three times—each time on the occasion of their wedding anniversary, February 11. Married in 1899, they had lived in many parts of the world, often in remote spots to which the President's mining-construction projects had taken him. A wealthy man, Hoover spent lavishly, paying for many of the comforts he added to the White House from his own pocket and leaving them for his successors to enjoy.

Lou Henry Hoover never questioned the amount of food consumed nor its cost. Her only stipulation was that it be the best; that it be well cooked and well served. The thirty-two servants at the White House included the chief cook, who did the cooking for the Presidential family and their guests; the second cook, who prepared the meals for the help; the third cook, who made the pastries and cakes and acted as consultant to the first cook; and three kitchen maids and a dishwasher whom everybody called "Pots and Pans."

There were three chambermaids; a bath maid, whose duty it was to keep the fourteen baths on the second and third floors spotless; seven housemen who cleaned the halls and corridors and washed the windows; a man who polished the floors, took care of the grate fires in winter and manned the ice-cream freezer in summer; the checker, whose duties included taking care of the White House dogs; a receiving clerk in charge of all incoming and outgoing parcels; the President's chauffeur, his valet, Mrs. Hoover's personal maid, and others.

President Hoover liked to discuss national problems at the breakfast table. His "Medicine-Ball Cabinet" met on the White House lawn before breakfast every morning—rain, snow, or shine—for a half-hour. They tossed a medicine ball back and forth, because the President thought it an excellent way of keeping fit. They then breakfasted on fruit, toast, and coffee under the huge, century-old magnolia tree on the south lawn when the weather permitted; otherwise in the China Room. Afterward the Chief Executive would bathe, dress, and announce a breakfast-table conference. Often enough guests would arrive at the last minute so that it was necessary to move from the private dining room to the State Dining Room. At the same time Mrs. Hoover would be entertaining wives

President Herbert Hoover.

of the President's guests at breakfast on the second floor.

Lou Henry Hoover was one of the most gracious of First Ladies, but both she and the President were unpredictable hosts. If she learned that the President had invited two extra persons for dinner, she might ask an additional dozen to make it a dinner party; or the President might turn such a meal into a semiofficial affair, which might swell to such proportions that the meal would have to be switched to the State Dining Room. These sudden changes threw the household staff into a dither, for they often didn't know how many persons were expected until they arrived.

In the September 1933 issue of the *Ladies' Home Journal,* Mrs. Ava Long, the housekeeper in the Hoover administration, wrote of how she went shopping at eleven o'clock one day when four guests were expected for lunch. She ordered twelve chops, which seemed quite sufficient. At twelve-thirty, shortly after she returned, a message came from the Executive wing, notifying her the number had increased to forty! The luncheon was to be served at one o'clock.

Mrs. Long was used to emergencies. She and Katherine, the chief cook, raided the White House refrigerators. They gathered up everything they could find, added the lamb chops, ran everything through a food chopper, and wound up with croquettes. These were garnished with mushroom sauce and a scattering of chopped parsley, and served with rice. Not only was there enough for everybody, but a distinguished foreigner was so intrigued he asked for the recipe. This necessitated another tour of the refrigerators to find out what had been used. The result was a recipe that included ham, beef, lamb, onions, and various condiments. To make it official, Mrs. Long christened the invention "White House Supreme."

But all the good recipes were not given out. Mary Rattley, who had been the family cook since Mr. Hoover was Secretary of Commerce, gained fame for her cleverness at concocting specialties, many of which had their origin at the White

Mrs. Herbert Hoover.

House. Among them was a cucumber sauce which she served with fish and crabs. A house guest who persistently sought this recipe learned only that "it calls for lemon juice, cream, and a lot of things which must be right to keep the cream from curdling." When Mary heard that the guest was still mystified about what ingredients could be turned into such an intriguing sauce, she remarked cryptically: "Well, just ask her how she thinks a black cow eats green grass and gives white milk." The Hoover household thus dubbed the cucumber sauce "black cow sauce," which became a sort of joke between Mary and the President.

"Laws, child, Mr. Hoover is the easiest man in the world to please," Mary once said. "In fact, I've never heard a cross word in this house in my life, unless some of the help had a little misunderstanding. The only time I've ever known Mr. Hoover to raise his voice was once when he came to the window and called me to tell me how much he liked something, and I said, well, I didn't know he could holler."

The President was fond of cherries, watermelon, corn soup, cream of potato soup, roast lamb, and—above all—of Virginia ham prepared by Mary's own recipe. Here it is, in her own words:

> I take a mildly cured ham, wash it and scrape it and soak it overnight, and then I put it on in cold water with the skin side down and add two cups brown sugar and two cups vinegar. I let it come to a boil and then simmer slowly until the skin puckers. Then I take it off the stove and let it cool in the water. That keeps the juices in the meat. Then I skin' it and rub it all over with currant jelly. And I always make my currant myself. Then I sprinkle the ham with bread crumbs and brown it in the oven.

Mary said she had the town beat at making vanilla wafers, but—"No, I never tell anybody how I make those cookies." Nor would she give the recipe for Mrs. Hoover's favorite oyster soufflé. She does tell her secret for asparagus soufflé and Maryland caramel tomatoes, favorite luncheon dishes:

ASPARAGUS SOUFFLÉ

Take one tablespoon butter and rub into it one and a half tablespoons flour and add it to one cupful cream. Cook until creamy and add the yolks of four eggs. Beat this mixture for five minutes and add salt and pepper to taste, then fold in one cup of asparagus tips, fresh asparagus preferred. Then add the whites of the four eggs beaten stiff, put into a hot buttered soufflé dish, set the dish in a shallow pan of water and bake for thirty-five minutes in a moderate oven. It will stand up and look beautiful. Before you take it out of the oven grease with butter and serve at once.

MARYLAND CARAMEL TOMATOES

Cut off tops of the tomatoes and make a cavity in the top, and fill each hole with a good-sized piece of butter (not a stingy piece) and put a tablespoon of sugar on each tomato. Sprinkle with salt and put in the oven to cook until the sugar is brown and the tomato done, but not flat. Stick a sprig of parsley in the top of each tomato and serve on rounds of toast with sauce of the tomato.

Mary had her own method of cooking peas to keep them from wrinkling:

I always put on my peas in a lot of water—float the peas—and cold (ice water OK). And I don't cover them, and when they're done they have retained their color and are nice and plump. Things that smell should be put on in boiling water and kept boiling and uncovered. That gets rid of the smell.

A tardy guest may or may not be fortunate enough to get his dinner if he makes the social blunder of being late for a White House dinner. On the occasion of one state dinner President and Mrs. Hoover had waited fifteen minutes for a couple who failed to appear until after the soup course had been served. "I'm sorry," said the chief usher, "but the President and Mrs. Hoover are at dinner. You may remain until they have finished or you may return later for coffee if you wish." The couple flounced out, the lady exclaiming: "Fancy dining at eight! At home we always serve dinner at eight-thirty."

The Hoovers entertained semiofficially at dinner several times a week. The First Lady preferred lace mats to a tablecloth on such occasions, and always used them on the table when there were twenty-two or fewer guests. The centerpiece on such occasions consisted of a gleaming brass bowl of roses or fruit, and brass candlesticks. She loved to show off the beautiful old highly polished mahogany table, which reflected the flowers like a mirror.

The first of their state dinners was given for British Prime Minister J. Ramsay MacDonald and his daughter, Ishbel, on October 7, 1929. There were ninety guests, including the diplomatic corps, members of the President's Cabinet, other high government officials, and high-ranking army and navy officers.

President Hoover and Mrs. Hoover entertained King Prajadhipok and the lovely Queen Rambai Barni of Siam in the White House April 30, 1931. The King and Queen arrived at the Executive Mansion a half-hour before the banquet. They were escorted to the Red Room, where the President and Mrs. Hoover awaited them. Here the two heads of state exchanged the usual courtesies. Then, preceded by the President's aides in full regalia, and followed by the King's entourage, equally if not more resplendent, the President and the King, followed by Mrs. Hoover and the Queen, went to the East Room. Here they slowly made the round of the great circle of dignitaries there to meet them. The King and Queen shook hands, American fashion.

The President with the Queen, and the King and Mrs. Hoover following, led the way to the State Dining Room. The horseshoe table was softly lighted by ivory tapers in golden candelabra, which were alternated with tall gold stands filled with California fruits. Clusters of purple grapes hung

Mrs. Hoover furnished this room with copies of some of the original Monroe pieces. The Monroe Room was used by George VI as a lounge when he visited the Franklin Delano Roosevelts in 1939, and Mrs. Eisenhower now uses it as a sitting room.

over the edges, some of them almost touching the tablecloth.

The Hoovers and their royal guests sat at the center of the table near the entrance door in high-backed tapestried chairs, the King on the right of the President, the Queen on his left, and the First Lady on the King's right. The Monroe plateau was laden with pink tulips, roses, spirea, and snapdragons.

The menu included a rare species of fish, cold lobster, cunningly devised beet baskets stacked with cucumbers, smothered chicken breast, endive in spring salad, fruits, ices, and candy. Each guest found two glasses at his place, one for water, the other for Apollinaris water. Coffee was served to the ladies in the Green Room and to the men in the Red Room.

There is no indication as to how long the dinner lasted, but usually if one lasted longer than an hour the President became impatient and signaled the housekeeper that he wanted the meal to end. Often she eliminated a course to shorten a meal.

President Hoover, like Teddy Roosevelt, had his troubles over protocol. There had been a social feud between Dolly Gann, Vice President Curtis' sister, and Alice Longworth, wife of the Speaker of the House, each claiming precedence over the other. The Vice President felt that his sister should have precedence over the Speaker's wife. The President settled the question by increasing the official dinners to five, the last of these to be the Vice President's dinner.

President Hoover's hopes for reelection proved to be futile indeed, and Franklin Delano Roosevelt, the first Democratic President since Woodrow Wilson, moved into the White House on March 4, 1933.

XXXI

New Deal in the White House

Franklin and Eleanor Roosevelt

The Franklin D. Roosevelts probably set and broke more precedents than any family that ever lived in the White House. Roosevelt was the first President to be inaugurated on the twentieth of January (this change was made by the twentieth amendment to the Constitution); the first to serve more than two terms; the first to entertain a ruling British monarch; and the first to abolish the New Year's Day reception, which had long been a burden and a bore to all concerned with its presentation. The Roosevelts reinstated the President's birthday ball, which Jefferson had discontinued. They entertained more guests, including royalty and heads of state, than any previous administration had done.

Though Franklin Roosevelt was seriously handicapped as a result of infantile paralysis, which he had contracted in 1921, he steadfastly refused to act the invalid. As a child he had had many interests—stamp collecting, ship models, sea lore, piano lessons, horseback-riding, sailing, swimming—and his

341

zest for activity and change sustained him throughout his life.

Franklin and Eleanor Roosevelt were married in 1905. She was given in marriage by her uncle, the former President Theodore Roosevelt. Eleanor and Franklin shared many interests, including politics and world affairs, and it was she, more than anyone else, who urged him not to retire from the world of affairs when his disease had left him permanently crippled.

Roosevelt's day in the White House began about nine o'clock, usually with breakfast in bed while conferring with his physician, secretaries, and General Watson, his military aide, who had charge of his appointments. These meetings with Watson were pleasant, for the General was jolly and a good storyteller, and they liked to match wits. Occasionally the President breakfasted with Mrs. Roosevelt in the glassed-in sun porch that jutted out on the roof. After reading or working until ten-thirty or eleven he went to the office in his wheelchair, remaining until around five-thirty. He then had a swim in the White House pool or a massage.

As a rule his lunch was served on trays at his desk with one or two members of his Cabinet or a guest. If he was alone, a member of the family often joined him. At times he lunched in his study (the second-floor Oval Room) or with Mrs. Roosevelt, who preferred lunching in the sun porch, garden, or in her sitting room.

The Roosevelts ate dinner in the family dining room. The President and Mrs. Roosevelt loved having their children and grandchildren with them; they were jolly and enjoyed one another. The President was "Pa"; Mrs. Roosevelt was "Ma" to the President and the children. They teased, joked, and argued—sometimes even the butlers left the dining room laughing over their quips.

The small, informal dinner that was customary before an official reception was another enjoyable meal. Guests entered at the Pennsylvania Avenue side, where ordinarily on formal

"My friends . . ."

occasions only those of great importance were admitted. After they removed their wraps, an usher led them through the long corridor into the Red Room, where each was introduced to those who had already entered and were standing in line. After a few minutes the erect Mrs. Roosevelt, stately in a tailored evening gown, would appear and greet each guest. "How nice that you are here!"; "I am so glad to see you"; or, "How are you?" she would say with her familiar warm smile.

Greetings over, she would ask her guests, usually numbering around sixteen (that was the comfortable seating capacity of the family table, though twenty-two have been seated by the use of smaller chairs), to come to the dining room. There the President, in black tie, seated at the center of one side of the table, greeted each as they passed. Mrs. Roosevelt took her seat opposite the President. No alcoholic cocktails were served and no wine glasses were on the table.

Sunday-night supper was an intimate occasion, invitations to which were highly prized. The President would sit at one end of the table and Mrs. Roosevelt at the opposite, where she scrambled eggs in a chafing dish. Among the guests would be artists, sculptors, writers, ambassadors, world travelers, friends, and others with whom the Roosevelts enjoyed chatting. Ham, bacon, or sausage, a salad, dessert, coffee, and Sanka, which the Roosevelts favored, were served.

Mrs. Roosevelt's day began early and ended late. It started with a horseback ride along the Potomac or a swim in the White House pool—an addition made early in Roosevelt's administration, and paid for by public subscription. She went from charity affairs to community meetings; she wrote a syndicated column, "My Day"; her articles appeared in magazines and she made speeches the country over; she held public welfare project conferences, sometimes presiding and sometimes sitting quietly with her knitting. She was her husband's confidante, his "eyes and ears" in many distant places. Her reports on her trips were filed for his information and use. With all her varied interests, she was always at the White House when she was needed there. If she had to be absent when a social function was scheduled, she made sure a substitute hostess would be there.

Never had there been so much entertaining in the Executive Mansion—nor has there been since, for that matter. The Roosevelt family was a big one, and the doors were always open to family, friends, and guests. Mrs. Roosevelt gave up her own bed one night and slept on a couch! All guests were honor guests and treated as such; they were made to feel at home and given whatever they requested. Breakfast was sent to their rooms on trays brightened with cheery flowers and cigarettes, from six in the morning until twelve noon.

Inauguration Days were probably the busiest days of all for the housekeeper. On January 20, 1941, she served a full luncheon—soup, ham, beef, tongue, a salad, cake, ice cream, and coffee—to twelve hundred guests within an hour. Two buffet tables were set, a long one in the East Room and another in the State Dining Room, each decorated with red carnations. The guests ate standing. Two and a half hours later four thousand guests were present for tea. Sandwiches and cakes were eaten along with one hundred and thirty gallons of tea and sixty gallons of coffee.

On other particularly busy days, especially in the spring, large conventions and organizations were honored at tea. At times there would be two teas in the garden during an afternoon, one following the other, serving possibly two thousand or more guests!

Mrs. Roosevelt had employed all colored men and women. Included among them were musicians, lawyers, teachers, and collegians. On special occasions a hundred and fifty extras were called in. Out of this group who worked under the Roosevelts was organized the Private Butlers' Association, Inc., which today has about seventy members. Only on the recommendation of an old member may a new one be admitted, and he has to pass about as rigid an examination as if he were joining the White House staff. Once accepted, he is taught carving and how to serve anything from an informal to the most formal dinner; he learns how to handle every type of party; and he receives the benefit of lectures by experts on subjects pertaining to his vocation.

Mrs. Nesbitt, the housekeeper, wished all guests were as honest as the house staff. Alonzo Fields, head butler, and his assistants cherished the historical pieces at the White House and handled them as if they were sacred. But many guests were guilty of walking off with ashtrays, ornaments, dishes, glassware, napkins—anything they could pick up and hide under their coats. So many spoons vanished at one large tea that it was decided none should be used at the next one! Twelve-inch trays were hard to keep. One afternoon two large silver trays and a specially made silver bowl, out of a set of four, vanished.

The housekeeper wanted White House guests to see and enjoy the benefit of the best the mansion afforded. She knew and appreciated the fact that many were disappointed at seeing ordinary plate and china in the President's House, but the loss of valuables had been so great that to keep expenses down she instituted the use of plated, unmonogrammed silver and either borrowed or rented government cafeteria china for large occasions.

The traditional pomp and ceremony that has always marked state functions at the White House was observed by the Roosevelts, and yet, with them, a delightful feeling of informality and real friendliness prevailed.

During Roosevelt's administrations, invitations were engraved on a card measuring 4¾ x 5½ inches, bearing the President's seal embossed in gold at the top. These dinner invitations were binding, for, according to official etiquette, they were not to be declined except in the case of sickness or absence from the city. In the early years of Franklin Roosevelt's administration they were sent out by messenger, a custom that had been in practice since George Washington's Presidency. But as the old "City of Washington" began bulging over its sixty-nine-square-mile District of Columbia area into the depths of the Maryland and Virginia hills (where many official families made their homes) it became necessary to mail them. Mailed three weeks in advance of either a luncheon or dinner, the invitations had to be acknowledged *immediately* in order that proper seating arrangements could be made. A typical acceptance, written on note paper by hand and in the third person, is as follows:

> Mr. and Mrs. ———
> have the honor of accepting
> the kind invitation of
> The President and Mrs. ———
> to dinner
> on Tuesday, February ———
> at eight o'clock

This was addressed to The Social Secretary, The White House, and mailed—not delivered, as had been the previous custom.

Formal dress was required for all evening affairs at the White House, unless attire was designated otherwise. The well-dressed women wore sleeveless gowns with long gloves, which were removed after sitting down at the table and put on again after dinner. For the men, tailcoats, white ties, and white gloves were the inviolable rule except in the case of military affairs, when many of the foreign representatives dressed in their full national regalia, medals and all.

High-ranking dignitaries attending a state dinner entered the White House at the wide Pennsylvania Avenue entrance, while the majority of guests entered by way of the east entrance and were met in the vestibule by aides. After presenting admission cards they were ushered into the coat rooms, where they left their wraps. They were then ushered to a desk to pick up envelopes—the gentleman's bearing the name of his dinner partner and the lady's the name of her escort. On the back of each card appeared a miniature diagram of the table showing where they were to sit. The seating was further simplified by an aide pointing out the guests' places on a large chart of the table, and a name card was at each cover.

After the guests ascended the stairs to the main floor, an aide proffered his arm to the wife and, the husband following, took the couple through a column of dress-uniformed army and navy aides, past the Marine Band, through the corridor, and into the East Room, where they were introduced to an aide who in turn announced them to senior military and naval aides. After the guests were greeted with handshakes by the military and naval aides, they were turned over to the aide who carried their names on his list; each list aide was responsible for ten guests.

The list aide proffered his right arm to the lady, her husband following, and led the couple to their place—a matter of protocol—in a circle, each gentleman standing to the left of his wife so that his name would be the first announced to the President. The aide then inquired of the husband whether he knew his dinner partner. If not, he was taken over for an introduction; otherwise he went to speak with her if he wished.

After the guests were assembled, President and Mrs. Roosevelt entered the East Room, stopping just inside the door. The line of guests, each woman behind her husband, filed by to greet the President and First Lady, the list aide repeating the guests' names to the senior aide, who made the introduction to the President and Mrs. Roosevelt. Then there was a temporary mixup as the men left their wives and began searching for their dinner partners. The circle soon re-formed, and as the Marine Band played a march, the President with the ranking lady guest, preceded by military and naval aides and followed by Mrs. Roosevelt on the arm of the ranking gentleman, led the procession through the long corridor into the State Dining Room.

The following order of protocol was observed for official entertainment during the Roosevelt administration:

TABLE OF PRECEDENCE

1. The President

   [No guest ever precedes the President. He precedes everyone, including his wife, in entering rooms, passing through doors, and getting into vehicles and the like. The only exceptions are aides and the Secret Service men, who may precede the President for security reasons.]

2. The Vice President
3. The Chief Justice of the Supreme Court
4. Ex-Presidents of the United States
5. Ambassadors of foreign countries, in the order of the date of their credentials
6. Widows of former United States Presidents
7. The Speaker of the House of Representatives
8. The Secretary of State
9. Ministers of foreign countries, in the order of the date of their credentials
10. Associate Justices of the Supreme Court
11. The Cabinet

    [Members of the Cabinet rank according to the date the departments were established.]

    (The Secretary of State ranks above foreign ministers.)

    Secretary of the Treasury

    Secretary of War

    Attorney General

    Postmaster General

    Secretary of the Navy

    Secretary of the Interior

    Secretary of Agriculture

    Secretary of Commerce

    Secretary of Labor

12. Governors of States

    [Governors rank according to the order in which their states were admitted to the Union.]

13. Senators
> [The president pro tem ranks with, but ahead of, his colleagues. Senators rank according to the length of their service. In the case of two or more whose years in the Senate are equal, precedence is given in the order of the dates of admission of their respective states to the Union.]

14. Ex-Vice Presidents
15. The Chief of Staff of the Army
16. The Chief of Naval Operations
17. Members of the House of Representatives, in the order of length of service
18. Undersecretary of State
19. Chargés d'affaires *ad interim* of foreign powers
20. Four-star generals
21. Four-star admirals
22. Undersecretaries of the executive departments
> [These follow the same sequence as the *Cabinet* listing.]

23. Assistant Secretaries of the executive departments
24. Counselors of embassies or legations of foreign countries
25. Brigadier generals and commodores

The Table of Precedence is subject to changes or variations in any new administration. At the time the above table was in use, the question was under debate as to which ranked higher, an ambassador or the Chief Justice of the Supreme Court. It was finally resolved in favor of the Chief Justice. The Truman administration brought on the change combining the War and Navy Departments under a single Secretary of Defense, whose rank took the place of the Secretary of War.

Guests were seated as they reached their places at the table, the ladies' chairs having been drawn by butlers in most cases, but if necessary by the gentlemen.

When guests entered the English oak dining room, they saw the horseshoe table set in practically the same manner as shown in the picture taken shortly after the enlargement of the dining room in the Theodore Roosevelt administration. (See page 293.) The most notable change was that the elk's head shown in the picture had been removed and the Healy portrait of Lincoln was in its place over the fireplace. The only other wall decorations were the silver girandoles which matched the silver chandelier.

The horseshoe table around which the company sat is of yellow pine and consists of twenty-two sections. When fully extended it stretches around three sides of the room, comfortably seating one hundred and four persons. When there were fewer than forty-four guests, a long straight table was used. The oval-backed, gilded bent-wood chairs, purchased to go with the table, were made more comfortable by the addition of removable gold plush cushions.

The tablecloth of white Irish linen, four yards wide, woven to special size, was divided into sections and cut on the bias at the turns of the table to fit the curves. The matching twenty-four-inch-square napkins bore the seal of the United States.

The President occupied the high-backed chair in the central position on the outer side of the curve near the entrance, and Mrs. Roosevelt sat opposite him. The ranking lady guest sat at the right of the President, and the ranking gentleman at the right of the First Lady. Other guests were seated accordingly, with the lowest in rank at the ends of the table.

In the center curve of the table, between the President and Mrs. Roosevelt, was the famed Monroe plateau.

The service plates were part of a seventeen-hundred-piece set of American Lenox china purchased by the Franklin Roosevelts. The President had a good sense of value and an eagle eye for detail, and always had the final say as to what was to be purchased in the way of china, glassware, rugs, and even draperies for the White House. When a sample of the new glassware that had been ordered etched in the President's crest was received for approval, the eagle looked over the wrong shoulder (the President's eagle looks to the left and the United States eagle to the right) and the President refused to accept the order until the necessary correction was made.

The Roosevelts chose china to harmonize with the gold service. It is the finest quality vitrified china, a practically unbreakable translucent ware. A rich ivory-toned border is rimmed with a narrow band of the Stars and Stripes motif in blue and gold, with an inner etching of the formal rose and triple-feather design of the Roosevelt coat of arms. The President's seal in gold is at the top of each piece.

The flatware service, except that required for the dessert course, was in place at the beginning of this dinner—the English pearl-handled knives with gold blades for the meat and fish courses, the gold soup spoon, and the cocktail fork at the right of the service plate, and three gold-beaded forks for fish, meat, and salad at the left.

The gold service at each cover was relieved by a heavy cut-glass water goblet and a small lightweight sherry glass, both bearing the United States coat of arms and relics of the Theodore Roosevelt regime, and a green beaded glass for sauterne. The green glass had been used for hock in the Cleveland administration. These two glasses constituted the wine service at the Franklin D. Roosevelt dinners; more than two wines were never served except on those occasions when royalty was entertained.

The food was prepared in the White House kitchen by the three cooks, each of whom had two assistants. It was served by the regular dining-room staff of ten colored butlers with well-trained helpers who were called in. A butler and an assistant were assigned to every eight guests, the butler passing one dish and his assistant following with another dish. As soon as everyone was seated, the President and First Lady were simultaneously served. As they started helping themselves, the other butlers began serving their special groups of guests.

The serving of the ice cream was a matter of clockwork precision. Although the cream was already sliced, it appeared to be in bulk form on the silver platter. As it was passed from

The diplomatic reception room is on the ground floor of the White House, under the Blue Room. President Roosevelt broadcast his "fireside chats" from here. The portraits are of Angelica Singleton Van Buren's official hostess, and Julia Gardiner Tyler.

one guest to another, the butler separated a slice from the bulk form, laying it between the serving fork and spoon in readiness for the guest to help himself. (No second helping is ever served at the formal dinners.)

When the dinner was finished Mrs. Roosevelt stood up— at which signal everyone present rose—and the ranking gentleman accompanied her to the door. The ladies then followed her into the Green Room, where coffee and cigarettes were passed to them. There was no smoking at the table during dinner. Coffee was poured in the pantry and the cups were passed on trays.

The men remained in the dining room, those nearest the President drawing their chairs up nearer to chat, and others bunching up at other places around the table for a demitasse, a smoke, and another glass of wine before joining their dinner partners in the Green Room, from which they would proceed to the East Room for the musicale.

Often as many as two hundred extra guests were invited to attend the musicales, which ordinarily began at ten o'clock. On such occasions the President joined the First Lady in the hall, and both stood at the right of the entrance to the East Room to receive the additional guests.

The artists never received remuneration for participating in the musicale. They were always entertained at supper in the family dining room afterward. When the evening's entertainment came to an end, the President took his leave first, and Mrs. Roosevelt stood alone near the door to the hall to bid good night to the guests as they left.

The Franklin Roosevelts were hosts to the first British monarch to set foot on American soil when King George VI and Queen Elizabeth arrived on the morning of June 8, 1939, to spend a full day and night with them at the White House. They demonstrated to the King and Queen the American way of entertaining, and served typical American food at all three meals.

The luncheon consisted of minted cantaloupe balls, green turtle soup, broiled sweetbreads, mushrooms, asparagus, saratoga chips, hearts-of-lettuce salad with Roquefort dressing, pineapple sponge shortcake, coffee, nuts, and candies. It was a quiet meal, served in the family dining room with only the Roosevelt family and their house guests present. The children came home for the occasion, but because of lack of room at the White House were obliged to sleep at hotels. Mrs. Roosevelt wrote that her boys were so subdued at the luncheon the President noticed it and remarked to the Queen that it was rare when something did not bring about a vociferous argument in their family.

The evening turned out to be one of the grandest occasions the mansion had ever witnessed. The whole place was a profusion of flowers sent from north, east, south, and west. Even on the south porch a vase of large purple gladioli stood by each column and, providing a homey touch, Franklin's Great Dane roamed the south lawn.

The State Dining Room was a fairyland! "It was a colorful sight," Mrs. Roosevelt wrote, "and her Majesty looked the part of the Fairy Queen." The ladies wore their prettiest gowns to the dinner—several wore tiaras—and every gentleman who had a decoration put it on.

Queen Elizabeth, a radiantly beautiful woman, wore a tiara of huge pearl-shaped rubies surrounded with diamonds, and matching necklace, long earrings, and bracelets. Her gown was a three-tiered white tulle sprinkled with golden flecks. Mrs. Roosevelt's gown was of natural Alençon lace, fashioned on princess lines. It had a wide flared skirt which formed into a train. Jeweled clips drew the neckline into a heart shape, and she wore an heirloom diamond necklace.

The gold service was, of course, used, with masses of giant white crimson-tongued orchids mixed with lilies-of-the-valley, baby's breath, and sprays of smaller orchids as table decorations. There were eighty-two covers. The menu consisted of clam cocktail, calf's-head soup, Maryland terrapin, corn bread, and sliced tomatoes, boned capon with cranberry sauce, peas, buttered beets, sweet-potato cones, frozen cheese and cress salad, maple and almond ice cream with white pound cake, and coffee. Wine was served with the dinner.

The President sat with the Queen at his right, and the First Lady opposite him with the King at her right. The President and the King were served simultaneously, and the First Lady and Queen thirty seconds later.

After dinner President and Mrs. Roosevelt entertained their royal guests with a variety show in the East Room. The program included such distinctly American features as Lawrence Tibbett's rendition of "The Pilgrim's Song," Kate Smith singing "When the Moon Comes Over the Mountain," Alan Lomax's folk song, "Git Along, Little Dogie," a spiritual, "My Soul's Been Anchored in the Lord," sung by Marian Anderson, and an example of authentic mountaineer dancing by the Soco Gap Square Dancers from the state of North Carolina.

To make it possible for the King and Queen to experience typical American home life, President and Mrs. Roosevelt took them for a visit to their country home at Hyde Park, New York. Their Majesties worshiped beside the President and Mrs. Roosevelt in the 128-year-old St. James Episcopal Church at Hyde Park; they bowed in prayer, joined in singing hymns, and heard a sermon on "Neighborliness" by the Reverend Henry St. George Tucker, bishop of the Protestant Episcopal Church in America. They rode through the Roosevelt Duchess Hill estate with the President at the wheel. They ate "hot dogs," which they apparently enjoyed, at a picnic, and they went swimming in an outdoor pool—all without the presence of reporters or photographers.

The visit, however, was not without incident. Mrs. Roosevelt, in her "My Day" column published in the Washington *Daily News* of June 14, 1939, wrote:

On June 8, 1939, President and Mrs. Roosevelt greeted Queen Elizabeth and King George in the Presidential Reception Room of the Union Station in Washington.

At Hyde Park the servants we brought from Washington suffered from a jinx which followed its course in three mishaps! My mother-in-law's serving table in the dining room has a center standard. Too many dishes were put on one side, and in the middle of the dinner the table tipped over. No one could think for a minute because of the noise of breaking china. Later in the evening, with a tray full of glasses, water, ginger ale, and bottles, one of our men going into the big library slipped and dropped the entire tray on the floor. And as a final catastrophe . . . my husband, moving backwards across the grass by the swimming pool, almost sat on another tray of glasses and pop bottles!

War clouds hovered over Europe at the time of the royal guests' visit, and four months later Germany invaded Poland. But it was not until December, 1941, when we went to war with Japan, that a quietus was put on social activities in the Executive Mansion. For the duration of World War II the White House was practically enveloped in a blackout; an air raid shelter was constructed off the East Wing.

There was a limited amount of entertainment, of course, chiefly of deposed royalty and foreign emissaries coming to the United States in connection with war problems. Among the visitors of the dark years of Roosevelt's administration were King George II of Greece; King Peter of Yugoslavia; Queen Wilhelmina of the Netherlands; Crown Prince Gustavus Adolphus of Sweden; Crown Prince Frederick and Princess Ingrid of Denmark; Crown Prince Olaf and Crown Princess Martha of Norway; Crown Princess Juliana and Prince Bernhard of the Netherlands; Grand Duchess Charlotte of Luxemburg, her consort, Prince Felix, and their son, Grand Duke Jean; also Madame Chiang Kai-shek of China; Prime Minister Winston Churchill of Britain; and presidents, heads of state, and a multitude of persons of lesser rank from all over the world. Most of these guests were entertained by the Roosevelts at either dinner or luncheon.

President Roosevelt was inaugurated for the fourth time on January 20, 1945. The country was still at war, and the

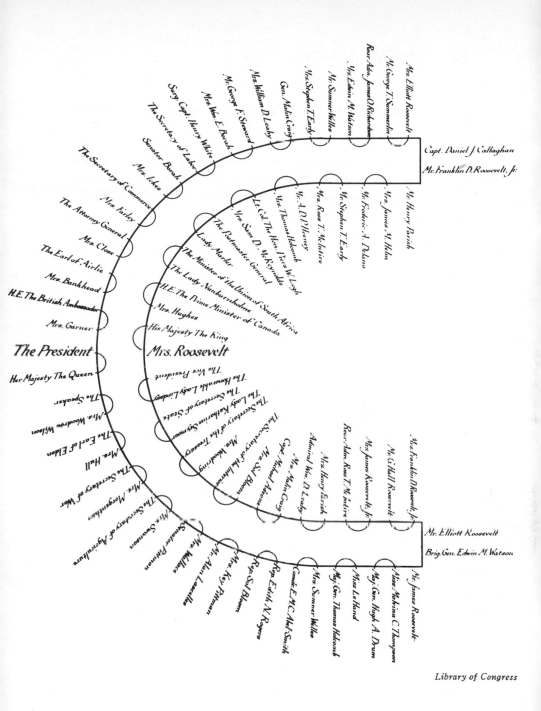

Mrs. Elliott Roosevelt
Mr. George T. Summerlin
Rear Adm. James O. Richardson
Mr. Edwin M. Watson
Mrs. Sumner Welles
Mrs. Stephen T. Early
Gen. Malin Craig
Mrs. William D. Leahy
Mr. George F. Steward
Mrs. Wm. E. Borah
Surg. Capt. Henry White
The Secretary of Labor
Senator Borah
Mrs. Ickes
The Secretary of Commerce
Mrs. Farley
The Attorney General
Mrs. Close
The Earl of Airlie
Mrs. Bankhead
H.E. The British Ambassador
Mrs. Garner

The President

Her Majesty The Queen
The Speaker
Mrs. Woodrow Wilson
The Earl of Eldon
Mrs. Hull
The Secretary of War
Mrs. Morgenthau
The Secretary of Agriculture
Mrs. Swanson
Senator Pittman
Mrs. Wallace
Mrs. Alben Lowden
Rep. Key Pittman
Rep. Sol Bloom
Rep. Edith N. Rogers
Comdr. E. M. C. Abel Smith
Mrs. Sumner Welles
Maj. Gen. Thomas Holcomb
Miss Le Hand
Maj. Gen. Hugh A. Drum
Miss Melvina C. Thompson
Mr. G. Hall Roosevelt
Mrs. Franklin D. Roosevelt, Jr.

Capt. Daniel J. Callaghan
Mr. Franklin D. Roosevelt, Jr.
Mr. Henry Parish
Mrs. James M. Helm
Mr. Frederic A. Delano
Mr. Stephen T. Early
Mrs. Ross T. McIntire
Mr. A. D. P. Heeney
Mrs. Thomas Holcomb
Lt. Col. The Hon. Piers W. Legh
Mrs. Sam D. McReynolds
The Postmaster General
Lady Marler
The Minister of the Union of South Africa
The Lady Nunburnholme
H.E. The Prime Minister of Canada
Mrs. Hughes
His Majesty The King

Mrs. Roosevelt

The Vice President
The Honorable Lady Lindsay
The Secretary of State
The Lady Katharine Seymour
The Secretary of the Treasury
Mrs. Woodring
The Secretary of the Interior
Mrs. Sol Bloom
Capt. Michael Adeane
Admiral Wm. D. Leahy
Mrs. Henry Parish
Rear Adm. Ross T. McIntire
Mrs. James Roosevelt, Jr.
Mr. Elliott Roosevelt
Brig. Gen. Edwin M. Watson
Mr. James Roosevelt

The U-table seating arrangement for the dinner given in honor of the King and Queen on the evening of June 8. The semicircles indicate dinner partners; six men are without partners.

inauguration took place on the south portico of the White House.

In the late afternoon of April 12 of that year, the news was flashed that President Roosevelt had died of a massive cerebral hemorrhage at Warm Springs, Georgia. That evening, in the Cabinet room of the executive offices of the White House, Vice President Harry S. Truman took the oath of office as the thirty-third President of the United States.

XXXII

Strawberry Festival

Harry and Bess Truman

Word of President Roosevelt's death reached Vice President Harry S. Truman while he was in his office in the Senate Office Building on the afternoon of April 12, 1945. At 7:09 that evening, with Mrs. Truman, their daughter Margaret, and Cabinet members in attendance, Truman was sworn in by Chief Justice Harlan Stone as the thirty-third President of the United States. "I pray God I can measure up to the task," said Truman.

Newspaper correspondents have described Truman as "the friendliest and kindest man ever to live in the White House." Though fiery-tempered, the new President—who called himself a Missouri clodhopper—was essentially a person of modesty and humility. He liked people and made friends easily, meeting them, he would say, "as if at a strawberry festival."

The Trumans were a close-knit family. Harry Truman had married the former Bess Wallace of Independence, Missouri, two years before he was elected to his first political office—

county judge at Kansas City. They had one daughter, Margaret, and the new President enjoyed nothing more than sitting down at the piano and playing a duet with his daughter, who was at that time a student at George Washington University.

Bess Truman quickly made herself loved by the entire White House staff. She was highly respected for her faculty of "knowing what she wanted, how a job should be done, and her ability to give specific orders in such a nice way." Truman often referred to her as "the boss."

It was not until World War II had ended that White House official entertaining began to return to normal. The diplomatic corps had increased so considerably in number by that time that two dinners had to be given in order to accommodate them in the State Dining Room. The corps was split into two groups: the odd numbers, as listed in the State Department's little blue book, received invitations to the first dinner, and the even numbers were invited to the second dinner.

On June 6, 1946, the Trumans honored President-elect and Señora Mariano Ospina-Pérez of Colombia at a luncheon. Sixty-five guests attended and were seated at the horseshoe table in the State Dining Room, which was decorated with a centerpiece of pink roses and white and lavender larkspur.

On April 29, 1947, President and Mrs. Truman entertained President Miguel Alemán of Mexico at a state dinner. In toasting President Alemán, President Truman remarked: "We are living in an age of friendship and unity in the Western Hemisphere." Then, turning to Secretary of State Marshall, he added: "I think that we can set an example for the other side of the world because our neighbors to the north and south are not afraid of us."

Truman presented an unusual gift to President Alemán— a book of mathematics which an American soldier had taken from the Military Academy of Mexico in 1847, during the

The Trumans: Margaret, Bess, and Harry.

Mexican War. New Hampshire's State Historical Society had discovered the volume in its collection, and felt it should be returned to Mexico.

The election of 1948, in which Harry Truman gained a four-year lease on the White House in his own right, was hardly over when the walls of the mansion all but caved in on the Trumans. It was necessary for them to move to Blair House, the nation's official guest house, while the White House was extensively renovated. Blair House was not adaptable to large-scale entertaining and the usual official state functions were discontinued. The nearby Carlton Hotel was used for entertaining foreign visitors.

It was at the Carlton that one of the most brilliant fetes of the Truman administration was staged, honoring President Gabriel Gonzáles Videla, his wife, and their daughter, Señora de Campos, of Chile. Sixty-eight guests sat around the traditional horseshoe table in the Carlton Room. The presidential party was seated in high-backed chairs at the center, the two Presidents sitting together, with Señora de Gonzáles on President Truman's right and Mrs. Truman on the left of the Chilean Chief Executive. Mrs. Truman wore silver-gray lace touched with cerise velvet; Señora de Gonzáles wore off-white taffeta, with a corsage of white orchids. Margaret Truman's dress was a ballerina-length white tulle sparkling with rhinestones.

The table was covered with a white damask cloth, and the service was off-white, gold-banded Bavarian china, with a gold-banded crystal water goblet and four matching wine glasses at each place. Silver candelabra (holding white candles and arrangements of pink carnations, roses, pink and white snapdragons, and blue delphiniums) were placed at intervals along the inner edge of the table, with fern connecting them and falling over the edge. The half-moon section directly in front of the presidential party was completely draped with the fern. Within the curve of the horseshoe, a garden of pink hydran-

Blair House was the President's residence from November, 1948, to March, 1952, while the White House was being renovated. This photograph was taken on November 1, 1950, when an attempt had just been made to assassinate President Truman.

geas and ferns surrounded a fountain sparkling under colored lights.

When President Truman toasted and presented his honor guest with a specially cast twenty-ounce solid gold medallion as "a token of the friendship and good feeling toward him by the President and the people of the United States," President González replied:

> I have followed your words with the greatest satisfaction. The people of Chile and their President have listened to the sincere voice of this friendly country, represented by its illustrious Chief Executive. For my part I repeat that the firm policy of Chile and its government is one of friendship and solidarity with the United States on the basis of equal sovereignty.
>
> On the American continent, there are no imperialistic nations, nor satellites. There are free nations which direct their own destinies and which act internationally and in conformity with a voluntary system, in the management of their common interests, as expressed in the pacts of Rio and Bogotá.

He congratulated President Truman on his five years in office and lifted his glass in a toast "for the enduring prosperity of the people of the United States and for the continued personal happiness of his excellency, President Truman, and his devoted wife and daughter."

President and Mrs. Truman were hosts at Blair House to Princess Elizabeth, the fifth member of British royalty to visit the United States, and her husband, Prince Philip, Duke of Edinburgh, from October 31 to November 3, 1951. (The Princess became Queen Elizabeth II, the sixth reigning Queen of England, on the death of her father, King George VI, three months and eight days later.)

There was pomp and ceremony, as befitted a future queen, at the small dinner given for her at the Blair House on Wednesday evening, October 31. The Princess wore a gown of white and gold lace in a diagonal pattern. A diamond tiara glittered above her dark hair, which was softly curled around

At the end of her four-day visit at Blair House in 1951, Princess Elizabeth presented to President Truman the over-mantel which now hangs on the wall of the State Dining Room. The gift, presented on behalf of her father, King George VI, is an heirloom dating from the eighteenth century.

her face and fell into a soft roll at the nape of her neck. She also wore a diamond necklace and the Order of the Garter— Star and Ribbon—a blue sash which is held to the left shoulder and crosses to the right at the waistline. On it were fastened miniatures of her grandfather, the late King George V, and her father, King George VI. When she appeared just before dinner, the President called her a "fairy princess."

Mrs. Truman wore blue brocade, and Margaret was dressed in shimmering pale-lavender satin. The Marine Band played to dinnertime conversation, and for the reception that followed. Only eighteen—the limit for the Blair House dining room—sat down at the damask-covered table, on which glittered the Monroe plateau. From the crown wells of the plateau glowed tall tapers; red roses, white snapdragons, and ferns filled the flower recesses.

Promptly at ten o'clock the doors of Blair House opened to the first of a hundred guests invited to meet the royal visitors at the after-dinner reception: the Cabinet, the Supreme Court, government officials, and their wives.

The next day, on a tour of the Capitol, the Princess told an aide she liked the way Southern Washingtonians say, "Howdy, Ma'am" and "Howdy, Sir."

Princess Elizabeth's last official ceremony was performed (in a typical London mist) on an elevated canopied platform in the White House rose garden at noon on the Friday she and Prince Philip were to begin their return trip to Canada. As she presented to President Truman an heirloom on behalf of her father, King George VI, she said:

> The renovation of the White House has attracted interest all over the world. Everyone knows how closely it has been bound up with the history of your country and how important it is to your people as a symbol of national pride. . . . We are glad to join with you in celebrating its restoration. My father, who has many happy memories of his own stay in the White House, has wished to mark the event with a personal gift. . . . It gave the King great pleasure when he

found the over-mantel which is before you now. The work of eight-eenth-century artists, and embodying the finest British craftsmanship, it seems perfectly suited for the place which it will occupy. . . . It is his hope, and mine, that it will be a welcome ornament to one of your proudest national possessions, and that it will remain here, as a mark of our friendship, so long as the White House shall stand.

President Truman replied:

It has been a very great pleasure to have you as our guests. I am sure I speak for all the people of the United States, and especially for the people of Washington. We have many distinguished visitors here in this city, but never before have we had such a wonderful young couple that so completely captured the hearts of all of us. You will leave many happy memories among the people who have greeted you here.

President Truman then said he was especially glad that Elizabeth's father, the King, had sent "something for this building which means so much to the people of the United States . . ." and that the over-mantel would be placed in the White House, and would be "greatly cherished as a mark of the close ties that bind our two countries together."

"Over the years," he said, "we have built these ties into a remarkable international friendship. We have had our differ-ences in the past, but today it would be just as hard to imagine a war between our countries as it would to imagine another war between the states of this country. It just couldn't hap-pen. . . . I hope the day will soon come when the same thing will be true among all the nations of the world, when war will be impossible in the world."

The President and First Lady returned to 1600 Pennsyl-vania Avenue on March 27, 1952, to find the servants lined up on the north veranda to greet them. The entire capital city, as well as the Truman family, was happy at this "homecom-ing." The original "President's Palace" now had an al-most entirely new interior. When they had moved out in 1949, the mansion had had 62 rooms and 14 baths. Its ceilings were sagging, its walls were in danger of cracking under the strain of the third floor and new roof which had been added in 1927, and the floor in Margaret's room had given way under the weight of her piano.

When they moved back, the White House had 132 rooms, 20 baths and showers, and five elevators instead of one. Only the sandstone outer walls had been retained intact, and these were now supported with a steel framework on concrete piers, the sinking of which required excavating to a depth of nearly thirty feet under the building; this excavation incidentally provided new basement space. The original rooms were copied as closely as possible, even to the extent of saving beautiful wood paneling and woodwork to use in the restored rooms and re-creating old cornices and moldings which had long since lost their original beauty. The main stair was given a new location which made it visible from the entrance foyer.

In the long corridor which connects the East Room with the State Dining Room hung two crystal chandeliers, older than the White House itself, which were anonymously presented to President Truman for the purpose. These are the most beautiful chandeliers in the White House.

The President and his family could now enjoy breakfast in the new top-floor solarium, which overlooked the Washington and Lincoln Memorials, the beautiful Potomac, and the Virginia hills. They could also enjoy the controversial ten-thousand-dollar balcony that Truman had added to the second floor in 1946. Altogether, Congress appropriated $5,761,000 for the renovation (the original White House cost less than half a million dollars).

President Truman had "curry-combed" the contractors to speed up the reconstruction of the mansion in preparation for the arrival of the Queen of the Netherlands on April 2, 1952, but the new electric kitchen was still not equipped to take care of a large dinner when she did arrive.

The handsome forty-two-year-old Queen Juliana and her

This photograph, taken from the vestibule, shows the Waterford chandeliers which were anonymously presented to President Truman for the renovated White House. The vestibule chandelier has now been replaced, but those in the corridor remain. The Seal of the President of the United States is above the Blue Room door.

consort, His Royal Highness Prince Bernhard, who were the first guests to visit in the newly resplendent White House, were there overnight, but were honored at a state dinner that evening at the Carlton Hotel. The table was set for ninety-six guests. No cocktails were served, but four wine glasses stood at each place.

Queen Juliana wore a diamond coronet on her chestnut hair, and a diamond necklace and bracelet. She wore no decorations on her pearl-gray chiffon gown, made with a pleated bodice and narrow draped skirt. A bolero of matching Chantilly lace covered the strapless bodice, and her long gloves were of the same color. Her slippers were silver.

Prince Bernhard, in white tie and tails, wore a string of medals across his chest, and the ribbon and medals of the American Legion of Merit around his neck. Mrs. Truman's gown for this occasion was of smoke-gray *mousseline-de-soie* over pale-gray taffeta, with sprays of embroidered lace cascading down the very full skirt.

The next day, after the Queen addressed the Congress, the royal couple was honored at a luncheon in the White House.

Following their departure, the First Lady began a series of five o'clock teas for Washington's officialdom so that they might have a look at the newly refurbished mansion. The diplomatic corps was the first to be received.

One of the most interesting parties given under Mrs. Truman's supervision at the White House took place on April 20, 1946, when it came her turn to entertain the Spanish class she belonged to. At nine o'clock that morning she, her Spanish teacher, Professor Ramon Ramos, Mrs. Dean Acheson, wife of the then Assistant Secretary of State, Mrs. Lester Pearson, wife of the Canadian ambassador, Representative Jessie Sumner of Illinois, and Mrs. Leverett Saltonstall, wife of the Senator from Massachusetts took over the White House kitchen to prepare a luncheon with a Latin-American flavor.

The chief dish served was *Picadillo,* a triumph of the Pro-

The top-floor solarium, overlooking the Potomac, is one of the most inviting of the rooms provided by the renovation.

fessor. Under his tutelage, the class chopped and mixed four varieties of meat with rice, seasoned the mixture with hot spices and plenty of garlic, and garnished it with almonds, pimiento, olives, and raisins, and made a vegetable salad to serve with it. The dessert was a mixture of Mexican cheese and guavas in syrup.

Waitresses for this occasion included Mrs. Dwight D. Eisenhower, wife of the Chief of Staff of the United States Army; Mrs. Hugo Black, wife of the Supreme Court Justice; Mrs. Robert P. Patterson, wife of the Undersecretary of War; Mrs. John L. Sullivan, wife of the Assistant Secretary of the Navy; Mrs. George Allen, wife of the head of the Reconstruction Finance Corporation, and Mrs. Brien McMahon, wife of the Connecticut Senator. Sixty-six classmates were served at the horseshoe table in the State Dining Room.

The Spanish luncheon was repeated by Mrs. Truman at the White House on April 18, 1947, to wind up Pan American Week. Other nationally known ladies helped to do the honors on this occasion.

This same Spanish-speaking group honored Mrs. Truman with a farewell tea just before she and the President returned to their home in Independence, Missouri. Mrs. Truman said it was the most beautiful tea she had ever attended. It was given in the brilliant crystal-chandeliered "Hall of The Americas" at the Pan American Union, the most lavishly beautiful building in Washington.

The tables were so odd and beautiful they are worth a description. The main tea table was about two-thirds as long as the width of the large hall and stood near one end of it. A white cloth was put on the table first, and then covered with a light-blue crinoline cloth. The centerpiece, of golden fall flowers, red leaves, fruits, and squash, was about two-thirds the length of the table. A seven-taper silver candelabrum, draped with grapes, stood at either end of the centerpiece. At one end of the table charcoal glittered in a large silver German samovar, keeping the water hot for tea; at the opposite end stood a silver antique English urn for coffee. A similarly "dressed-up" table standing lengthwise in the hall held two silver bowls of punch, one at each end.

The food consisted of small, steaming-hot rolls with slivers of Virginia ham inserted in them, assorted sandwiches, cookies, nuts, mints, coffee, tea, and punch. It was placed on the tables on old-fashioned silver cake-tazzas.

Chocolate dessert was almost a "must" on the menu during Truman's time, because Margaret was so fond of it; she liked chocolate ice cream, chocolate cake, and chocolate candy. At any time of the day or evening ham sandwiches were in order, and the third-floor refrigerator was always stocked with snacks for her and her college friends.

The Truman family had simple meals. The following is a typical menu:

Minted Orange Cup

Pork Roast
Apple Sauce
Creamed Peas   Buttered Carrots
Mashed Potatoes

Baked Chocolate Alaska
Chocolate Sauce

Here is a recipe for the dessert:

BAKED CHOCOLATE ALASKA

Bake a sponge cake in the shape of a loaf of bread. Cut off the top, scoop out the inside, pack the shell with hard chocolate ice cream, and replace the top. Put into the freezing compartment of the refrigerator to harden. Just before serving, place on a paper-covered board, cover entirely with meringue, and brown quickly in a 450° oven.

President Truman described himself as a "meat-and-potato

man," which would lead one to believe that he was a big eater, but he was known to his friends as a very light eater. He doesn't smoke, doesn't drink coffee, and doesn't touch alcoholic beverages except to be sociable.

President Truman would not permit himself to be "fenced in" at any meal. In good weather, breakfast, luncheon, and often dinner were served on the south-side porch; otherwise the family took their meals in the family dining room, one of the most beautiful and homelike rooms in the building. The entire room, including the vaulted ceiling, is off-white, and is set off by stately, highly polished antique mahogany furniture; the table has a seating capacity of sixteen. Over the table hangs a crystal chandelier which holds candles; candlelight is the only illumination used in this room. Glistening antique silver in the china closet and on the buffet and serving table add brilliance to the room. The mantel is of marble, and has a mirror above it.

The Truman family breakfasted at about a quarter of eight. From year to year the President chose practically the same menu: a glass of orange, grapefruit, or tomato juice; hot cereal in winter and dry at other times; two pieces of wholewheat toast, and a glass of milk. He was particularly fond of buttermilk. Eggs or hotcakes were never a part of his breakfast. He was also indifferent to salads, and, like many Midwesterners, he and his family were not too fond of fish.

When there was no Cabinet or stag luncheon in the State Dining Room, the President would usually join his family for lunch; occasionally he lunched at the Capitol with Senate cronies or with his staff at the Executive Office. These were sometimes very jovial get-togethers, with the President leading the banter.

President Truman and Justice Bennett Champ Clark of the Court of Appeals had a common love for baked ham and greens with cornbread. When Truman was a newcomer, the Senate's "little man" from Missouri, Senator Clark, was al-

The East Room was restored in white and gold; the two Chippendale sofas, which were donated, are blue. Portraits of George and Martha Washington (the former is the Gilbert Stuart saved by Dolly Madison in 1814) are set in gold frames fitted into the wall panels. Compare this picture with one of the East Room made before the 1902 renovation.

ready famous as a connoisseur of Missouri ham and greens, often going to the market himself to select the tenderest leaves. The recipe for this dish was given to the author by Mrs. Clark when her husband was senior Senator:

HAM AND GREENS

Take a combination of any two or more of the following greens:
Turnip
Mustard
Kale
Collards
Rape
Poke (Poke must be parboiled)
Wash them in about ten waters, or until clean and free of all sand. Put on in boiling water, and add three fair-sized pieces of hog's jowl, or enough salt pork to season if hog's jowl is not available. Cook slowly about 2½ hours. Season with salt to taste.

When done, drain and place in serving dish and top with slices of the meat. Serve with cornbread and a dish of sliced tomatoes and finely chopped raw onions.

When Harry Truman decided to withdraw from the 1952 presidential race and return to Missouri, the hectic years that saw the renovation of the White House, the ending of World War II, and the greater part of the Korean War were over. The retiring President, with honor and distinction, relinquished the reins of government to the popular and beloved "Ike"—Dwight David Eisenhower.

XXXIII

A Soldier, and a
Soldier's Wife

Dwight and Mamie Eisenhower

After twenty years of Democratic occupancy the White House took on a new look when World War II hero Dwight D. Eisenhower moved in on January 20, 1953, after winning a landslide victory over Governor Adlai Stevenson of Illinois.

The new First Lady, Mamie Doud Eisenhower, immediately revealed herself to be a charming, warm-hearted person. The White House was to hold few surprises for her in the way of social obligations and the entertainment of foreign dignitaries; as the wife of General Eisenhower, Supreme Commander of NATO, she had traveled extensively and had entertained every manner of "Very Important Person" abroad. Her early years as the wife of an army lieutenant—Eisenhower was a recent West Point graduate when they married in 1916—had also taught her to adapt to many types of environment, chiefly army posts!

President Eisenhower began his term in office by introducing the "Knife and Fork" series—breakfasts, luncheons, and dinners at which he made the acquaintance of the members of Congress. Within four months he played host to five hundred and twenty-seven Senators and Congressmen—only four House members were unable to attend. The first of these sessions was held in February, and the last on the twelfth of May.

The "get-acquainted-with-Congress" phase of his social program completed, the President began to give small stag dinners for business leaders, administration officials, publishers, editors, writers, educators, Republican party leaders, scientists, artists, sportsmen, religious and labor leaders, and his old soldier friends. His purpose was, of course, to familiarize himself with the latest information and opinions in many fields. The dinner hour was seven-thirty. Guests were invited to wear business suits, but usually appeared in dinner jackets because the invitation noted that the President would probably wear a black tie.

Eisenhower is an early riser, and usually breakfasts alone in his dressing room at about seven o'clock. He seldom has more than grapefruit, toast, and coffee, though he will occasionally take bacon or sausage and eggs. While eating, he scans the news or is briefed by an aide on the day's program.

Mrs. Eisenhower's day begins at eight-thirty with breakfast in bed. She then goes over such details as menus, questions pertaining to the running of the household, and her schedule of engagements for the day. There is no secrecy about the fact that Mamie Eisenhower dislikes to cook—but the President's enthusiasm for cooking more than makes up for her lack of interest.

When no official guests are scheduled for luncheon or dinner, the President and Mrs. Eisenhower lunch and have dinner together in their second-floor living room, which is usually bedecked with flowers. In such cases, dinner is a leisurely meal, after which the President relaxes in his favorite wing chair and Mrs. Eisenhower—probably with her shoes off—watches television. If friends join them for dinner, as they often do,

"Ike" may take them to the glass-walled solarium at the top of the White House and prepare charcoal-broiled sirloin and corn roasted in the husk. Afterward they may play bridge or canasta, watch a movie, or just sit and talk. The President's other specialties are vegetable soup, cornmeal flapjacks, potato salad, trout, chili, and cake.

Both the Eisenhowers enjoy hobbies. Mamie collects autographs, plays the electric organ (a gift from her mother), and enjoys a game of canasta or Scrabble. Once when she and the President were returning from a visit with her mother in Denver, and he was scheduled to stop off in Indianapolis and make a speech, Mamie had the plane radio ahead to Indianapolis to have a Scrabble set waiting at the airport so that she and her friends could while away the time with a game while waiting for him to return to the plane.

President Eisenhower, too, has more than one hobby. Aside from cooking, he paints, hunts, fishes, and plays a fair game of golf and a better one of bridge. He will play with Republicans or Democrats, so long as they are good players. Usually he gets together a stag foursome and they start playing at about five o'clock on a Saturday afternoon. With time out for dinner, perhaps ordered from a Chinese restaurant, they play until ten or eleven in the evening. Sunday mornings are reserved for church, but sometimes an afternoon game is possible while Mamie and her friends play canasta.

Mamie Eisenhower is a friendly, hospitable person, and as personally popular as her husband, but the White House social season is far less elaborate in this administration than it has been in the past. The First Lady receives a great many guests—Girl Scouts, delegations of Republican women, church societies, patriotic organizations—and sponsors many charity drives, benefit teas, and fashion shows. There is an air of breezy informality about these receptions. On one occasion an elderly woman in the line told Mrs. Eisenhower that it was her birthday. The woman couldn't have been more pleased when the First Lady planted a kiss on her cheek. After that, birthdays became a commonplace among elderly guests, all of whom probably hoped for the same attention.

Mrs. Eisenhower soon changed the old system of receiving a long, unbroken line of guests. Instead, she had an aide usher a small group at a time into the Red Room, where a second aide was on hand to introduce each guest to her. She cordially shook hands and chatted for a moment; when she reached the last guest, the group was ushered into the corridor and another was brought in to meet her.

The Eisenhowers have entertained an unprecedented number of heads of state and high-ranking officers of foreign governments. President José Antonio Remón of Panama and his wife were overnight guests on September 28, 1953, and were the first to be entertained at a full-fledged state dinner in the newly renovated White House. The table was covered with white damask, and the venerable Monroe plateau was decked with bowls of yellow roses, daisies, and snapdragons to harmonize with the light-green paneling, green chenille rug, and gold silk damask window draperies of the State Dining Room. The floral arrangements were alternated with eleven-tapered candelabra and *epergnes* overflowing with black grapes.

On this occasion the white-and-green-bordered Truman china was used with the flatware inherited from the Monroe administration: fish, dinner, and salad forks were at the left of the plates, and an oyster fork, soup spoon, and the beautiful old pearl-handled fish and dinner knives were at the right. Three wine glasses were grouped about each water goblet.

King Paul and Queen Frederika of Greece were the next visitors to the White House. They were honored with a state dinner on October 28 of the same year, at which time the table was formed in a U-shape. The President and King sat side by side, with the Queen at the President's right and Mrs. Eisenhower at the left of the King. A glittering fountain, banked in ferns, splashed in the well of the "U."

The Red Room is done entirely in red and white: walls, draperies, rug, and sofas are red; chairs are white.

Queen Frederika was dressed in cream satin heavily en-
crusted with ivory beading, her skirt falling in soft folds to
the floor; she wore a tiara and a diamond-and-emerald necklace. Mrs. Eisenhower wore coral *peau de soie* covered in
black lace, with a strapless bodice; a black net dust ruffle edged
the full skirt. Her gloves were of black net.

When the champagne was poured, President Eisenhower
presented to King Paul the Legion of Merit—the highest
decoration the United States can confer on a citizen of another country in time of peace. The King responded with
thanks from his people for American aid and support during
the war years and the postwar period.

After dinner, Mrs. Eisenhower led the ladies to the Red
Room for coffee and seated her Majesty on the sofa according
to protocol. To avoid any stiffness at the party, she shelved
the traditional rule that no one sit while the President and his
wife stand, and planned beforehand with the Cabinet wives
that they sit down and converse with the Queen to make her
feel at ease. As soon as her royal guest was engaged in conversation, the First Lady left her and began moving among
the other groups of ladies.

The Queen unwittingly revived a long-standing controversy
which kept telephones buzzing long after she had departed.
It centered about the sixteen- to twenty-button-length white
gloves that are a "must" for official occasions. At the pre-
dinner reception given by the President and Mrs. Eisenhower
to introduce Cabinet and Little Cabinet members to the royal
couple, the wives presented trimly gloved hands to her Majesty. In the meantime, guests not invited to the reception
gathered in the East Room. When they were placed in line
according to protocol and waiting for the President and his
guests to enter, a dictum went down the line: "Take off your
right-hand glove before presenting your hand to the Queen."

The next day, King Paul and Queen Frederika entertained
at a reception for two thousand guests at the Army and Navy

*The State Dining Room was painted light green in the Truman renovation,
harmonizing with the verde-antique marble mantel and green chenille rug.
Healy's portrait of Lincoln is framed in gold, and draperies and upholstered
chairs are gold. The chandelier over the Hepplewhite table dates from 1902.*

Courtesy National Park Service

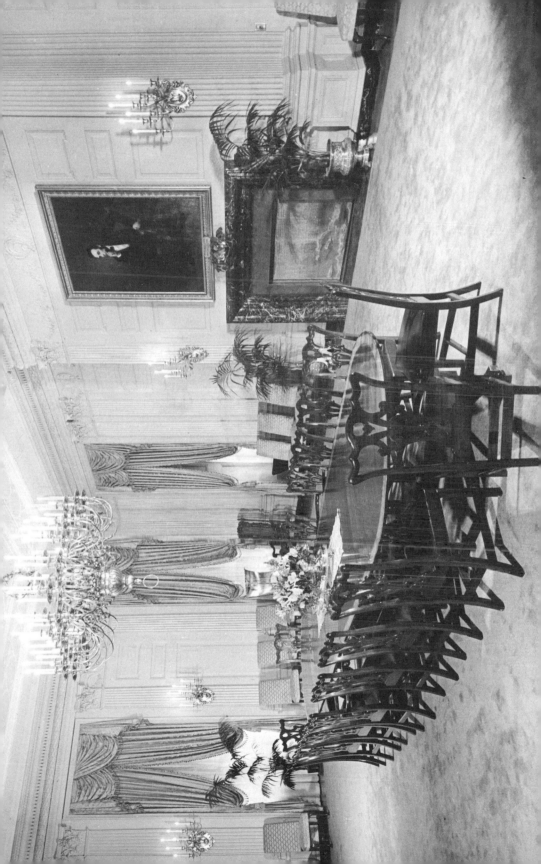

Country Club, and the Queen received in a gloveless right hand. The Greek, Norwegian, French, and British embassies were deluged with calls: "Do you or don't you remove your glove before shaking hands with visiting royalty?" The official reply was, "In Greece it is not considered polite to present anything but a bare hand to royalty." The Norwegian Embassy, whose ambassador was dean of the diplomatic corps in Washington, made this reply: "It is the custom for women in Continental Europe to remove the glove from the right hand when meeting royalty or other important people."

The British Embassy, after poring over all available books of etiquette for the Court of St. James's, found that an Englishwoman "never, never takes off her right glove going down a receiving line, not even for a Greek Queen or an American First Lady."

The White House, of course, received its share of calls, most of which were inquiries as to whether Mrs. Eisenhower prefers to shake a gloved or ungloved hand. The reply was that she has no preference, but, speaking for herself, feels it is more friendly to shake hands without a glove. (Mrs. Roosevelt and Mrs. Truman always shook hands in gloves, because they found it less tiring.)

In the first social season of the Eisenhower administration there were six official dinners—for the Cabinet, the Supreme Court, the first and second diplomatic corps, the Vice President, and the Speaker of the House—and five receptions. These were for the diplomatic corps, the judiciary, government department heads, the army and navy, and Congress. The dinners and receptions were given on alternate weeks, with the exception of the two diplomatic dinners, which followed in succession. The dinners were at eight o'clock and the receptions at nine.

In arranging the 1953–54 social calendar it was designated that two "pool reporters" from the White House press room would be invited, in turns, for the purpose of covering the news and passing it on to colleagues for publication. As it happened, the wines and liqueurs served at the Cabinet dinner (first of the season) turned out to be the biggest news for the reporters, for it had been announced only a short time before that alcoholic beverages would be served only when required by protocol for exchange of toasts with foreign dignitaries. The furor caused by this revelation led to a slight change in procedure: the reporters who were to cover the Supreme Court dinner two weeks later were notified at their homes that the President and Mrs. Eisenhower would welcome them as dinner guests but not as reporters.

Just before the first diplomatic dinner was to take place, Mrs. Eisenhower was ordered to bed with a bronchial infection. Of course she could not attend the dinner, and the question arose as to who would serve as hostess in her place. Mrs. Nixon, wife of the Vice President, was in the Far East. If Mrs. Dulles sat opposite the President at the table, where would her husband, the Secretary of State, sit? Traditionally, the Secretary of State and his wife attend diplomatic dinners and are placed in the normal line of protocol. The outcome was that at this function the role of hostess went unfilled.

When President Celal Bayar—the first Turkish chief of state to visit America—and his wife were overnight guests on January 27, 1954, and were honored with a state dinner, the problem of communication arose. Mrs. Eisenhower spoke no Turkish and Mme. Bayar no English. The problem was solved, however, when pictures of the Eisenhower grandchildren and Mme. Bayar's children were brought out; the women managed to discuss them in French!

Haile Selassie, Emperor of Ethiopia, was a guest on May 26, and at the state dinner given that evening there was another "communications" problem. The Emperor remarked to Secretary of the Treasury George M. Humphrey that he could not understand why more Americans did not speak French—but then he added: "The reason Americans don't learn to speak French is that they are proud of their country, and they think that eventually everyone else in the world will learn to speak English!"

In 1956, the White House entertained President Giovanni Gronchi—Italy's first chief of state to visit America—and President Sukarno of Indonesia, and in 1957 Queen Elizabeth II of England and her husband, Prince Philip, Duke of Edinburgh, arrived for a visit on October 17.

That evening, at the state dinner given to honor the royal guests, the Queen did not remove her long white glove to shake hands. Although the White House and State Department had made it known that for American women to curtsy to rulers of foreign countries "is not our democratic way" to greet them, a few did curtsy. For British guests, of course, it was obligatory for the women to curtsy and the men to bow.

The next ruling monarch to walk down the red carpet at the National Airport was King Mohamed V of Morocco, on November 25, 1957. The President escorted the King to the door of the President's Guest House and departed, expecting to see him and his entourage at the state dinner being given in his honor that evening. But President Eisenhower returned to the White House with a chill (later diagnosed as a mild stroke), and, despite his protests, was confined to bed. Vice President Richard M. Nixon was pressed into service, and for the first time played host at a White House state dinner. Mrs. Eisenhower attended, and entered the State Dining Room on the arm of Mohamed V.

Although every effort was made to mask concern about the President's health, the dinner was subdued and strained. Vice President Nixon again substituted for the President at the dinner given by the King on the last day of his visit.

As time brought improvement in the President's health, he and the First Lady again took on important entertainment duties. In May of 1959, Sir Winston Churchill arrived in Washington for a visit with his old friend of the war years.

The President's broadcasting room, on the ground floor, was formerly the White House kitchen. On either end of the room is a large sandstone fireplace, and the alcoves in which doors have been placed were originally baking ovens. Adjoining this room is a modern electric kitchen.

An informal family dinner on the evening of his arrival was Sir Winston's first scheduled entertainment; the next day the President took him to the Gettysburg farm by helicopter.

Shortly after the Churchill visit, the twenty-eight-year-old King of the Belgians paid a three-day official visit to the capital city. King Baudouin stayed at Blair House and that evening a dinner was given for him in the State Dining Room. The dessert served was called *Betty Brune de Pommes,* and it drew a tongue-in-cheek comment on the editorial page of the Washington *Daily News* the next day: "You don't need a French-English dictionary to recognize . . . plain, old, respectable, uninspired Brown Betty. . . . We don't know what kind of dessert the White House cooked up for Winston Churchill, but that was the time for Brown Betty, if ever such time must be. The British are raised on Bird's custard, bread pudding, trifle, junket, and something known as 'grey shape.' Brown Betty would put them in ecstasy. But for the King of the Belgians, a people with a civilized palate, no, no, no!"

The year 1959 was a historically momentous one so far as entertaining was concerned. Churchill, King Baudouin, Princess Beatrix of the Netherlands, and Nikita Khrushchev visited the White House. Princess Beatrix was entertained at a White House luncheon on September 14. The visit of the pink-cheeked, twenty-one-year-old Princess was a short one. She spent only one day in Washington, but found it "thrilling."

The next day, at half-past noon, a giant Soviet jet aircraft landed at Andrews Air Force Base, and Chairman Nikita S. Khrushchev of the Council of Ministers of the U.S.S.R. stepped out to greet the President of the United States, the Secretary of State and Mrs. Christian Herter, the United States Representative to the United Nations and Mrs. Henry Cabot Lodge, the Chairman of the Joint Chiefs of Staff and Mrs. Nathan Twining, the dean of the diplomatic corps of seventy-eight embassies and six legations in Washington, Mrs.

The Chartran portrait of Mrs. Theodore Roosevelt is one of those adorning the marble walls of the ground floor corridor. The library, china room, broadcasting room, and diplomatic reception room open into the corridor.

Guillermo Sevilla-Sacasa of Nicaragua, and many others.

After luncheon and a brief rest at the President's Guest House (Blair House, just across the Avenue from the Executive Mansion), the Soviet Premier and President Eisenhower conferred for nearly two hours in the President's office in the White House. At eight o'clock that evening Premier Khrushchev and his entourage were entertained at a formal dinner at the White House, where some one hundred guests were seated at the E-shaped table in the State Dining Room. Although the dinner was a "white tie" affair, the Premier appeared in a dark business suit, and Mrs. Khrushchev wore a simple teal-blue gown with a diamond-and-emerald brooch at the neck. Mrs. Eisenhower wore a gown of gold brocade, diamond earrings, and a necklace of diamonds and pearls.

On the eighteenth, Premier and Mrs. Khrushchev entertained the Eisenhowers at the Soviet Embassy. The President's dinner for Mr. Khrushchev had featured curry soup, roast turkey with cranberry sauce, sweet potatoes, and a tossed salad. The Premier's menu for the President was:

Fresh Caviar and Assorted Fish Fillets
Vodka

———

Stuffed Partridges
Vodka

———

Choice of Perch Soup or Ukrainian Borscht
Wine

———

Sterlet (Flounder) in Champagne
Caucasian Shashlik

White Sec   Red Sec

Asparagus

———

Baked Alaska   Fresh Macaroons
Mints, Nuts, Demitasse
Champagne

———

Assorted Fresh Fruits after Dinner

Soviet Premier and Mrs. Nikita Khrushchev were guests of honor at a dinner given at the White House on September 15, 1959. Photographed with the President's party here are cadets and midshipmen assigned as White House social aides for the dinner.

The following morning, Thursday, Mr. Khrushchev and his party boarded an early train for New York, first stop on a whirlwind cross-country tour. He returned ten days later, stayed overnight at Blair House, and the following day left with President Eisenhower for Camp David, a mountain retreat about twenty miles south of Gettysburg. On the first of October, the Premier returned to Washington, held his final news conference at the National Press Club, made a farewell telecast at the National Broadcasting Company's Washington studio, and left Washington in his jet plane at about ten o'clock.

Many White House events of the Eisenhower administration have, of course, been concerned with people and things related only to "home." Mrs. Eisenhower received the final addition to the collection of china used by the Presidents over a period of nearly two hundred years; this was a sugar bowl, two saucers, and a serving plate which had belonged to President Andrew Johnson. Presentation of this "missing link" was made by Johnson's granddaughter, Margaret Johnson Patterson Bartlett of Greenville, Tennessee. Five Presidents must remain unrepresented, since they purchased no special china—Jackson, Taft, Harding, Coolidge, and Hoover. The one piece of china that has remained in the White House ever since its purchase is the Dolly Madison punch bowl. This charming French porcelain bowl is about thirty inches high, and is blue with a gold-dotted border and shield. It is upheld by figures of the three graces.

Mrs. Eisenhower herself has presented twenty-six gold-framed plates, with portraits of former First Ladies in the centers, to the collection now housed in the White House China Room.

In May, 1959, another event with nostalgic connotations took the form of a White House tea at which descendants of former Presidents were the guests. Eight children, and a number of relations further removed, attended, and for most of

The White House collection of china belonging to American Presidents was completed when Mrs. Margaret Johnson Patterson Bartlett, a descendant of Andrew Johnson, presented to Mrs. Eisenhower a Lyons sugar bowl that had belonged to him. The china room adjoins the diplomatic reception room on the ground floor.

them the White House held very specific memories. There was a good deal of comparing done, but all agreed that the rooms are much "lighter and brighter" today than they used to be.

Heirlooms and descendants form strong links with the past, but the White House itself is stronger than either. It has been "home" to thirty-two of the thirty-three men who have held the office of Chief Executive, and it would have been "home" to George Washington if it had existed in his time. As a building it is subject to deterioration and heedless abuse. As a symbol it will never lose its power, so long as the prayer of John Adams is taken to heart by his successors. This prayer is engraved on the mantel over the fireplace in the State Dining Room:

I Pray Heaven to Bestow
The Best of Blessings on
THIS HOUSE
and on All that shall hereafter
Inhabit it. May none but Honest
and Wise Men ever rule under This Roof!

NOV. 2, 1800
JOHN ADAMS

INDEX

Page numbers in italics refer to illustration captions.

397